WOMEN'S QUICK FACTS

WOMEN'S QUICK FACTS

Compelling Data on Why Women Matter

#womensquickfacts

NEW YORK

NASHVILLE MELBOURNE

Women's Quick Facts
Compelling Data on Why Women Matter

Published in New York, New York, by Morgan James Publishing. Morgan James and The Entrepreneurial Publisher are trademarks of Morgan James, LLC.
www.MorganJamesPublishing.com

The Morgan James Speakers Group can bring authors to your live event. For more information or to book an event visit The Morgan James Speakers Group at www.TheMorganJamesSpeakersGroup.com.

Shelfie

A **free** eBook edition is available
with the purchase of this print book.

ISBN 978-1-68350-226-5 paperback
ISBN 978-1-68350-227-2 casebound
ISBN 978-1-68350-228-9 eBook
Library of Congress Control Number:
2016915227

CLEARLY PRINT YOUR NAME ABOVE IN UPPER CASE

Instructions to claim your free eBook edition:
1. Download the Shelfie app for Android or iOS
2. Write your name in **UPPER CASE** above
3. Use the Shelfie app to submit a photo
4. Download your eBook to any device

Morgan James
The Entrepreneurial Publisher™

Builds

with...

Habitat for Humanity®
Peninsula and
Greater Williamsburg

In an effort to support local communities, raise awareness and funds, Morgan James Publishing donates a percentage of all book sales for the life of each book to Habitat for Humanity Peninsula and Greater Williamsburg.

Get involved today! Visit
www.MorganJamesBuilds.com

Edie Fraser
CEO, STEMconnector

Michael DuBois
Director, Innovation &
Development

Reaa Chadha
Contributor

Junlin Du
Graphic Designer

Matthew Pilsbury
Contributor

Li Zeng
Graphic Designer

Lorena Fimbres
Contributor

Zhihui Xiong
Contributor

Matthew Gonsalves
Graphic Designer

Justin Spizman
Editor

Sheila Boyington
Contributor

Carolyn Fischer
Editor

Kayla Brown
Contributor

"Women's Quick Facts has so many uses to "up our game" for all women and girls. Women are agents of change and as males we step up our support and commitment."
Michael Norris, Senior Adviser, STEMconnector
Vice Chair, Million Women Mentors

"Higher education is the best pipeline for high skill and in-demand careers. Data proves that the number of women students is surging at undergraduate and graduate levels all across the nation. Congratulations on Women's Quick Facts. We need to make certain that every school, college, and university uses this book to build the case for increased investment in this crucial segment of our skilled workforce."
Rob Denson, President, Des Moines Area Community College and Chair
STEMconnector Higher Education Council

"As founder and CEO of GoldieBlox, the children's multimedia company, our mission has always been to level the playing field and empower girls to be whatever they want to be. We believe that together we can make this happen! Congratulations on the book, Women's Quick Facts, and your focus on the importance of entrepreneurship, mentoring and STEM. It's great to see us all united and working towards the same goal."
Debbie Sterling, Founder and CEO, Goldiblox

WOMEN'S QUICK FACTS

TABLE OF CONTENTS

Acknowledgments

Producing *Women's Quick Facts* would not have been possible without the contributions of Li Zeng, Michael DuBois, Justin Spizman, Carolyn Fischer, Junlin Du, Reaa Chadha, Matthew Pilsbury, and Matthew Gonsalves. All the infographics for this book were designed by Junlin Du and Li Zeng.

I owe a special debt of gratitude to Lorena Fimbres, Sheila Boyington, Talmesha Richards, Jordan Bullock, and Latifa Cooper—all in Washington, D.C. and Kayla Brown, Zhihui Xiong, our Million Women Mentors team for the states.

For helping to drive ideas, I'd like to thank Ted Wells, Tommy Cornelis, Jeff Terhune, and all the STEMconnector® colleagues, including our interns Max Abraham, Carly Jean-Louis, Tevin Ali, and Ishmael King. My thanks also goes to the leaders of Diversified Search, especially our chairman, Judee von Seldeneck.

In addition, I want to express my great appreciation for the stellar work of our publisher, David Hancock of Morgan James Publishing. David believed in two of our other publications and did the same with this important book. The team at Morgan James worked tirelessly on this project, and a special thanks goes out to Justin Spizman and Carolyn Fischer, who served as the editors.

There are so many people who continue to inspire and contribute to this worthy endeavor, especially Balaji Ganapathy and the team at TCS; Joan Perry of My College Options/NRCCUA; Heidi Kleinbach-Sauter of PepsiCo and chair of the Global STEM Talent Summit; Monica Smiley of Enterprising Women; Michael Norris of Sodexo North America; and countless others.

Many of the organizations in Million Women Mentors® stimulate us to drive the needle and thread the facts and you will see these organizations sourced throughout this publication.

As our team deserves applause, we never forget to thank our partners and the thousands of sources holding us accountable.

Sincerely,

Edie Fraser, CEO, STEMconnector®, Million Women Mentors®

Overview

Women count. *Women's Quick Facts* is the only resource of its kind. It is a powerhouse compilation of statistics, research, in-depth numbers, and resources that support women's status and contribution. Page by page, chapter by chapter, this amazing resource paints an intricate and comprehensive picture of the strong and promising drive to equity and economic prowess through data and rich models. Hundreds of resources and sources are cited. Use them. Progress? Yes! Enough? No! Join the Call for Action! We have so many colleagues as champions; galvanize them and others.

Now, more than ever women are leaders, decision-makers, game-changers, drivers of growth, development, and making progress in our economy and our society at large. Women are literally the backbone of the economy as wage earnings, spenders, and wealth creators. Women are moving up in business, government, education, and organizations both in the United States and globally. Even then, we are far from equity. There is a fervent fight to close the gap of disparity and recognize the basic right of economic and societal equality—one we advocate for, each and every day.

We still have miles to go before we can rest easy whereby establishing equity with our male counterparts. We salute all women and males who join us in the women's upward movement. We should celebrate our history of achievement, while continuing to forge the path ahead. There are thousands of individual opportunities in the United States and globally to elevate women in business, entrepreneurship, organizations, education, and government. *Women's Quick Facts* highlights these compelling prospects, and helps us put the wheels in motion. We must jump-start greater progress, execution, and all be advocates for change.

Women and girls are making strides in STEM; however, when we look at technology or engineering, we must move faster so as to not get left behind. We salute the millions of us engaged in driving upward and with that, delivering results.

Women are change leaders who are making an exceptional impact on the economy and society at large. Women are the torch holders. This book will help you ensure each torch is burning bright, while motivating others to pass the torch. The gap is shrinking as we continue analyzing the data, research, crunching numbers, and then using our valuable takeaways to promote the remarkably important changes. You cannot ignore the data. Listen to the facts, consider them, and use *Women's Quick Facts* as a powerful accelerator, needle-mover, and game-changer.

Chapter 1: Demographics - Overview

More than anything, the numbers assist us in describing a remarkably accurate picture of the current demographics in the workplace. In fact, demographics are clearly beginning to tell the story of equality. By the year 2050, the U.S. population will have more than a majority of females. As this book goes to press, we're close to 50/50 now on a global basis. Thus, the story of the real demographics has to be reflected in that marketplace. When we look at the workforce in the United States, white women still lead the way. Nevertheless, the numbers of black, Hispanic, Asian, and others, as well as the impact of lesbian, gay, bisexual, and transgender (LGBT), are rising strongly. By 2040, these minorities will be the majority face of America. Therefore, we must put diversity and inclusion extremely high on the priority list. The trends support both this effort and growth, and we should celebrate and join the exciting restructuring and changes presently occurring in the marketplace. With women and minorities, the nation is rapidly transforming, and we are marching into leadership roles in every area of society.

The data and statistics found within this book show the labor force is impacted in an exciting way. Gone are the days of pushing the boulders up the mountain. We are so close to reaching the same pinnacle our male counterparts have reached. It may have taken us longer, but we are indeed rising to the top. The impact is not just from female executives and business professionals, it also includes married women and stay-at-home mothers, as well as single women. Women as an entirety are contributing to the continued growth and development of our society and our economy. It is truly a team game, and we are all carrying the torch in one way or another. In 2014, women accounted for 47% of the labor force and total employment in the United States. Approximately 75.6 million women consider themselves professionals, and their hard work impacts the workforce each and every day. Compared to our male counterparts, we are still only about 79% in median income—a chasm that needs to be closed. Science, technology, engineering, and math (STEM) jobs pay far better. Parity is forming, but the pay gap is still not close enough, or even close at all. Our reality is we make approximately $11,000 less per year while serving in the same positions as males do. Disappointing, to say the least.

But that which is measured can be improved. And this book offers you the numbers and research that simply cannot be ignored. Share these demographics and travel through each chapter of *Women's Quick Facts*. Pull those statistics that resonate and use them to set the bar ever higher than it rests today. Using the data shared in this book, will help you to come together and work toward change not only by 2020, but also on a decade-by-decade basis.

How can we reach total equity by 2050, if not before? This is a clarion call to step up with the demographics and cite and use these facts to ensure that the demographic story will be one of a celebration of women leaders and women in the workplace and marketplace. The goal of this book is to crunch the numbers and show you the research that supports our continued growth as women. It will inspire you, motivate you, and help you to take the necessary steps to generate change and bridge the gap in the forthcoming years.

Call to Action:

- Take notes and highlight the statistics and research you find to be most compelling. This data tells a story and builds a case for use to move the needle in a major way.

- Share the data with your colleagues and champions, women and men alike. All change starts with education and a basic understanding of the facts underlying the issue. Build a plan for what you and others can do to drive the numbers upward.

- Distribute books.

- Galvanize support for raising the bar.

- Establish how far we can move forward parity by 2020.

- Give credit to all the organizations initiatives you can, individually and collectively we drive action and results.

CHAPTER 1: DEMOGRAPHICS

Population

U.S. Population

Global Population

- 50.8% of the U.S. population is female as of July 2014. Equating to 162 million females, 157 million males.
- Globally, 49.6% of the population is female.
- 2 to 1: At age 85 and older, the approximate ratio by which women outnumbered men in 2014 (4.1 million to 2.1 million).

Source: U.S. Census Bureau (2015).

- Projected Population Growth: In 2050 - 197,727,000 males and 200,601,000 females. Females are projected to be 50.4% of the population.

Source: U.S. Census Bureau (2014).

U.S. Population

2050   197,727,000 Males
        200,601,000 Females

Age

Population by Age and Sex: 2013						
(Numbers in thousands. Civilian noninstitutionalized population.)						
	Both		Male		Female	
Age	Number	Percent	Number	Percent	Number	Percent
All ages	311,116	100.0	152,335	100.0	158,781	100.0
Under 5 years	19,917	6.4	10,176	6.7	9,741	6.1
5 to 9 years	20,536	6.6	10,490	6.9	10,046	6.3
10 to 14 years	20,640	6.6	10,558	6.9	10,082	6.3
15 to 19 years	20,970	6.7	10,672	7.0	10,299	6.5
20 to 24 years	22,153	7.1	11,134	7.3	11,019	6.9
25 to 29 years	21,138	6.8	10,628	7.0	10,510	6.6
30 to 34 years	20,659	6.6	10,189	6.7	10,470	6.6
35 to 39 years	19,221	6.2	9,461	6.2	9,759	6.1
40 to 44 years	20,657	6.6	10,162	6.7	10,495	6.6
45 to 49 years	21,060	6.8	10,319	6.8	10,742	6.8
50 to 54 years	22,386	7.2	10,926	7.2	11,460	7.2
55 to 59 years	20,880	6.7	10,099	6.6	10,781	6.8
60 to 64 years	17,611	5.7	8,224	5.4	9,387	5.9
65 to 69 years	14,437	4.6	6,900	4.5	7,537	4.7
70 to 74 years	10,264	3.3	4,704	3.1	5,561	3.5
75 to 79 years	7,598	2.4	3,233	2.1	4,364	2.7
80 to 84 years	5,692	1.8	2,490	1.6	3,202	2.0
85 years and over	5,296	1.7	1,971	1.3	3,325	2.1
Median age	37.3	N/A	36.1	N/A	38.5	N/A

Footnotes:

Plus armed forces living off post or with their families on post.

Note: Details may not sum to totals because of rounding.

Source: U.S. Census Bureau, Current Population Survey,

Annual Social and Economic Supplement (2013). Internet release date: March 2016.

Ethnicity

As of July 2014, the U.S. female population was:

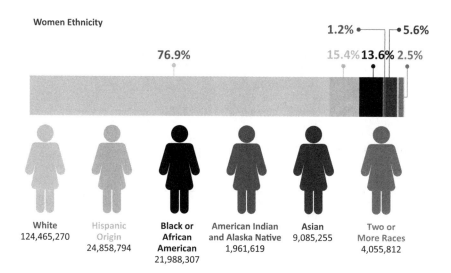

Women Ethnicity

1.2%   5.6%

76.9%   15.4% **13.6%** 2.5%

| White 124,465,270 | Hispanic Origin 24,858,794 | **Black or African American** 21,988,307 | American Indian and Alaska Native 1,961,619 | Asian 9,085,255 | Two or More Races 4,055,812 |

As of July 2014, the U.S. female population was:
- White - 124,465,270 - 76.9%
- Black or African American - 21,988,307 - 13.6%
- American Indian and Alaska Native - 1,961,619 - 1.2%
- Asian - 9,085,255 - 5.6%
- Native Hawaiian and Other Pacific Islander - 331,721 - 0.2%
- Two or More Races - 4,055,812 - 2.5%
- Hispanic Origin - 24,858,794 - 15.4%*

For reference, the total U.S. female population at the time was 161,920,569.
Source: U.S. Census Bureau (2015).

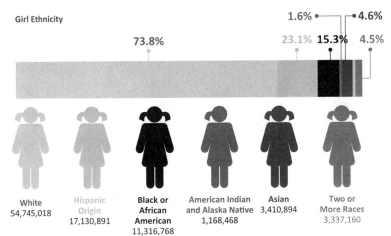

Girl Ethnicity

73.8%   23.1% **15.3%** 4.5%
1.6% •   • 4.6%

| White 54,745,018 | Hispanic Origin 17,130,891 | Black or African American 11,316,768 | American Indian and Alaska Native 1,168,468 | Asian 3,410,894 | Two or More Races 3,337,160 |

Girls under the age of 18:
- Total - 74,181,467
- White - 54,745,018 - 73.8%
- Black or African American - 11,316,768 - 15.3%
- American Indian and Alaska Native - 1,168,468 - 1.6%
- Asian - 3,410,894 - 4.6%
- Two or More Races - 3,337,160 - 4.5%
- Native Hawaiian and Other Pacific Islander - 203,159 - 0.3%
- Hispanic Origin - 17,130,891 - 23.1%*

Source: U.S. Census Bureau (2015).

Diversity

69%   31% **15%** 6.4%
1.2% •   • 8.2%

| White | Hispanic Origin | Black or African American | American Indian and Alaska Native | Asian | Two or More Races |

- White - 69%
- Black or African American - 15%
- American Indian and Alaska Native - 1.5%
- Asian - 8.2%
- Two or More Races - 6.4%
- Native Hawaiian and Other Pacific Islander - 0.3%
- Hispanic Origin - 31%*

Source: U.S. Census Bureau (2012).
Hispanic Origin is calculated separately from other ethnicities.

- Diversity Woman – The magazine and programs are designed for women business leaders, executives, and entrepreneurs of all races, cultures, and backgrounds, who have unique interests and concerns. Diversity Woman is the only magazine on the market designed exclusively to help smart, savvy diverse and multicultural women leaders achieve their career and business goals. Diversity Woman also plays a mentorship role. Both the magazine and web site serve as a forum and membership directory to connect aspiring businesswomen directly with other women in leadership roles.
Source: Diversity Woman.

LGBT

Population

2%-4%
U.S. Adults Are LGBT

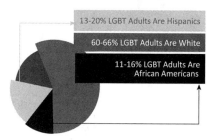

13-20% LGBT Adults Are Hispanics

60-66% LGBT Adults Are White

11-16% LGBT Adults Are African Americans

- Among all adults, not just females, the proportion who identified as LGBT varies from 2.2% in the NHIS to 4% in the Gallup data.
- These estimates imply that between 5.2 and 9.5 million adults in the United States identify as LGBT.
- Among all adults, between 52% and 60% of LGBT respondents were female.

Ethnicity (Male & Female):
- Approximately 60-66% of LGBT adults identified as White and non-Hispanic.
- African Americans comprised between 11% and 16% of LGBT adults.
- Hispanics comprised between 13% and 20%.
Source: The Williams Institute (2014).

Employment

- Women account for 47% of total employment in the United States in 2014.
Source: U.S. Bureau of Labor Statistics (2015).

- Female unemployment rate = 4.2% in May of 2016.
Source: U.S. Bureau of Labor Statistics (2016).

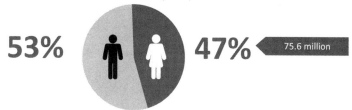

53%   47% ◄ 75.6 million

Labor Force

- 75.6 million: The number of females age 16 and older who participated in the civilian labor force in 2014. Women comprised 47.4% of the civilian labor force in 2014.

Source: U.S. Census Bureau (2015).

Labor Force Participation Rate

57%
Female Labor Force

76.2%
Unmarried mothers
with children under 18

68.4%
Married mothers with
children under 18

- 57% of women were considered to be in the labor force in the United States in 2014.
- Labor rate based on marital status and children.
  - Divorced women = 64.2% in 2014.
  - Married women = 58.4% in 2014.
  - All women with children under 18 = 70.8% in 2014.

Source: U.S. Bureau of Labor Statistics (2015).

Labor Force Participation Among Mothers

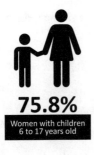

75.8%
Women with children
6 to 17 years old

64.3%
Women with children
under 6 years old

70.8%
Women with children
under 3 years old

- Women with children 6 to 17 years old = 75.8% in 2014.
- Women with children under 6 years old = 64.3% in 2014.
- Women with children under 3 years old = 61.8% in 2014.

- Unmarried mothers with children under 18 = 76.2% in 2014.
- Married mothers with children under 18 = 68.4% in 2014.

Source: U.S. Bureau of Labor Statistics (2015).

Earnings

Median Annual Earnings

Earning Difference

- $39,621: The median annual earnings of women 15 or older who worked year-round, full time in 2014. In comparison, the median annual earnings of men were $50,383. Average weekly earnings of $719 in 2014.
- 79¢ is the amount that female year-round, full-time workers earned in 2014 for every dollar their male counterparts earned.

See Chapter 6 for a discussion of how STEM jobs pay more.

Percentage of Increase

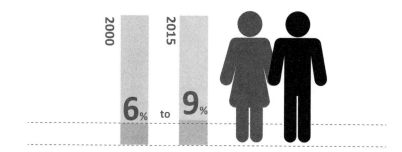

- 3% points of increase — from 6% to 9% — where the wife in married couples earned at least $30,000 more than the husband between 2000 and 2015.

Source: U.S. Census Bureau (2015).

Occupations

Employed Women 16 Years and Older, by Detailed Occupation: 2004 & 2013				
	(Thousands)		(Percent Female)	
Occupation	2004	2013	2004	2013
All occupations	64,728	67,577	46.5	47.0
Management, professional, and related occupations	24,396	28,114	50.3	51.4
Management, business, and financial operations occupations	8,517	9,896	42.1	43.4
Professional and related occupations	15,879	18,218	56.1	57.1
Architect	50	S	24.2	S
Biological and life scientist	122	156	43.3	47.0
Chemist	S	S	S	38.8
Dietitian	75	99	89.3	90.0
Economist and market and survey researcher	69	158	46.3	56.8
Engineering and related technologist or technician	141	96	20.1	17.6
Engineer	186	238	10.2	11.7
Health technologist or technician	1,639	1,971	78.3	77.8
Lawyer or judge	316	388	31.0	33.4
Mathematical or computer scientist	848	1,039	27.0	26.1
Pharmacist	110	155	47.2	56.0
Physician	244	332	29.4	35.5
Physicians' assistant	S	83	S	64.3
Psychologist	124	138	67.0	74.2
Registered nurse	2,271	2,606	92.2	90.1
Science technician	120	119	41.0	44.7
Teacher, except postsecondary (college and university)	4,128	4,524	75.9	76.3

Teacher, postsecondary (college and university)	541	660	46.0	50.3
Therapist	427	567	74.4	74.8
Other healthcare professional	112	277	29.8	50.4
Other natural scientist	66	84	28.4	30.0
Other social scientist or urban planner	S	S	S	S
Other professional or related occupation	4,156	4,392	61.9	62.3
Other occupations	40,332	39,463	44.5	44.2

S = suppressed for data reliability reasons.

Source: U.S.Bureau of Labor Statistics, *Current Population Survey* (2015).

25 Most Common Occupations for Employed Women by Selected Characteristics: (2014 Annual Averages)					
Occupations	Number of Women Employed Full Time (thousands)	Women as a Percentage of Total Employed in the Occupation*	Women's Median Weekly Earnings	Men's Median Weekly Earnings	Women's Earnings as a Percentage of Men's
Total, full-time wage and salary workers	47,076	47%	$719	$871	82.5%
Secretaries and administrative assistants	2,215	94%	685	811	84.5%
Elementary and middle school teachers	2,196	81%	956	1,096	87.2%
Registered nurses	2,064	90%	1,076	1,190	90.4%
Nursing, psychiatric, and home health aides	1,200	89%	466	528	88.3%
First-line supervisors of retail sales workers	1,022	44%	595	793	75.0%
Customer service representatives	1,014	65%	606	698	86.8%

Managers, all other	983	33%	1,153	1,412	81.7%
Cashiers	921	72%	387	412	93.9%
Accountants and auditors	910	63%	999	1,236	80.8%
Receptionists and information clerks	825	91%	532	616	86.4%
First-line supervisors of office and administrative support workers	775	67%	763	919	83.0%
Office clerks, general	753	85%	626	662	94.6%
Bookkeeping, accounting, and auditing clerks	745	90%	660	732	90.2%
Retail salespersons	733	50%	491	698	70.3%
Maids and housekeeping cleaners	685	89%	400	404	99.0%
Financial managers	606	53%	1,127	1,671	67.4%
Social workers	563	82%	839	892	94.1%
Secondary school teachers	549	57%	984	1,108	88.8%
Waiters and waitresses	542	72%	415	501	82.8%
Personal care aides	534	84%	425	465	91.4%
Teacher assistants	492	90%	494	580	85.2%
Preschool and kindergarten teachers	486	97%	625	-	-
Education administrators	451	63%	1,171	1,439	81.4%
Licensed practical and licensed vocational nurses	451	89%	737	868	84.9%
Janitors and building cleaners	438	33%	415	540	76.9%

Source: U.S. Bureau of Labor Statistics (2014).

- Women account for 52% of all workers employed in management, professional, and related occupations in 2014.

Source: U.S. Bureau of Labor Statistics (2015).

- 20% of software developers
- 26% of chief executives
- 33% of lawyers
- 90% of registered nurses
- 81% of elementary and middle school teachers
- 63% of accountants and auditors
- 16% of all the directors, executive producers, producers, writers, cinematographers and editors who worked on the top-grossing 250 domestic films of 2013.
- 28% of all off-screen talent on broadcast television programs during the 2012-2013 primetime season.

Source: Center for American Progress (2014).

Sectors in 2014
- Financial activities = 53%
- Education and health services = 75%
- Leisure and hospitality = 51%
- Agriculture = 25%
- Mining = 13%
- Construction = 9%
- Manufacturing = 29%
- Transportation and utilities = 23%
- Other services = 53%

Source: U.S. Bureau of Labor Statistics (2015).

14% - Percentage of employed women 16 and over in 2014 who worked in management, business, and financial occupations compared with 15.6% of employed men in the same year.

Source: U.S. Census Bureau (2015).

- 26% of employed women usually worked part time in 2014.
- Of all women who worked at some point during 2013, 61% worked full time and year-round in 2014.
- In 2014, 5.3% of employed women held more than one job.
- In 2014, 5.3% of working women in nonagricultural industries were self-employed compared with 7.4% for their male counterparts.
- 5.3% of women held more than one job; men = 4.5% in 2014.
- 40% of self-employed workers were women in 2014.

Source: U.S. Bureau of Labor Statistics (2015).

Motherhood & Marriage

43.5 million
15-50 year old mothers in the United States

67.1 million
married women 18 and older

- 43.5 million: Estimated number of mothers age 15 to 50 in the United States in 2014.
- 2.0: Average number of children that women age 40 to 44 had given birth to as of 2014, down from 3.1 children in 1976.
- The percentage of women in this age group who had ever given birth was 85% in 2014, down from 90% in 1976.

Source: U.S. Census Bureau (2015).

Stay-at-home Parent

199,000 VS. 5.2 million
stay-at-home fathers in the United States stay-at-home mothers in the United States

- 5.2 million: Number of stay-at-home mothers nationwide in 2015, compared with 199,000 stay-at-home fathers.
- 67.1 million: Number of married women 18 and older (including those who were separated or had an absent spouse) in 2015.

Source: U.S. Census Bureau (2015).

Chapter 2: Corporations - Overview

As far as time can dictate, corporations have always been the lifeblood of the marketplace. They leave the greatest impact, and can make the most lasting shifts. If we look at the basic facts of the Fortune 500, we see that women comprise 45% of that workforce. While we're moving up as executive officials in mid-level management, we still only account for 19.9% of board seats within these large organizations. Thus, we should stop and look at this data and the charts that follow to show that the disparity remains unnerving. A 2016 CNN study indicates that women account for only 5% of the chief executive officers (CEOs) leading all S&P 500 companies. While we account for almost half of the entire workforce, we still leave a small imprint on C-suite executive positions.

Throughout this chapter, there are lists provided by Fortune, Forbes, Catalyst, The Center for American Progress, and others that reveal the top women serving large corporations. These are just a snippet of the role models, but we must work to raise many more to these coveted and highly respected positions. As we study the different industries hiring women as their CEOs, it is no surprise the leaders are the consumer product companies and the telecom industry. Why? As we will see in our chapter focused on the marketplace, women not only control the marketplace, but also are the predominant economic spenders.

While we still have work to do to bridge the gap of women in leadership positions, it's exciting to see that female chief financial officer's (CFO's) salaries are growing faster than our male colleagues. The change is dramatic. When we look at female chief technology officers (CTOs) and chief information officers (CIOs) in large corporations, we can pause for a moment and enjoy knowing that of the top 100 companies, 24% of their CEOs are women. Within the Fortune 500, that number lowers to 17.4%, but it is still indicative of progress, especially as technology impacts every company and every consumer across the globe. Women are quickly rising in the technology sector, a topic we will review in greater detail in our chapter on women and technology.

When we begin to look at women as chief marketing officers (CMOs), women comprise nearly 33% of the total market, with 32% of females globally serving as CMOs for their respective corporations. Again, those growing numbers make sense when we consider the skill women bring to the realm of marketing. In terms of chief human resource officers (CHROs), women are enjoying almost a 50% market share. Referencing human resource managers (HRMs), women account for 76% within the United States. Women get it. They understand how to identify and hire talent, and are the trailblazers in this space. As we look at the growth of lawyers and general counsels, we see that the Fortune 500 recognize 21% female general counsels—and that number continues to grow.

But what do these numbers really represent? Looking at the desire for continued advancement, this chapter will show each of you how women care desperately about their progress. Women have a place in the boardroom and the corner offices. They are the leaders, the movers, the shakers, and the C-suite juggernauts. There is no denying the continued influx of women at the top of the corporations which shape our everyday life with their products and services. Women are not only impacting networking and innovation, but also leadership development and mentoring opportunities. They are putting their stamp on talent acquisition, customer relations, and community and corporate brand. Corporations can attribute much of their success to the females both in the trenches and in the C-suites diligently working to build on their own credentials and the victories of their respective organizations.

Call to Action:

- Seek to work at a corporation advancing women in general and minority women. Find one with a culture you love. Educate others about those "good" companies and push the bar even higher where you are. Get the support of male colleagues and leaders.

- Think of the most impactful organizations in your life. Maybe a brand you admire, a service you regularly use, or a product you often buy. Visit their websites and review their C-suite leadership to determine who is running the show.

- Push the envelope for companies to champion more women at the top. For example, accounting firms are now asking that one-third of their partners be women, and they are achieving it. This should be a minimum threshold across the board for all companies. Be a corporate advocate and seek others in the process.

CHAPTER 2: CORPORATIONS

Overall United States
Women in the S&P 500

Source: CNN (2016).
See Chapter 3, Women on Boards.

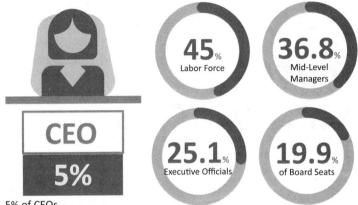

- 5% of CEOs
- 19.9% of Board seats
- 25.1% Executive officials
- 36.8% Mid-level managers
- 45% Labor force

Source: Catalyst (2016) and McKinsey (2015).

The 2016 McKinsey Report will be released Sept. 27, 2016.

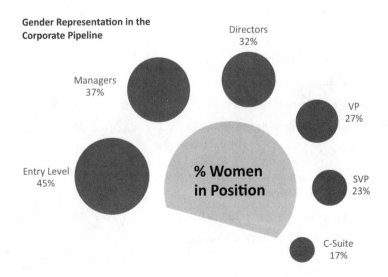

Female CEO at Fortune 1,000 Companies

The visibility of CEOs like IBM's Ginni Rometty, General Motors' Mary Barra and Hewlett Packard's Meg Whitman may give the impression that America's largest companies are finally embracing female leadership. But as a recent Fortune report reveals, that couldn't be further from the truth. Women comprise less than 7 percent of chief executives at Fortune 1000 companies — America's largest corporations based on revenue — according to a recent survey conducted by sales analytics software company DiscoverOrg. "That means that for every [Rometty, Whitman, or Barra], there are a dozen male chief executives," said Fortune. Of the almost 10,000 C-level executives DiscoverOrg surveyed, just 18 percent were women. Only 6.7 percent of all chairs of the board, 7.2 percent of chief operating officers and 8.8 percent of chief financial officers were women. Women are well-represented in two C-level positions, however: They make up almost half of chief marketing officers and more than 60 percent of chief human resources officers, according to the survey.
Source: Discovery and Huffington Post (2016).

Women in the C-Suite

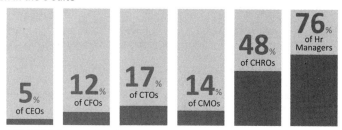

Source: CNN (2016), Fortune (2015), The Suite Magazine (2015), Forbes (2015), Spencer Stuart (2015), and McKinsey (2015).

- 17% of CTOs/CIOs
- 48% of CHROs
- 76% of HR managers

- 5% of CEOs
- 12% of CFOs
- 14% of CMOs/CCOs/CSOs

- In 1980, there were no women in the top executive ranks of the Fortune 100; by 2001, 11% of those corporate leaders were women.
Source: Center for American Progress (2014).

Powerful Women in Corporate World

Fortune 2015 List of the 50 Most Powerful Women

- Mary Barra, 53   CEO, General Motors Co.
- Indra Nooyi, 59   CEO and Chairman, PepsiCo Inc.
- Ginni Rometty, 58   CEO, Chairman, and President, IBM Corp.
- Marillyn Hewson, 61   CEO, Chairman, and President, Lockheed Martin Corp.
- Abigail Johnson, 53   CEO and President, Fidelity Investments

- Meg Whitman, 59   CEO, Chairman, and President, Hewlett-Packard Co.
- Sheryl Sandberg, 46   COO, Facebook
- Irene Rosenfeld, 62   CEO and Chairman, Mondelez International Inc.
- Phebe Novakovic, 57   CEO and Chairman, General Dynamics Corp.
- Carol Meyrowitz, 61   CEO and Chairman, TJX Companies
- Safra Catz, 53   Co-CEO, Oracle Corp.
- Lynn Good, 56   CEO and President, Duke Energy Corp.
- Helena Foulkes, 51   President, CVS/pharmacy; EVP, CVS Health
- Rosalind Brewer, 53   CEO and President, Sam's Club, a division of Wal-Mart
- Angela Ahrendts, 55   SVP, Retail and Online Stores, Apple
- Ursula Burns, 56   CEO and Chairman, Xerox Corp.
- Marissa Mayer, 40   CEO and President, Yahoo Inc.
- Susan Wojcicki, 47   CEO, YouTube, Google
- Pam Nicholson, 55   CEO and President, Enterprise Holdings
- Cathy Engelbert, 50   CEO, Deloitte LLP
- Heather Bresch, 46   CEO, Mylan Inc.
- Debra Reed, 59   CEO and Chairman, Sempra Energy Corp.
- Denise Morrison, 61   CEO and President, Campbell Soup Co.
- Susan Cameron, 56   CEO and President, Reynolds America
- Ruth Porat, 57 SVP   CFO, Google and Alphabet
- Carrie Tolstedt, 55   Senior EVP of Community Banking, Wells Fargo
- Sandra Peterson, 56   Group Worldwide Chairman, Johnson & Johnson
- Mary Erdoes, 48   CEO, JP Morgan Chase Asset Management, JP Morgan Chase & Co.
- Judith McKenna, 49   EVP and COO, Wal-Mart U.S., Wal-Mart
- Marianne Lake, 46   CFO, JP Morgan Chase & Co.
- Kathleen Murphy, 52   President, Personal Investing, Fidelity Investments
- Margaret Keane, 56   CEO and President, Synchrony Financial
- Barbara Rentler, 58   CEO, Ross Stores
- Bridget Van Kralingen, 52 SVP, IBM Global Business Services, IBM
- Carolyn Tastad, 54   Group President, North America, Procter & Gamble
- Ann-Marie Campbell, 50   President, Southern Division, Home Depot
- Michelle Gloeckler, 49   EVP, Consumables and Health and Wellness; U.S. Manufacturing Lead, Wal-Mart
- Shari Ballard, 49   President of U.S. Retail and CHRO, Best Buy
- Crystal Hanlon, 50   President, Northern Division, Home Depot Inc.
- Jane Fraser, 48   CEO of Citigroup Latin America, Citigroup
- Kathleen Kennedy, 62   President, Lucasfilm, Walt Disney Co.
- Diane Bryant, 53   SVP and General Manager, Data Center Group, Intel
- Lynne Doughtie, 52   CEO and Chairman, KPMG U.S.
- Ilene Gordon, 62   CEO, Chairman, and President, Ingredion
- Debra Crew, 44   President and CCO, R.J. Reynolds Tobacco, Reynolds American Inc.
- Kim Lubel, 51   CEO, Chairman, and President, CST Brands
- Beth Mooney, 60   CEO and Chairman, KeyCorp
- Sheri S. McCoy, 56   CEO, Avon Products
- Beth Comstock, 55   Vice Chair, General Electric

Source: Fortune (2015).

- Vicki Hollub became the first female CEO of an oil company (Occidental Petroleum Corp.) in 2016.

Source: Bloomberg (2016).

Women CEOs

 4%
Consumer
Discretionary

 2%
Healthcare

 13%
Consumer
Staples

 3%
Industrials

 0%
Energy

 8%
IT

 4%
Financials

 3%
Materials

Source: CNN (2016).

 17%
Telecom

 7%
Utilities

Today, 21 women are serving as CEOs of Fortune 500 companies (5.2%).
Source: Fortune (2016).

Women CEOs in the S&P 500

- Mary T. Barra, General Motors Co.
- Heather Bresch, Mylan Inc.
- Ursula M. Burns, Xerox Corp.
- Debra A. Cafaro, Ventas Inc.
- Susan M. Cameron, Reynolds American Inc.
- Safra A. Catz, Oracle Corp. (co-CEO)
- Lynn J. Good, Duke Energy Corp.
- Marillyn A. Hewson, Lockheed Martin Corp.
- Vicki Hollub, Occidental Petroleum Corp.
- Lauralee E. Martin, HCP Inc.
- Gracia C. Martore, TEGNA
- Marissa Mayer, Yahoo Inc.
- Beth E. Mooney, KeyCorp
- Denise M. Morrison, Campbell Soup Co.
- Indra K. Nooyi, PepsiCo Inc.
- Phebe N. Novakovic, General Dynamics Corp.
- Debra L. Reed, Sempra Energy Corp.
- Barbara Rentler, Ross Stores Inc.
- Virginia M. Rometty, IBM Corp.
- Irene B. Rosenfeld, Mondelez International Inc.
- Meg Whitman, Hewlett-Packard Co.

Source: Catalyst (2016).

Women CEOs in the Fortune 500

- Mary T. Barra, General Motors Co.
- Meg Whitman, Hewlett-Packard Co.
- Virginia M. Rometty, IBM Corp.
- Indra K. Nooyi, PepsiCo Inc.
- Marillyn A. Hewson, Lockheed Martin Corp.
- Safra A. Catz, Oracle Corp. (co-CEO)
- Irene B. Rosenfeld, Mondelez International Inc.
- Phebe N. Novakovic, General Dynamics Corp.
- Lynn J. Good, Duke Energy Corp.
- Ursula M. Burns, Xerox Corp.
- Deanna M. Mulligan, Guardian Life Insurance of America
- Barbara Rentler, Ross Stores Inc.
- Debra L. Reed, Sempra Energy Corp.
- Kimberly Lubel, CST Brands
- Sherilyn McCoy, Avon
- Susan M. Cameron, Reynolds American Inc.
- Denise M. Morrison, Campbell Soup Co.
- Kathleen M. Mazzarella, Graybar Electric
- Ilene S. Gordon, Ingredion
- Lisa Su, Advanced Micro Devices
- Jacqueline Hinman, CH2M Hill

Source: Fortune (2016).

One-sixth (16.9%) of MSCI USA Index companies had at least one woman serving as CEO or CFO, as of August 15, 2015; at non-U.S. companies, the figure was only 11.4%. *Source:* MSCI USA Index.

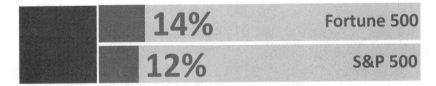

| 14% | Fortune 500 |
| 12% | S&P 500 |

Women CFOs

- Female CFOs' salaries are also growing faster than those of male CFOs; last year, women's earnings increased by 11%, while men's earnings increased by 7%.
- The median pay for these women was $3.32 million last year, while the median pay for male S&P 500 CFOs was $3.3 million.
- About 14% of CFOs in the Fortune 500 were women as of the end of 2015.
  - Up from just over 12% in 2014.
  - More than double the percentage 10 years earlier.

Source: Fortune (2015).

  - Meanwhile, 6% were male or female minorities
  - Up from 4.7% a year earlier and just 3.3% in 2006.

Source: Wall Street Journal (2016).

Top 50 Female CFOs in 2015

1. Pat Yarrington, Chevron Corp.
2. Cathie Lesjak, Hewlett-Packard Co.
3. Marianne Lake, JPMorgan Chase & Co.
4. Amy Hood, Microsoft Corp.
5. Carol Tomé, Home Depot Inc.
6. Ruth Porat, Google and Alphabet
7. Kelly Kramer, Cisco Systems Inc.
8. Kathy Waller, The Coca-Cola Co.
9. Sharon McCollam, Best Buy
10. Gina Wilson, TIAA-CREF
11. Karen Hoguet, Macy's
12. Carol Roberts, International Paper Co.
13. Robin Washington, Gilead Sciences Inc.
14. Kimberly Ross, Baker Hughes Inc.
15. Laura Bishop, United Services Automobile Association
16. Christine Komola, Staples Inc.
17. Kathleen Quirk, Freeport-McMoRan Inc.
18. Kathryn Mikells, Xerox Corp.
19. Cheryl Miller, AutoNation Inc.
20. Beth Bombara, Hartford Financial Services Group Inc.
21. Tammy Romo, Southwest Airlines Co.
22. Laura Thompson, The Goodyear Tire & Rubber Co.
23. Daphne Foster, Global Partners LP
24. Sabrina Simmons, The Gap Inc.
25. Kimberly Allen Dang, Kinder Morgan Inc.
26. Carol Yancey, Genuine Parts Co.
27. Mindy West, Murphy USA Inc.
28. Glenda Flanagan, Whole Foods Market Inc.
29. Teresa Gendron, Leucadia National Corp.
30. Ann Ziegler, CDW Corp.
31. Teresa Madden, Xcel Energy Inc.
32. Marta Stewart, Norfolk Southern Corp.
33. Susan Lattmann, Bed, Bath & Beyond Inc.
34. Tracey Thomas Travis, The Estée Lauder Companies
35. Caroline Dorsa, Public Service Enterprise Group Inc.
36. Karla Lewis, Reliance Steel & Aluminum Co.
37. Karen McLoughlin, Cognizant Technology Solutions Corp.
38. Shawn Hagel, Precision Castparts Corp.
39. Martina Hund-Mejean, MasterCard Inc.
40. Jody Feragen, Hormel Foods Corp.
41. Theresa Wagler, Steel Dynamics Inc.
42. Stacy Loretz-Congdon, Core-Mark Holding Co.
43. Patty Bedient, Weyerhaeuser Co.
44. Maryann Seaman, FMC Technologies Inc.
45. Carol Lowe, Sealed Air Corp.
46. Laurie Brlas, Newmont Mining Corp.
47. Lauren B. Peters, Foot Locker Inc.
48. Barbara Smith, Commercial Metals Co.
49. Barbara Niland, Huntington Ingalls Industries Inc.
50. Kathy Willard, Live Nation Entertainment Inc.
Source: Business Insider (2015).

Women CTOs & CIOs

17%
of CIOs are women

17.4%
of CIOs are women

24%
of CIOs are women

- As of November 2015, 17% of CIOs of S&P 500 companies were women. *Source:* Forbes (2015).

- 17.4% of Fortune 500 CIOs are women.
- 24% of the top 100 companies have female CIOs.
- 25% of the technology industry's workforce is composed of women.
Source: Boardroom Insider (2016).

Women CIO Globally

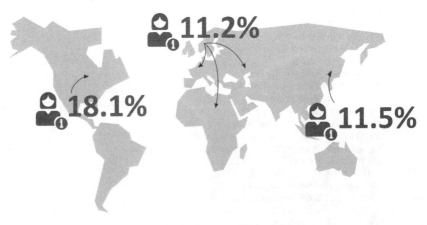

For more information on women in technology, see Chapter 7.

- 14% of CTOs worldwide are women. (This number has stayed static for the past decade.)
- North America has women making up 18.1% of CIOs.
- Women make up only 11.5% of CIOs in Asia.
- 11.2% in Europe, Africa, and the Middle East.
Source: BizWomen (2014).

Five of the Top 10 Companies on the Fortune 500 List Have Female CIOs
- Wal-Mart
- ExxonMobil
- Ford Motor
- GE
- Valero Energy

Source: Boardroom Insider (2016).

12 Female CTOs to Watch in 2016
- Camille Fournier, Rent the Runway
- Elissa Murphy, GoDaddy
- Gerri Martin-Flickinger, Starbucks
- Selina Tobaccowala, SurveyMonkey
- Megan Smith, United States
- Rebecca Parsons, ThoughtWorks
- Susie Wee, Cisco
- Raji Arasu, StubHub
- Kimber Lockhart, One Medical Group
- Bridget Frey, Redfin
- Farnaz Ronaghi, NovoEd
- Santhi Analytis, Moxxly

Source: Women 2.0 (2016).

Top Female CIO/CTO Leaders in STEM
- Janne Sigurdsson, CIO, Alcoa
- Mary Heger, VP & CIO, Ameren Corp.
- Pam Parisian, CIO, AT&T
- Archie Deskus, VP & CIO, Baker Hughes
- Angela Yochem, Global CIO, BDP International
- Kim Barrier, CIO, Bio-Rad Laboratories Inc.
- Tanya Arthur, Associate CIO & VP of Strategy & Business Operations, Catholic Health Initiatives
- Kathleen Brandt, President & CIO, CSX Technology
- Jan Marshall, VP & CIO, Cubic Corp.
- Paula Tolliver, CIO & Corporate VP of Business Services, The Dow Chemical Co.
- Kim VanGelder, CIO, Eastman Kodak
- Ina Kamenz, SVP & CIO, Ebay Inc.
- Rhonda Vetere, CTO, Estée Lauder Companies
- Maureen Osborne, Global CIO, EY
- Marcy Klevord, VP & CIO, Ford Motor Co.
- Patty Hatter, VP & General Manager of Intel Security and Softward Group IT & CIO of Intel Security Group; Intel Corp.
- Kim Stevenson, Corporate VP & CIO, Intel Corp.
- Cara Carbody, SVP of Information Technology, Jacobs
- Kathy McElligott, Executive VP, CIO, and CTO, McKesson Corp.
- Cynthia Stoddard, SVP & CTO of Customer Solutions, NetApp
- Kathy Fish, CTO, Procter & Gamble
- Jane Wachutka, EVP & CTO, Qualcomm Inc.
- Robin Beinfait, Chief Enterprise Innovation Officer, Samsung
- Shelia Jordan, SVP & CIO, Symantec
- Nicola Palmer, SVP & Chief Network Officer, Verizon Wireless
- Sophie Vandebroek, CTO & President of Xerox Innovation Group, Xerox Corp.

Source: STEMconnector's 100 CIO/CTO Leaders in STEM (2015).

Women CMO/CSO/CCOs

- 14% of CCOs are women domestically.

Source: The Suit Magazine (2015).

Women CMO/CSO/CCOs

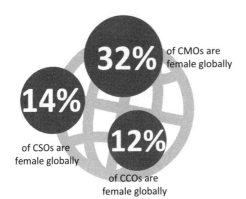

32% of CMOs are female globally

14% of CSOs are female globally

12% of CCOs are female globally

CMO - Chief Marketing Officer; CSO - Chief Sales Officer; CCO - Chief Commercial Officer

Top Three Most Successful Female CMOs

- Karen Walker, SVP & CMO, Cisco
- Beth Comstock, Former CMO & Vice Chair of Business Innovations, GE
- Anne Finucane, Vice Chairman & Global Chief Strategy and Marketing Officer, Bank of America

Source: Business Insider (2016).

Top 10 Most Influential CMOs Who Are Mothers

- Meagen Eisenberg, MongoDB
- Marisa Thalberg, TacoBell
- Kristin Lemkau, JPMorgan Chase & Co.
- Heather Deason Zynczack, DOMO
- Shannon Duffy, VP Marketing, Pardot, Salesforce
- Lauren Crampsie, Ogilvy & Mather Worldwide
- Lauren Wagner Boyman, Morgan Stanley
- Morgan Flatley, Gatorade & Propel, PepsiCo Inc.
- Gail Galuppo, Aflac
- Ann Simonds, General Mills

Source: Traackr (2016).

Women CHROs

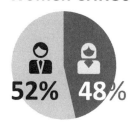

52% **48%**

76%
HR managers in the U.S. are women

Source: Bureau of Labor Statistics (2015)

- 48% of CHROs in the Fortune 250 are women.
Source: Spencer Stuart (2015).
- 76% of HR managers in the United States are women.
Source: Bureau of Labor Statistics (2015).
- Women held 30% of federal government HR jobs in 1969.
- By 1988, that number had more than doubled to 71%.
Source: Human Resource Executive (2012).

Women General Counsels

From the Fortune 1000 by Gender

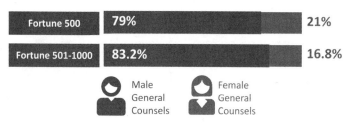

| Fortune 500 | 79% | 21% |
| Fortune 501-1000 | 83.2% | 16.8% |

Male General Counsels
Female General Counsels

There are 79% male and 21% female general counsels in the Fortune 500 and 83.2% male and 16.8% female general counsels in the Fortune 1000.
Source: American Bar Association (2014).

General Counsels in the Fortune 1000 by Race

	Caucasian	African American	Hispanic	Asian / Islander	Middle Eastern
Fortune 500	81.9%	10.5%	5.7%	1.9%	0%
Fortune 501-1000	91.7%	7.1%	1.2%	0%	0%

Source: American Bar Association (2014).

Women Stay Longer

- With the exception of director positions, men are more likely to leave their position when compared to women.
- In the C-suite, men are almost twice as likely than women to leave their position.

Source: McKinsey (2015).

Desire for Advancement

Gender Representation in the Corporate Pipeline

Gender & Pipeline	Entry Level	Manager	Director	VP	SVP	C-Suite
Leave Rate (Men)	11.5%	9.5%	8.6%	9.5%	11.1%	8.7%
Leave Rate (Women)	10.9%	8.9%	9.2%	9.1%	8.9%	4.5%
Advancement Rate (Compared to Men)	82%	79%	85%	86%	93%	N/A
Women's Desire to Be Top Level	39%	53%	53%	72%	72%	N/A
Men's Desire to Be Top Level	47%	63%	63%	72%	72%	N/A

Source: McKinsey (2015).

Reasons for Not Wanting to Be a Top-Level Executive

	Men + Child	Women + Child	Men w/o Child	Woman w/o Child
Stress of Role	58%	58%	49%	55%
Family Balance	62%	65%	42%	35%
Not Interested	48%	38%	54%	46%
Unsure Success	23%	19%	24%	19%
No Support	12%	11%	12%	10%

- Black, Hispanic, and Asian women are 43% more interested in becoming a top executive than white women and 16% more interested than white men.

Source: McKinsey (2015).

Impact of Gender on Advancement

Impact of Gender on Opportunities & Advancement

Women Have Opportunities Compared to Men	More	The Same	Fewer
Men's Responses	16%	72%	12%
Women's Responses	2%	55%	43%

Source: McKinsey (2015).

Is Gender Inhibiting Your Success?

% Who Responded Yes	Men	Women	Men (Future)	Women (Future)
Entry Level	9%	23%	13%	28%
Middle Management	10%	31%	15%	36%
Senior Management	11%	40%	15%	36%

- 28% of senior-level women are very happy with their careers, compared with 40% of senior-level men.

Source: McKinsey (2015).

Is Gender Diversity a Priority? - 74% of Companies Respond "Yes"

	Men	Women
Believe CEO Is Committed to Gender Diversity	49%	37%
Believe Direct Manager Is Committed to Gender Diversity	35%	31%

- 1 in 9 men believe that women have fewer opportunities than men.
- 13% of men believe it is harder for men to advance because of gender-diversity programs.
- 70% of men think gender diversity is important, but only 12% believe women have fewer opportunities.
- 40% of companies hold managers accountable for performance on gender-diversity metrics.

Source: McKinsey (2015).

Pay Gap in the Russell 3000

Median Compensation	Men	Women	Women % of Men's Comp.
All Top Compensated Executives	1.5M	1.1M	70%
Non-CEO Top Compensated Executives	1.2M	0.96M	79%

Source: ION (2014).
See Chapter 4 for more information.

Manufacturing

Total Employed in Thousands	Women	Black/African American	Asian	Hispanic/Latino
15,338	29.1%	9.7%	6.6%	16.2%

Source: Bureau of Labor Statistics (2015).

Which Industries Are Most Attractive to Women in Manufacturing?

82% Life Sciences	**72%** Technology, Media, and Telecommunications	**69%** Energy	**28%** Industrial products	**26%** Automotive	**19%** Process

- 82% - Life sciences
- 72% - Technology, media, and telecommunications
- 69% - Energy
- 28% - Industrial products
- 26% - Automotive
- 19% - Process (i.e., chemicals)

Manufacturing Pipeline

- 12% of respondents believe the K-12 educational system actively encourages female students to pursue careers in manufacturing.
- 35% say it does not encourage or discourage.
- 53% believe it does not encourage females.

What Do Women in Manufacturing Say About Organizational Diversity?

- 1% Overrepresented
- 26% Sufficiently represented
- 73% Underrepresented

Compared to Other Sectors, Respondents Cite the Following Factors as Contributors to Underrepresentation of Women in Manufacturing

- 74% - Industry bias toward men for leadership positions
- 53% - Organizational cultural norms
- 47% - Lack of mentorship
- 46% - Perception of manufacturing overall

Source: Deloitte (2015).

Woman in Retail

- Women represent more than half of the retail workforce.
  - Women represent 18% of the retail industry's executive officers.
  - And less than 2% of its CEOs.

Source: Network of Executive Women (2013).

- Women and men are nearly equally represented in the retail sector, with women slightly more represented in retail than in the workforce as a whole.

Source: Workforce Strategies Initiative at the Aspen Institute (2012).

Latinos and African Americans

- In 2011, almost 11% of workers in retail were African American, 5% were Asian, and 15% were Hispanic/Latino.
- However, both women and minorities are underrepresented in higher paying retail management positions with women also overrepresented in lower paying front-line jobs.

Source: Workforce Strategies Initiative at the Aspen Institute (2012).

- Like the overall retail workforce, the vast majority of black retail workers are adults. More than half have some education after high school, and about one-third are working parents.
- Black and Latino retail workers are more likely to be working poor, with 17% of black and 13% of Latino retail workers living below the poverty line, compared to 9% of the retail workforce overall.
- Black and Latino retail workers are underrepresented in supervisory positions like managers or first-line supervisors. Black workers make up 11% of the retail labor force but just 6% of managers.
- Black and Latino retail sales workers are overrepresented in cashier positions, the lowest paid position in retail.
- Retail employers pay black and Latino full-time retail salespersons just 75% of the wages of their white peers, amounting to losses up to $7,500 per year.

41

- Retail employers pay black and Latino full-time cashiers about 90% of the wages of their white peers, amounting to $1,850 in losses per year.
- Retail employers pay 70% of black and Latino full and part-time retail sales workers less than $15 per hour, compared to 58% of white retail workers.
- Black and Latino retail workers are more likely to be employed part time despite wanting full-time work. One in five black retail workers are employed involuntarily part time, compared to less than 1 in 7 white workers.

Source: Demos (2015).

Best Companies for Women

Top Companies for Executive Women 2016

- Abbott
- Accenture
- Aetna
- Allstate Insurance
- American Express
- Aon
- AstraZeneca
- AT&T
- Avon Products
- Bank of America
- BDO USA
- Boehringer Ingelheim USA
- Bristol-Myers Squibb
- CA Technologies
- Capital One Financial
- Cardinal Health
- Cisco
- Citi
- Colgate-Palmolive
- Diageo North America
- DuPont
- Edelman
- Eli Lilly and Co.
- EY
- First Horizon National
- FleishmanHillard
- Freddie Mac
- General Mills
- General Motors
- Grant Thornton
- IBM
- Intel
- JLL
- Johnson & Johnson
- Kellogg
- KPMG
- Marriott
- International MassMutual Financial Group
- MasterCard
- McKinsey & Co.
- MetLife
- Moss
- Adams
- New York Life Insurance
- Northern Trust
- Pillsbury Winthrop Shaw Pittman
- PNC Financial Services Group
- Principal Financial Group
- Procter & Gamble
- Prudential Financial
- PwC
- Sodexo
- State Farm
- Target
- Texas Instruments
- The Advisory Board Co.
- Verizon
- Viacom
- Wal-Mart
- Zurich North America

Top Nonprofit Companies for Executive Women 2016

Source: National Association for Female Executives (2016).

- Bon Secours Virginia
- Children's Healthcare of Atlanta
- March of Dimes Foundation
- Mercy Health System
- Northwestern Memorial HealthCare
- Scripps Health
- TIAA
- TriHealth
- WellStar Health System
- Yale-New Haven Hospital

Top 10 Best Companies for Working Mothers 2015

Source: CNN (2015).

- Abbott
- Deloitte
- EY
- General Mills
- IBM
- KPMG
- McKinsey & Co.
- PwC
- WellStar Health System
- Zoetis

Best Companies for Multicultural Women 2016

Source: Working Mother (2016).

- Accenture
- ADP
- Allstate Insurance
- American Express
- Bon Secours Health System
- CA Technologies
- Cisco
- Citi
- Colgate-Palmolive
- Deloitte
- General Mills
- General Motors Co.
- Horizon Blue Cross Blue Shield of New Jersey
- IBM
- JPMorgan Chase & Co.
- KPMG
- Morgan Stanley
- New York Life Insurance
- Procter & Gamble
- Prudential Financial
- PwC
- Sodexo
- State Farm
- Verizon
- WalMart Stores

DiversityInc.'s Top 50 Best Companies for Diversity

Source: DiversityInc. (2016).

1. Kaiser Permanente
2. Novartis Pharmaceuticals Corp.
3. EY
4. AT&T
5. PricewaterhouseCoopers
6. Sodexo
7. MasterCard
8. Johnson & Johnson
9. Marriott International
10. Prudential Financial
11. Deloitte
12. Wells Fargo
13. Procter & Gamble
14. Abbott
15. Accenture
16. KPMG
17. Merck & Co.
18. Cox Communications
19. Cummins
20. IBM
21. ADP
22. Target
23. New York Life
24. BASF
25. Anthem
26. Eli Lilly and Co.
27. Wyndham Worldwide
28. Dell
29. Comcast NBC Universal
30. Kellogg Co.
31. Northrop Grumman
32. Aetna
33. TIAA
34. Toyota Motor North America
35. Allstate Insurance Co.
36. Colgate-Palmolive
37. Time Warner
38. Walt Disney Co.
39. TD Bank
40. General Mills
41. Nielsen
42. Hilton Worldwide
43. Monsanto
44. KeyCorp
45. AbbVie
46. Southern Co.
47. MassMutual Financial Group
48. General Motors Co.
49. Genentech
50. Medtronic

LATINA*Style* 50's Top 12 Companies 2015

- Comcast NBC Universal
- AT&T
- Marriott International, LLC
- Accenture
- Prudential Financial
- Johnson & Johnson

- Sodexo USA
- Wells Fargo and Co.
- FCA US LLC
- United Technologies Corp.
- Pepsico Inc.
- General Motors Co.

Source: LATINAStyle 50 (2015).

Corporate Women's Affinity/ Network Groups

Women's Internal Networks (WINs).

- 90% of Fortune 500 companies have employee resource groups.

Source: Jennifer Brown Consulting (2015).

The Financial Women's Association survey of corporate women in the financial industry found that

- 66% of respondents have a Women's Internal Network (WIN) in their firm.

- 67% of which have joined their WIN.

- 77% of respondents at firms without a WIN would join if their organizations had one.

- 39% of respondents believe these groups could contribute to their reasons for staying with their current firm.

- Millennials and newer employees who have worked in their firm for only a few years (up to 4) are more likely to say that their WIN contributes to their reasons for staying at their firms.
    - Meaning, the presence of women's groups contributes to employee retainment.
    - 41% of women said time was a reason for not participating.

- "The schedules are during family time," noted one respondent.

- 39% of respondents agree that men should join a WIN.

- The key reason cited was to increase men's understanding of women's needs for advancement and avoid segregation of female employees.

Source: Financial Women's Association (2015).

Top 10 Companies for Employee Resource Groups

1. Merck & Co.
2. EY
3. PricewaterhouseCoopers
4. Dell
5. KPMG
6. AT&T
7. Novartis Pharmaceuticals Corp.
8. Kellogg Co.
9. MasterCard
10. Caterpillar

Source: DiversityInc. (2015).

Benefits of Employee Resource Groups

- **Connections and Networking** offered with "like others", with employees at all levels, and with leaders and decision makers.

- **Innovation** promoted by creating opportunities for diverse and culturally sensitive ideas to develop, and informed decision making with input from employees knowledgeable about specific demographics or populations.

- **Leadership Development and Career Promotion Opportunities** provided for employees at all levels.

- **Mentoring Opportunities** given from the top-down and bottom-up (e.g., younger employees mentoring senior leaders on social media).

- **Talent Acquisition, Talent Management, and Recruitment** efforts expanded to include a diverse employee base through the connections and networks of employee resource group members.

- **Professional and Personal Development Opportunities** surface through involvement with and visibility within employee resource groups.

- **Engagement, Commitment, Retention, and Job Satisfaction** strengthened by offering employees a voice in decision making as a direct contributor to the business outcomes of the organization.

- **Culture of Diversity and Inclusion** achieved from the work of individual employee resource groups and the synergy of employee resource groups working together.

- **Culturally Sensitive Marketing and Product Development** created with input from employees with expertise in specific demographics or regions.

- **Customer Retention** boosted from hiring diverse employees who create culturally sensitive marketing and products.

- **Community Brand** enhanced by increasing visibility in the community as a diverse and inclusive employer represented by employees who work to benefit the   community.

Source: Boston College (2015).

Minorities

Hispanics
- 68% have seen their Hispanic employee resource groups grow in the past two years.
- 79% expect their Hispanic employee resource groups to grow larger in the next two years.
- Over 95% of Hispanic employee resource groups indicated that top Hispanic executives at their companies are engaged with the Hispanic employee resource groups.
- 74% identified that these top Hispanic executives serve as mentors to Hispanic employee resource group leaders.

Source: Hispanic Association of Corporate Responsibility (2013).

Employees Who Feel the Need to Cover at Least Some Aspect of Their Identity in the Workplace in Order to Retain Employment or Advance in Their Careers
- 94% of African Americans
- 91% of lesbian, gay, and bisexual individuals
- 66% of women
- 45% of white men also cited the compulsion to cover along at least one of the axes.
- Employee resource groups can help to ease these concerns by providing a group where individuals are among their peers.

Source: Jennifer Brown Consulting (2015).

How to Start an Employee Resource Group
- **Formalize:** Create a document that details the role of employee resource groups in your organization and how they can impact recruitment/retention, organizational culture, and business outcomes. Define a structure for the organization as well.
- **Make the Business Case:** Describe and articulate the value proposition/business case of your organization's employee resource group. Define your group's mission and goals.
- **Customize:** Start with the employee resource groups that align with your business needs.
- **Get Members:** Recruit employees from various areas of the organization and articulate the benefits of participating (interacting with employees from all levels within the organization, leadership opportunities, mentoring possibilities).
- **Develop Leadership:** Determine how you will recruit executive sponsors and provide mentoring/leadership opportunities.
- **Communicate:** Determine how the voices/data from the employee resource groups will be shared with executives/leaders and other members of the organization to provide diverse and informed opinions that can drive business decisions.
- **Assess Outcomes:** Figure out how you will measure success.

Source: Boston College (2015).

Chapter 3: Boards - Overview

As we dive even deeper into corporate America and the S&P 500, the numbers quickly demonstrate the reality: although there is a plethora of talented women, why are there not more serving on corporate boards? Where is the parity? Women hold 19.9% of the S&P board seats. Compare that to the current market rate of 26.9% of new directorships in those companies choosing to select women onto their boards. Yet, if we look back just 10 years ago, the growth rate has been just an unremarkable 7%. Even worse, women of color are not moving up quickly enough as board directors. Diverse women hold only 3.1% of board seats amongst the Fortune 500 companies. This is not only concerning, it is sad. As much as we have developed and evolved as a society, the statistics still show us our work is just beginning. If balance is the goal, we are a long way from our destination.

We have a tremendous journey ahead, especially when black women account for only 1.9% and Latinos just over 1% of the S&P 500 board seats. From a pure business perspective, we see that diverse boards add enormous value and bring better stock prices to their organizations. Globally, the good news is we've seen the European horizon recognizing the changing trends, and celebrating them by mandating for progressive balance. Sweden enjoys 33.7% of women residing in their board seats. France is about the same, at 33.5%. But even then, we are still outweighed by almost three to one. To that end, we pose the question: should board seats have quotas? In the United States, we're allowing the market to dictate the times, while also allowing the market performance to influence our roles on corporate boards. That attitude is consistent with a free market, but it takes time.

This chapter shows numerous examples of groups advocating for and advancing women on their boards. Their services are specific in drawing up slates of women and proposing them for boards of directors. The progressive companies are moving toward diversity as an accurate representation of the society they serve. Leadership amongst boards and board committees is being impacted in a major way. Today, 14.5% of board governance committees are held by women, 14% of nominating chairs are by women, and audit committees include women at the rate of 12.5%.

These are powerful positions. The numbers might seem miniscule related to the opposite gender, but the rates are constantly improving and moving in the right direction. In fact, studies show that companies with three or more female corporate directors significantly outperform those with a lower representation of females leading the charge. The numbers don't lie, and it should be noted that you can actually improve the bottom line of your business by simply celebrating diversity. We embrace the evolution, and recognize that changing data will make a difference to create good governance and positive stock price returns over the long haul. To continue to promote diversity amongst boards, we suggest you:

Call to Action:

- Support companies and organizations with strong corporate board female leadership, and do all you can to increase the numbers so that these corporate boards reflect a 25 to 30% women representation.

- Align yourself and support organizations like Women in the Boardroom, 2020 Women on Boards, Corporate Women Directions International, Boardroom Bound, Catalyst, and the National Association of Corporate Directions to continue the goal of emerging with a more balanced and diverse board.

- Share the information with your peers and galvanize those who can serve on boards. Advance others and build your own case for board membership within your organization.

CHAPTER 3: BOARDS

Statistical Overview

Boards Seats

As of 2016, 19.9% of the S&P 500 board seats were held by women. *Source:* Catalyst (2016).

S&P 500 Board Seats

19.9%
of S&P500 board seats were held by women

Boards Seat in S&P 500

8 Firms
in the S&P500 have no women on their board

3.4%
of board chairs are female

25%
of firms in the S&P500 have one female board member

S&P 500

17.9%
of Fortune 1000 board seats are held by women

- 14% of boards have 30% women or more.
- 25% of firms in the S&P 500 have one female board member.
- There are 8 firms in the S&P 500 with no women on their board.
Source: Catalyst (2015).

- 3.4% of board chairs are female.
Source: Deloitte (2015).

- 17.9% of Fortune 1000 board seats are held by women.
- 26.9% of new directorships at S&P 500 companies are women.
- *Source:* 2020 Women on Boards (2016).

26.9%
of new directorships at S&P 500 companies are elected to women

Top Five Industries for Female Board Representations

 16%
Consumer Businesses

 11%
Energy and Resources

12%
Life Services
and Healthcare

11%
Technology, Media,
and Communications

 12%
Financial Services

Top Five Industries

- Consumer Businesses - 16% of board seats are held by women.
- Life Services and Healthcare - 12% of board seats are held by women.
- Financial Services - 12% of board seats are held by women.
- Energy and Resources - 11% of board seats are held by women.
- Technology, Media, and Communications - 11% of board seats are held by women.

Source: Deloitte (2015).

Board Seat Increase

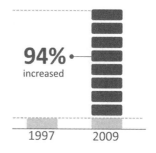

94%
increased

1997   2009

Committees

Female Committees Representations

14.8%	15.1%	14.8%	13.8%
Board Seats	Board Seats	Board Seats	Board Seats
Audit	**Governance**	**Nominating**	**Compensation**
Chairs	Chairs	Chairs	Chairs
12.5%	14.5%	14%	10.9%

- Audit - 14.8% of board seats; 12.5% of chairs.
- Governance - 15.1% of board seats; 14.5% of chairs.
- Nominating - 14.8% of board seats; 14% of chairs.
- Compensation - 13.8% of board seats; 10.9% of chairs.

Source: Deloitte (2015).

- From 1997 to 2009, women's share of board seats in S&P 500 companies increased by 94%.
- The percentage of women on all U.S. corporate boards has been stuck in the 12.1% to 12.3% range over the past decade.

Source: Center for American Progress (2014).

Women on Corporate Boards

**12.1%
to
12.3%**

In the past year has your board had conversations about the following types of board diversity?

Women of Color

Diverse Women on Boards

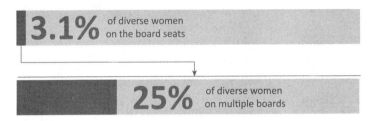

3.1% of diverse women on the board seats

25% of diverse women on multiple boards

Diverse Women as Board Directors

- Diverse women hold 3.1% of the board seats at Fortune 500 companies.
  - 25% of diverse women who serve on a board, serve on multiple boards (Twice as likely as white women.)
- More than two-thirds of Fortune 500 companies have no women of color as board members.
Source: Catalyst (2015).

2.2% of Fortune 100 seats

1.9% of Fortune 500 board seats

Black Women

- Currently, black women hold 1.9% of Fortune 500 board seats.
  - And 2.2% of Fortune 100 board seats.
Source: Executive Leadership Council (2016).

- As of 2013, Latinas hold less than 1% of Fortune 500 board seats.
Source: Hispanic Association on Corporate Responsibility (2013).

Return on Investment

- 25% is the average return on equity for companies with a diverse (ethnicity and gender) corporate board, compared to only 9% for a uniform board.
Source: EY (2013).

- Companies with three or more female corporate directors significantly outperformed those with lower representation of female corporate directors by
  - 84% on return on sales;
  - 60% on return on invested capital; and
  - 46% on return on equity.
- Companies ranked in the highest quartile of those with female directors outperformed those with the least by
  - 16% on return on sales; and
  - 26% return on invested capital.

- Companies in which women comprise more than 30% of the board seats fare better in periods of greater economic volatility than companies where women hold less than 10%.

Source: Glenmede, Nancy Carter, Mary Curtis (Catalyst 2016).

Glenmede Investment Managment has its women in leadership fund.

Glenmede Paper adding value with a gender investment lens.

Globally

Women Board members

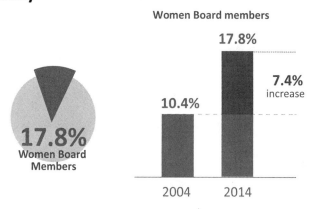

17.8%

10.4%

17.8%
Women Board Members

7.4%
increase

2004   2014

On average, 18% of board members are women:
- From 2004 – 2014, the percentage of women board members has increased by 7.4%.
  - From 10.4% in 2004 to 17.8% in 2014.
  - Equating to an increase of less than 1% annually.
- 7% are ethnic minorities and 13% have been appointed in the past 12 months.

Source: Women Corporate Directors (2016).

Emerging Markets   **Women Board Seats**

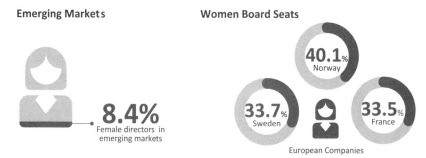

8.4%
Female directors in emerging markets

40.1%
Norway

33.7%
Sweden

33.5%
France

European Companies

- Female directors comprised 8.4% of board seats in companies in emerging markets (up from 7.1% in 2014).
- Norway (40.1%), Sweden (33.7%), and France (33.5%) have the highest percentage of board seats filled by women.

Global Boards

- 73.5% of boards globally have at least one female director.
  - 20.1% have boards with three or more women.
- Companies that had strong female leadership generated a return on equity of

Appointing Women to Board Seats

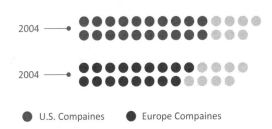

2004 ⟶

2004 ⟶

● U.S. Compaines   ● Europe Compaines

10.1% per year versus 7.4% for those without (on an equal-weighted basis).
Source: MSCI (2015).

The United States has lost its lead in appointing women on boards to Europe:
- In 2004, 20 of 27 best performing companies were U.S.-based.
- In 2014, 17 of 25 companies with the best percentages of women directors are based in Europe.
- With U.S. companies reduced to only 7 in the top 10 listing.
Source: Women Corporate Directors (2016).

From 2004-2014, these countries posted the lowest rates of increase in the percentage of women directors:

Global Women Directors' Rate of Increase

- China at 3.6%.
- Japan at 4.5%.
- United States at 4.9%.
- European countries' rates of increase averaged 16%.
- Italy posting the highest rate of change at 24%.
Source: Corporate Women Directors International (2015).

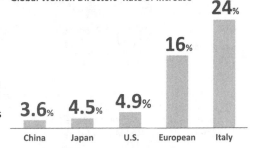

The majority of companies with all-male boards are based primarily in the Asia-Pacific region:
- 16 of China's 28 largest companies in the Fortune Global 200 do not have a single woman director.
- Japan and South Korea still have minimal women's presence on their boards, despite some recent improvements.

Source: Corporate Women Directors International (2015).

Latin America's Board Room

Women remain locked out of the board rooms of Latin America's largest companies:
- Men hold 93.6% of board seats at the 100 largest companies in the region, leaving women only 6.4% of board seats.

Source: Corporate Women Directors International (2015).

6.4%
of women on board seats

Women Board Representation by Region

- Europe - 5%
- Middle East and Africa - 5%
- Americas - 4%
- Asia-Pacific - 4%

Source: Deloitte (2015).

Europe	**5%**
Middle East and Africa	**5%**
Americas	**4%**
Asia-Pacific	**4%**

Global Representation by Industry

Female representation is highest (20% or more) in the following industries:
- Consumer staples.
- Financial services/professional services.
- Consumer discretionary sectors.

Representation is lowest in IT/telecom (13%).

Source: MSCI (2015).

Top 4 Global Industries for Female Board Representation

≥20%   **13%**

Consumer staples   Financial services/   Consumer   IT/telecom
                professional services   discretionary sectors

Source: Corporate Women Directors International (2015).

Strategies to Increase Women's Representation

Quotas

Some countries, such as Germany and Norway, among several other countries, have government quotas to increase the percentage of women on boards.
- For example: Germany requires that 30% of board seats at certain public companies be allocated for women.
- Norway requires that 40% be allocated for women.

Source: Government Accountability Office (2015).

- Since 2004, the number of countries with legislative quotas for publicly listed or state-owned companies has increased from 7 to 24 in 2014.
- During the same time period, the number of countries, which have amended their corporate governance codes requiring or recommending board or gender diversity on boards, has increased from 4 to 26.

Source: Corporate Women Directors International (2015).

- Fortune Global 200 companies based in countries with quotas averaged 25.3% women's representation on boards.
  - Compared to 15.6% in countries without quotas.
- In 2014, the top three countries with the highest percentage of women board directors all have legislative quotas.
  - France has 30.2%; up from 7.2% in 2004.
  - Italy has 25.8%; up from 1.9% in 2004.
  - Netherlands has 23.6%; up from 8.6% in 2004.

Source: Corporate Women Directors International (2015).

Disclosure Policies

Other countries, such as Australia and Canada, have adopted "comply or explain" disclosure arrangements. Under such arrangements, if companies choose not to implement or comply with certain recommendations or government-suggested approaches related to board diversity—such as establishing a diversity policy—they must disclose and explain why.

Source: Government Accountability Office (2015).

Voluntary Approaches

The United Kingdom has aimed to increase the representation of female directors through a voluntary, target-based approach rather than through the use of government-mandated interventions. The government worked with leading companies, investors, and search firms to encourage the adoption of a set of recommendations to increase representation of women on boards.

These recommendations included that certain companies:
- Achieve a minimum of 25% women on boards by 2015.
- Publicly disclose the proportion of women on the company's board, management, and workforce.

Executive search firms were, additionally, encouraged to create a voluntary code to

address gender diversity and best practices covering relevant search criteria for board directors, including trying to ensure that at least 30% of proposed candidates are women.
Source: Government Accountability Office (2015).

Groups Advocating for Women on Boards

Boardroom Bound

Boardology™ is the art and science of quality corporate governance, which means that board directors focus on balancing the profit factor by considering the environment and corporate social responsibility impact into policy decisions. Boardroom Bound's Mission of "fostering quality governance through inclusive leadership in America's boardrooms" predates the U.S. Securities and Exchange Commission's (SEC's) effort to address the ways board directors are identified and selected in 2009. Today, the SEC requires publicly traded companies to report on their board diversity policies in their annual proxy statements.
Source: Boardroom Bound (2016).

Catalyst

Catalyst is the leading nonprofit organization with a mission to accelerate progress for women through workplace inclusion. Catalyst is dedicated to creating workplaces where employees representing every dimension of diversity can thrive. Its studies and services are significant.

2020 Women on Boards

A national campaign dedicated to increasing the percentage of women on corporate boards to 20% by 2020. The campaign redefines successful corporate governance, gender diversity standards, and creates a cultural imperative for corporate action.

Corporate Women Directors International

Corporate Women Directors International (CWDI) promotes the increased participation of women in corporate boards globally, fosters national and international networks to connect women directors, and seeks to hone directors' skills in corporate governance.

Women Corporate Directors

World Corporate Director (WCD) members are among the world's most powerful and influential women in business today. They are the global business elite who are at the top of their organizations serving as directors, CEOs, COOs, divisional presidents, and other executive positions. WCD members are on boards of public and/or large private-ly held companies, as well as large family businesses.

Boardroom Diversity - SAIS Center for Transatlantic Relations

The SAIS Center for Transatlantic Relations is Washington, D.C.'s premier academic think tank focused on finding solutions to the difficult policy issues facing Europe and North America. It works to strengthen and reorient transatlantic relations to the dynamics of the globalizing world. The website provides the text or links to legislation, codes, regulations, and best practices on boardroom diversity; academic and corporate research; plus articles and events on this topic.

Women in the Boardroom

Women in the Boardroom (WIB) is committed to translating the intellect, skills and expertise of their members into inaugural or additional powerful corporate director roles. WIB focuses on ensuring its members have a board portfolio that highlights their skill set for board positioning, and teaching them how to network their way to a corporate board seat and how to maintain strong and connected relationships with boards through WIB's virtual platform. Other WIB offerings designed to connect our members with board contacts include WIB's Matchmaking Program, board opening notifications, and exclusive invites to events such as the Annual Board Assembly. Senior-level executive women are encouraged to join as a member of WIB to accelerate their path into the corporate boardroom.

National Association of Corporate Directors

The National Association of Corporate Directors (NACD) helps more than 17,000 directors lead with confidence. As the recognized authority on leading boardroom practices, NACD aspires to a world where businesses are sustainable, profitable, and respected, and where stakeholders trust directors to develop strategies that create long-term value and provide effective oversight.

Diversity-Specific Organizations Examples

Executive Leadership Council

The Executive Leadership Council is the preeminent member organization for the development of global black leaders. Its mission is to increase the number of successful black executives—both domestically and internationally—by adding value to their development, leadership, and philanthropic endeavors throughout the life cycle of their careers thereby strengthening their companies, organizations, and communities.

Hispanic Association on Corporate Responsibility

Founded in 1986, the Hispanic Association on Corporate Responsibility (HACR) is one of the most influential advocacy organizations in the nation representing 16 national Hispanic organizations in the United States and Puerto Rico. Its mission is to advance the inclusion of Hispanics in corporate America at a level commensurate with our economic contributions. To that end, HACR focuses on four areas of corporate social responsibility and market reciprocity: employment, procurement, philanthropy, and governance.

Leadership Education for Asian Pacifics

Envisioned as a vehicle to develop future leaders, Leaership Education for Asian Pacifics (LEAP) is a national nonprofit organization whose mission is to achieve full participation and equality for Asian and Pacific Islanders (APIs) through leadership, empowerment, and policy. LEAP works to meet its mission by: developing people, because leaders are made, not born; informing society, because leaders know the issues; and empowering communities, because leaders are grounded in strong, vibrant communities. Unmatched in vision and scope, LEAP offers leadership training and programs, publishes leadership research and conducts community education to advance a comprehensive strategy of API empowerment. With more than 30 years of experience, LEAP has delivered more than 2,700 leadership development programs, workshops, and presentations to over 125,000 participants across the country.

CalPERS

CalPERS is committed to a work environment that promotes and supports diversity and inclusion. The Investment Office Targeted Investment Programs team works with the CalPERS Diversity Outreach Program to engage and promote a diverse workforce and extend that philosophy to its stakeholders. It hosts the CalPERS Diversity Forum, which explores the representation of women and minorities in business.

Chapter 4: Entrepreneurship - Overview

Today, there are more women entrepreneurs than ever before. On the global basis of 10 economies, women are as likely as men or more likely to become entrepreneurs. As a society, we enjoy the stories of those hard-working individuals who have built a successful career and business through pure grit and determination. Women-owned businesses and women entrepreneurs are changing the face of this country, and the world around it. In the United States alone, we have 11.3 million female-owned businesses. In fact, there are well over 1,000 businesses started by women each day, and that number continues to grow. In the United States, women are starting businesses 1.5 times the average rate of men. To that end, women-owned businesses generate revenue of over $1.6 trillion.

Women account for one-third of all active businesses. This growth survived our great recession, and the surge will continue as women secure the capital they need. When it comes to access to loans and funding, we cry out for equality. Only 4% of commercial loan dollars are given to women. The access to capital and the support for venture capital issues will drive the growth of businesses that can be scaled up to above the billion-dollar threshold. To do this, we need commercial banks and venture firms to recognize and appreciate that growth.

The statistics show that women-owned businesses have a proven track record for growth and thus, make for good investments. Next, women business owners are building markets overseas. About 95% of consumers living outside the United States now represent two-thirds of the world's purchasing power. Women-owned businesses are enjoying an exciting opportunity to grow with exports and businesses around the world.

There are over five million minority women-owned firms, which accounts for almost half of all women-owned businesses. They are often small in size, but ever growing, as women of color own 79% of new women-owned firms. This is quite a change from just a decade ago, and projected to increase in the forthcoming years. The economic impact of women-owned firms is particularly strong in the states and the metropolitan areas we cite. We refer to these areas as the hotbeds of entrepreneurship. Use these supports and references to consider where you have the best opportunity to build your businesses.

Call to Action:

- Recognize that a high percentage of young women, as well as those leaving the corporate space, want to be entrepreneurs. Support and encourage this entrepreneurship movement.

- The resources in this chapter will help you to obtain accelerators, training, and certification, and also encourage networking and advocacy.

- Support small- and medium-size businesses owned by minority women within your community. Familiarize yourself with the Top 50 female entrepreneurs in the United States, and support their endeavors and share their websites, articles, and blogs with your friends and loved ones.

CHAPTER 4: ENTREPRENEURSHIP

Number of Firms

- Women entrepreneurs have started approximately 11.3 million businesses in the United States.

Source: American Express OPEN (2016).

- Up from 9.9 million firms in the United States in 2012 - a 14% increase.
- Up from 7.8 million firms in 2007 - a 26.9% increase.

Source: 2012 Survey of Business Owners (2012).

- Since 2007, there have been 1,072 net new women-owned firms started each day .

Source: American Express OPEN (2016).

- 1,143 per day from 2007 to 2012.
- 983 per day from 2012 to 2016.
- For an increase total of approximately 3.5 million firms.
- Women are now the majority owners of 38% of the country's businesses.

Source: American Express OPEN (2016).

- Up from 35.8% in 2012.
- Up from 29% in 2007.
- Women start companies at 1.5 times the average rate in the United States.
- The absolute number of startups in Crunchbase with at least one female founder has more than quadrupled in the last five years, from 117 in 2009 to 555 in 2014.
- Women entrepreneurs in the United States rank their happiness at nearly three times that of women who are not entrepreneurs or established business owners.
- The United States ranks No. 1 among 31 countries considered by Dell on the support of women's entrepreneurship.
- Today, 18% of all startups have at least one female founder.
- There are just over 9 million women-owned companies in the United States.
- A net new 340,000 jobs were added by woman-owned businesses between 2007 and 2015. At the same time, men-owned businesses shed 1.2 million jobs, according to a 2015 study by WomenAble and American Express.
- 46% of the privately held companies in the United States are now at least half owned by women.

Source: Inc. 2015.

Julie Weeks of WomenAble.com has worked to produce valued research for AMEX as well as many valued studies and materials.

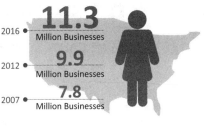

2016 — **11.3** Million Businesses

2012 — **9.9** Million Businesses

2007 — **7.8** Million Businesses

+1,072
Women-owned Businesses
started each day since 2007

Women-owned Firms

2016 — **38%** of All Businesses

2012 — **35.8%** of All Businesses

2007 — **29%** of All Businesses

- The National Association of Women in Real Estate Businesses is a leading voice for women in the housing ecosystem. NAWRB is dedicated to providing women the tools and opportunities for economic growth and expansion, while advocating and promoting women-owned businesses. NAWRB is the only third-party industry-specific certifier of Women-Owned Businesses (WOB) and Minority Women-Owned Businesses (MWOB) in the housing economy. NAWRB provides a unique platform for uniting Women in Housing and Women in Government including educational training on contracting opportunities both government and private, to expand our members' business growth.

Source: National Association of Women In Real Estate Businesses (NAWRB).

Revenue

- Women-owned firms generate over $1.6 trillion in revenues.

2016 • **1.6T** in Revenues

Source: American Express OPEN (2016).

- Up from $1.4 trillion in 2012 - a 14.3% increase.

2012 • **1.4T** in Revenues

Source: 2012 Survey of Business Owners (2012).

2007 • **1.2T** in Revenues

- Up from $1.2 trillion in 2007 - an 18.7% increase.

Source: 2012 Survey of Business Owners (2012).

- Business revenues among women-owned firms have increased by a total of 35% since 2007, compared to 27% among all U.S. firms.

- Contributing 4% of the nation's business revenues.

Source: American Express OPEN (2016).

- A study by Barclays on unlocking the female economy found that the gender pay gap was reversed for wealthy entrepreneurs and business owners, with men trailing behind their female counterparts. "This suggests that women will tend to achieve greater financial success in an environment that is purely market-driven, rather than a more traditional job in which pay must be negotiated."

Source: Open Mind (2016).

- One analysis by Quantopian hedge-fund researcher Karen Rubin showed that women CEOs outperform peers three to one in the S&P 500, further developing the conversation over women driving top financial returns.

- Businesses with a woman on the executive team are more likely to have significantly higher valuations at Series A—as in, 64% higher.

- Businesses with a woman on the executive team are more likely to have significantly higher valuations in their last funding round—49% higher.

- Financially, women entrepreneurs outperform everyone but blue chips over time. In the last couple decades, the growth in the number of women's businesses (up 68%), employment (up 11%), and revenues (up 72%) blows past the growth rates of all but the largest publicly traded businesses, and tops growth rates among all other privately held businesses over this period.

- Female-founded or co-founded "unicorn" companies, those with a billion or more in valuation, include Theranos, Eventbrite, SunRun, and Houzz.

Source: Inc. (2015).

Growth

- Between 2007 and 2016, the number of women-owned firms increased by 45%, compared to just a 9% increase among all businesses.
  - Over the past nine years, the number of women-owned firms has grown at a rate five times faster than the national average.
  - The rate for women of color is even higher, at 126%, equaling nearly 2.9 million firms.

Source: American Express OPEN (2016).

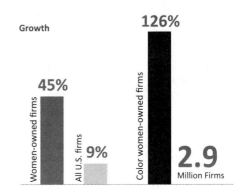

According to the EY *Global Job Creation Survey 2016*, entrepreneurs are more than twice as likely to be hiring new staff this year as large corporates. The survey of nearly 2,700 entrepreneurs globally also finds that disruptive entrepreneurs (who change some or all of the rules of their sector) and innovative entrepreneurs (who have created a brand new product or service in the past year) are also growing their workforces at a much faster rate than more conventional entrepreneurs. The research has been launched ahead of the EY World Entrepreneur Of The Year™ event. *Source*: EY (2016).

WIPP Overview

Women entrepreneurs are an economic powerhouse. Making up one-third of all businesses, women-owned firms are growing at four times the rate of men-owned firms and contribute $1.6 trillion to the American economy. This growth not only survived the Great Recession, but has propelled recovery in communities nationwide.

Women business owners are not getting the capital they need. Only 4% of all commercial loan dollars go to women. The cumulative regulatory burden on community banks—a traditional source of capital for women entrepreneurs—has increased costs and made it difficult for these institutions to rationalize smaller loans. The unmet needs of women entrepreneurs total billions of dollars each year.

Despite significant barriers, women-owned firms compete for and win government contracts. Reaching the goal of awarding 5% of contracts to women-owned firms in 2015 effectively set the floor for the federal market. To ensure women have access and can bring innovative solutions to government problems, more needs to be done. Parity in federal procurement opportunities is essential for women-owned businesses.

Women businesses are a good investment. The track record of growth for women business owners is proven, yet only 3% of all venture capital goes to companies run by women. The limited number of women fund managers is a factor in this statistic. A study from the Diana Project, found that venture capital firms with women partners are three times more likely to invest in companies with women CEOs. The next Administration can use the Small Business Investment Company (SBIC) Program among other tools to ensure more women fund managers have the experience needed.

Women business owners seek markets beyond U.S. borders. With 95% of consumers living outside of the United States representing two-thirds of the world's purchasing power, women's growth must be fueled by access to international markets. Strengthening the existing support of the federal government for small firms should complement nonprofit and private export assistance to small businesses. Our government must continue its efforts strengthening intellectual property (IP) rights and protections at home and abroad to encourage more entrepreneurship and the global expansion of women-owned firms.
Source: WIPP (2016).

Top 4 Industries

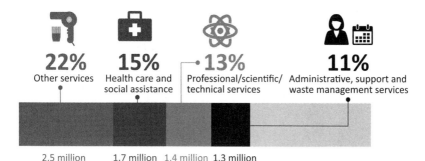

22%	15%	13%	11%
Other services	Health care and social assistance	Professional/scientific/ technical services	Administrative, support and waste management services
2.5 million	1.7 million	1.4 million	1.3 million

- Six in 10 (61%) women-owned firms are found in 4 industry sectors:
  - Other services (home to hair and nail salons and pet care businesses): 2.5 million firms accounting for 22% of all women-owned firms;
  - Healthcare and social assistance (including child day care and home healthcare services): 1.7 million firms, 15%;
  - Professional/scientific/technical services (including lawyers, accountants, architects, public relations firms, and management consultants): 1.4 million, 13%; and
  - Administrative, support, and waste management services (including janitorial and landscaping services, as well as office administrative support and travel agencies): 1.3 million, 11%.

Source: American Express OPEN (2016).

Women Presidents' Organization's (WPO) 50 Fastest-Growing Women-Owned Businesses

- S'well
- Pinnacle Technical Resources
- Orangetheory Fitness
- Morning Star Financial Services
- E2 Optics
- Aerial Development Group
- BlackLine
- Matisia Consultants
- BrightStar Franchising
- Legion Logistics
- Ivie & Associates
- Akorbi
- Erkunt Tractor Industries
- Strategy and Management Services
- TransPerfect
- Xtreme Solutions
- Tribal Tech
- Atrium Staffing
- Point 2 Point Global Security
- NuGate Group
- OpTech
- Quantum Health
- Swoon Group
- MegaCorp Logistics
- Maximum Games
- Blink Reaction
- Protea Group International
- InGenesis
- Xclusive Staffing
- Zero Waste Solutions
- Excellence Engineering
- Design To Delivery
- The Revel Group
- ORI
- ICON Information Consultants
- Home Care Assistance
- Atlantic Infra
- The Greene Group
- Boost Technologies
- Ampcus Inc
- Merrimak Capital Company
- Social Media Link
- The Bakery Cos.
- J Curve
- Imagine Technology Group
- Anserteam Workforce Solutions
- Walker-Miller Energy Services
- Overture Promotions
- Technology Group Solutions
- Vivere Health

Source: Fortune: Women Presidents' Organization (2015).

Jobs/Organizations

- Employment in women-owned businesses has increased by 18% since the 2007, while overall businesses employment has declined 1% since 2007.
- These firms employ 8% of the nation's private-sector workforce.
- WPO (Women Presidents' Organization) members employ nearly 9 million people.

Source: WPO (2016).

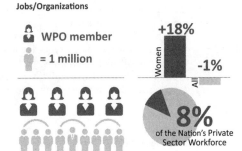

- National Association of Women Business Owners (NAWBO) is the unified voice of over nine million women-owned businesses in the United States representing the fastest growing segment of the economy.
  - NAWBO represents the interests of all women entrepreneurs across all industries; and with chapters across the country.
  - NAWBO is a one-stop resource to propelling women business owners into greater economic, social, and political spheres of power worldwide.
  - It's an Institute for entrepreneurial development.

Source: NAWBO (2016).

- The National Women's Business Council (NWBC)
  - A non-partisan federal advisory council created to serve as an independent source of advice and counsel to the president, Congress, and the U.S. Small Business Administration on economic issues of importance to women business owners.
  - The council is the government's only independent voice for women entrereneurs. Members are prominent women business owners and leaders of women's business organizations. NWBC is composed of 15 members who are appointed to three-year terms.

Source: NWBC (2016).

- TechCrunch
  - TechCrunch is a leading technology media property, dedicated to obsessively profiling startups, reviewing new Internet products, and breaking tech news.
  - Founded in June 2005, TechCrunch and its network of websites now reach over 12 million unique visitors and draw more than 37 million page views per month. The TechCrunch community includes more than two million friends and followers on Twitter, Facebook, LinkedIn, Google, and other social media.

Source: TechCrunch (2016).

2016 Best Public Accounting Firms for Women and Best Firms for Leadership Equity

The Bonadio Group | Pittsford, NY
While 36% female partners and principals is an accomplishment in its own right, The Bonadio Group manages to accelerate more women to leadership even as the firm grows rapidly, currently topping 577 employees. The Bonadio Group reinforces collaboration with its policy of providing equal credit for new businesses brought in to both the referring employee and the employee working the account.

Burr Pilger Mayer | San Francisco, CA
In one of the toughest talent markets in the world, Burr Pilger Mayer has boosted its proportion of women partners by concentrating coaching, professional development, and internal networking to help senior managers fine-tune their vision of personal success. The firm is cross-pollinating best practices among its offices to foster mentoring and sponsorship.

Clark Nuber | Bellevue, WA
Leadership is both "caught" and "taught," which is why Clark Nuber invests heavily in training top leaders to be effective performance managers. Among the skills they must master: advocating for candidates, ferreting out the right opportunities at the right time in candidates' careers, and never putting career goals on automatic pilot. It's working: 38% of the firm's partners and principals are women.

CohnReznick | New York, NY
Try it, track it, evaluate success, repeat. That's how CohnReznick reinvests in the precise programs that make the biggest differences to retaining and advancing women: backup child care, women's networking events customized for each office, and top-level coaching for executive sponsors to amplify their results.

Frazier & Deeter | Atlanta, GA
Frazier & Deeter retains women in its partnership pipeline better than most, with women comprising 31% of partners and principals and 57% of female senior managers. The firm just introduced a 100% childcare reimbursement for all Georgia employees, a move designed to retain millennials who are starting families and add an additional resource for mid-career women.

Lurie | Minneapolis, MN
When your CEO and COO are both women, you actively demonstrate how to lead by example. Lurie is increasing market share by sharing with clients and prospects in the Twin Cities business community the firm's dedication to retaining women. Strong female leadership at the firm increases credibility with the entire Minneapolis business community.

MCM CPAs and Advisors | Louisville, KY
MCM CPA and Advisors achieves what most firms consider to be impossible: it gains women at higher levels, with women comprising 60% of the firm's managers, 57% of senior managers, and 50% of directors. To help increase referrals within the firm, MCM held a business development program for employees to learn more about cross-selling and how to identify client's needs for other services.

Moss Adams | Seattle, WA
With women comprising 27% of its partners, Moss Adams is gaining momentum as it aims for 30% by 2022, and its clients are rooting for it. One tactic: a year-long leadership development program for high-potential women senior managers. The program is based on a comprehensive analysis of data on what it takes to succeed: personal brand
definition, team building, and business development.

Plante Moran | Southfield, MI
When the firm's first pay equity audit discovered some anomalies, the women's initiative leadership was drawn into the analysis. The resulting insights helped Plante Moran
better understand the intersection of culture and compensation, and how to evolve all of its renowned programs to ensure holistic equity.

Rehmann | Troy, MI
Women early on in their careers don't have to wait their turn for leadership development opportunities. Rehmann's leadership development programs, as well as its Women's Initiative Network, offer tracks that help associates and senior associates gain traction with a variety of business skills and self-evaluation.

Source: Accounting a Financial Woman's Alliance: Accounting MOVE Project Report.

Small and Medium Enterprises (SMEs)

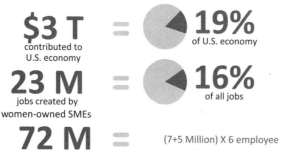

$3 T = 🥧 **19%**
contributed to
U.S. economy
of U.S. economy

23 M = 🥧 **16%**
jobs created by
women-owned SMEs
of all jobs

72 M = (7+5 Million) X 6 employee
jobs will be created by Women-owned SMEs over the next 5 years.

- Women-owned SMEs in the United States are expanding at more than double the rate of all other firms.

Source: EY (2015).

  - Contributing nearly $3 trillion to the U.S. economy (totalling 19%).
  - Directly delivering 23 million jobs (16% of all jobs).
- A projected seven million female entrepreneurs and five million female established business owners plan to grow their businesses by at least six employees over the next five years.
- Globally, there are roughly 8 million to 10 million formal SMEs with at least one woman owner.
- Women's Business Centers (WBCs) represent a national network of nearly 100 educational centers throughout the United States and its territories, which are designed to assist women in starting and growing small businesses. WBCs seek to "level the playing field" for women entrepreneurs, who still face unique obstacles in the business world.
  The Association of Women's Business Centers (AWBC) works to secure economic justice and entrepreneurial opportunities for women by supporting and sustaining a national network of more than 100 WBCs.
- WBCs help women succeed in business by providing mentoring and opportunities to over 140,000 women entrepreneurs each year.

Source: Association of Women's Business Centers (2016).

- U.S. Small Business Administration's (SBA's) Office of Women's Business Ownership (OWBO) oversees the WBC network, which provides entrepreneurs (especially women who are economically or socially disadvantaged) comprehensive training and counseling on a variety of topics in several languages.

Source: U.S. Small Business Administration (2015).

Women-Owned Family Business

Family Business

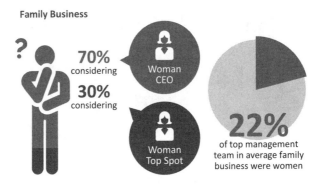

70% considering

30% considering

Woman CEO

Woman Top Spot

22%
of top management team in average family business were women

- 25 of the largest family businesses in each of the 21 largest global markets, average $3.48 billion in sales and 12,000 employees.
- Leadership
  - They average about five women in the C-suite.
  - 70% of family businesses are considering a woman for their next CEO, and 30% are strongly considering a woman for the top spot.
  - And 4 women being groomed for top leadership positions.
- Women compose 22% of the average family business top management team.
- Globally:
  - Developed Economies - Average of 5.5 women in the C-suite.
  - Developing Economies - Average of 3.5 women in the C-suite.

Family Businesses

5.5 women in the C-suite in developed economies.

3.5 women in the C-suite in developing economies.

Boards of Family Businesses
- 55% have at least one woman on their board.
- Boards average 16% women, which is more than one woman per board.
- 8% of their boards are 50% or more composed of women.
- Globally, Family Businesses in:
  - Developed Economies - 60% have at least one woman on the board.
  - Developing Economies - 49% have at least one woman on the board.
  - Developed Economies - 10% of boards are at least half women.
  - Developing Economies - 4% of boards are at least half women.

Source: EY & Kennesaw State University (2015).

55%
of the boards have at least one woman

16%
Women board owners

Capital Access

- Access to finance remains a hurdle for female entrepreneurs.
Source: EY (2015).

- Women's Business Development Center hosts the Entrepreneurial Women's Conference (EWC), the largest entrepreneurial business conference in the Midwest, which has been going on for nearly 30 years.
    - It aims to help female entrepreneurs by helping them get access to resources, contracts and capital.
- SBA sets a goal for the federal government to grant 23% of business opportunities to women.
    - Focus on minority- and veteran-owned businesses, as well as those in certain economically disadvantaged areas.
Source: Access to Capital, Dun & Bradstreet (2015).

- One of the biggest obstacles women led businesses are facing is access to capital. Groups assisting women overcome these issues include:
    - SBA Loans: The SBA offers a variety of loan programs for many different needs. According to the Urban Institute, SBA loans are three to five times more likely to go to women than non-SBA loans.
    - SBA backed venture capital programs including the PRIME program and the SBIC program.

Business USA's Access Financing Wizard

- The Access Financing Wizard, female business owners receive lists of loan programs, financing resources, and information for local lenders based off of their business profile. It is a great way to find loans and grants that may be available to your business.

Women's Initiative for Self Employment

- This nonprofit organization provides business education and financing to high-potential, low-income women. In order for women to have access to one-on-one consultations, networking events, seminars, and business loans they must complete the SIMPLE STEPS business management course.
- This 11-week course teaches female entrepreneurs how to write a business plan, analyze the competition, price a product or service, keep accurate records and manage finances, and business promotion, among other skills.
- Completion of this course will allow female business owners to apply for a loan of up to $25,000, as well as apply for Individual Development Accounts.

Banks

- Wells Fargo has pledged to lend a cumulative $55 billion to female business owners by 2020.
Source: Wells Fargo (2016).

- Citi Women is a company-wide effort designed to achieve these objectives. It offers two core programs, Women Leading Citi and the Women's Leadership Development Program, along with other work focused around advancing women across our businesses, fostering a global network, and engaging clients in the effort.
Source: Citigroup (2016).

- JP Morgan's exciting introductory program for undergraduate women, the Winning Women Program, provides an entry into financial services and a meaningful overview of the many opportunities for female leadership at the firm.

Source: JP Morgan (2016).

- PNC loans nearly $1 billion dollars annually on average, to female business owners. PNC offers a wide range of services for all our customers, from individuals and small businesses, to corporations and government entities. No matter how simple or complicated your needs, they are sure to have the products, knowledge and resources necessary for financial success.

Source: PNC (2016).

- All banks feature women-centered lending programs for business owners. These traditional lenders are definitely viable options for female business owners looking to partner with big banks.

Opportunity Funding

- The largest nonprofit microfinance lender in California and has been helping small businesses find funding since 1995. They have invested over $200 million locally in California with 51% of their loans going to woman-owned businesses.

Source: Access to Capital, Dun & Bradstreet (2015).

- Women-owned small businesses have an inability to compete with large businesses as well as general lack of new business opportunities are most frequently cited as the most significant barriers to lack of business growth.

- Outside funding for women-owned small businesses is secured after an average of 2.7 attempts, up from 1.6 last year.

- 2015 research revealed a significant shift in funding sources from collateralized bank loans to lines of credit.

- Median loan sizes for women in 2015 are $332,000.

  - Outside funding, when secured, is most often used to finance the existing business. Those who do not seek outside funding are either self-funding or feel they do not need outside funding.

  - When asked what they would do if they had additional funding, most often they said they would use it to hire more employees.

Source: Women Impacting Public Policy (WIPP) (2015).

- The proportion of businesses seeking outside funding remains steady, at about 4 in 10.

- Outside funding has been sought by higher revenue companies, who were more successful in obtaining funding, and by minority-owned businesses who were generally unsuccessful in finding funding.

- 2015 research identified an increase in the number of attempts required to obtain funding.

Source: Women Impacting Public Policy (WIPP) (2015).

- Among the most successful companies, men start their businesses with six times as much capital as women do, according to the most recent National Women's Business Council (NWBC) Annual Report.

Source: Inc. (2015).

Women and Venture Capital

Between 4% and 10% of venture capital funds go to women:
(Babson, 2014)
- Between 2010 and 2015, 10% of venture dollars globally funded startups that reported at least one female founder.

Capital Access for Women

2010   2015

$31.5 Billion = 3,265 funding rounds, 12% of all venture funding rounds

$2.35 Billion = 4,852 funding rounds, 17% of all seed rounds

- A total of $31.5 billion.
- This represented 3,265 funding rounds or 12% of all venture funding rounds.
- During the same time period, 17% of seed/angel rounds globally funded startups that reported at least one female founder.

From 2011–13, just 15% of U.S. companies receiving venture capital funding had a woman on the executive team.
- This is up 10 % since 1999.
- But all-men teams in 2013 are still more than four times more likely to receive funding from venture capital investors.

Source: EY (2015).

Capital Access

2011   2013

- The percentage of funded startups with at least one female founder increased from 9% to 18% between 2009 and 2014.

A total of $2.35 billion. This represents 4,852 rounds or 17% of all seed rounds. *Source:* TechCrunch (2016).
Data regarding the percentage of venture funding women-founded firms receive varies from 4%-10% depending on its source.

- Out of the top 100 venture firms, 7% of the partners, or 54 of 755, are women, and 38% of the top 100 firms have at least one female partner.
- At the 29 firms founded by at least one female co-founder in the last five years, fully half of the investing partners are women.

Female Representation in Venture Firms

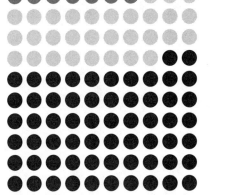

Source: TechCrunch (2016).

- 12% of venture rounds and 10% of venture dollars globally between 2010 and 2015 went to startups with at least one woman founder.
- 17% of seed rounds and 15% of seed dollars globally between 2010 and 2015 went to startups with at least one woman founder.

Source: TechCrunch (2016).

Venture Rounds and Dollars

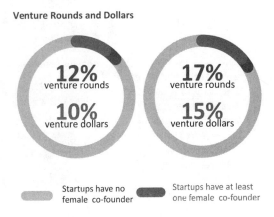

- No matter which crowdfunding platform they choose, female founders perform equal to or better than their male counterparts when raising money online.
- Offline, it's a different story. Only 10% of startups which raised Series A last year had female founders. Today's venture capital environment clocks some 305 active funds over $100 million. These funds collectively put $114 billion to work. Ninety percent of it never sees a female founder.
- That said, venture capital firms with women partners are more than twice as likely to invest in companies with a woman on the executive team.
- Venture firms with a woman partner are more than three times as likely to invest in companies with women CEOs.
- 94% of decision makers at venture capital funds are male.
- Even so, there is more venture for women, and the women's entrepreneurial ecosystem is gaining traction, as angel investor Kelly Hoey points out in Inc.

Source: Inc. (2015).

Organization Examples

Women's Venture Capital Fund

- Women's Venture Capital Fund backs businesses with women entrepreneurs and gender-diverse teams within the digital media and sustainable product and service sectors.

Golden Seeds

- An early-stage investment firm that backs women-led companies across all sectors. The firm looks at whether the female entrepreneur (founder, CEO, or other c-level role) has influence on the company and owns a fair amount of equity.

Source: Pitchbook (2015).

Springboard Enterprises

- A highly-vetted expert network of innovators, investors, and influencers who are dedicated to building high-growth technology-oriented companies led by women.
- The programs and initiatives are how they source, qualify, advise, showcase and support the most promising businesses seeking capital or partnerships for product development and expansion.
- 627 women-led companies have participated in Springboard's accelerator programs; raising $7.2 billion, creating tens of thousands of new jobs, and generating billions of dollars in annual revenues. 81% of Springboard companies are still in business as independent or merged entities, including 12 IPOs and many are the technology engines of publicly traded companies.

BBG Ventures

- An early-stage fund born out of AOL's #BUILTBYGIRLS effort to encourage young women to pursue tech careers. Launched in September 2014, the fund backs companies with at least one female founder, typically investing between $100,000 and $250,000. BBG Ventures focuses on the consumer Internet and consumer tech sectors.

BELLE Capital USA

- An early-stage angel fund that targets companies with at least one female founder or c-level executive, or businesses that are willing to recruit women for the c-level team and board of directors. The fund focuses on four sectors: IT, digital health, cleantech, and technology-enabled products and services. BELLE Capital USA generally invests $100,000 to $1.5 million in tranches based on milestone achievements.

Female Founders Fund

- Female Founders Fund backs female-led companies in ecommerce, media, web-enabled products and services, marketplaces, and platforms.

Finomial

- A financial services automation company that offers products to aid the hedge fund subscription process among investors, fund managers, and administrators. As of February 2016, Finomial has raised about $1.6 million for a new financing round.

Publication Example

Enterprising Women

- Enterprising Women of the Year - The annual Enterprising Women of the Year Awards is widely considered one of the most prestigious recognition programs for women business owners. To win, nominees must demonstrate that they have fast-growth businesses, mentor, or actively support other women and girls involved in entrepreneurship, and stand out as leaders in their communities. Many of the honorees also serve as leaders of the key organizations that support the growth of women's entrepreneurship.
- International magazine that inspires and educates women entrepreneurs to grow their businesses to the next level, with one million readers in 185 countries in a global community sharing best practices.
- Enterprising Women is a partner in the Million Women Mentors Project and has committed to bringing a focus on opportunities in STEM to high school girls who may not have role models or mentors.
- STEMpreneurs program: Washington, D.C. area's leading women entrepreneurs and business leaders from diverse industries work together to build up entrepreneurship within the STEM field for women.
- The Enterprising Women Foundation has embarked on a major initiative to connect high school girls with outstanding women entrepreneurs in their communities to educate, inspire, and mentor them on entrepreneurship, with a special emphasis on STEMs.
  - The foundation has a five-year goal to host mentorship events in 100 U.S. cities over the next five years.

Source: Enterprising Women Magazine (2016).

Minority Women Enterprising Firms & Growth

There are five million minority women-owned firms (4,992,200), comprising fully 44% of women-owned firms.

Firms & Growth

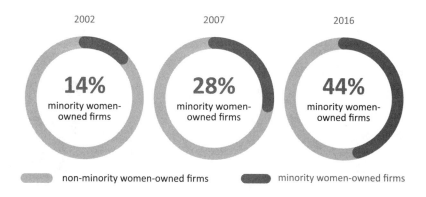

2002 — **14%** minority women-owned firms

2007 — **28%** minority women-owned firms

2016 — **44%** minority women-owned firms

non-minority women-owned firms   minority women-owned firms

- In 2007, 2.2 million minority women-owned firms accounted for 28% of all women owned businesses.
- In 2002, less than one million firms were owned by women of color, comprising just 14% of women-owned firms.

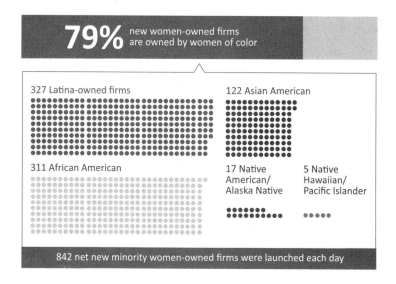

79% new women-owned firms are owned by women of color

327 Latina-owned firms

122 Asian American

311 African American

17 Native American/ Alaska Native

5 Native Hawaiian/ Pacific Islander

842 net new minority women-owned firms were launched each day

Since 2007, there have been 1,072 new women-owned firms started each day and 79% of these firms are owned by women of color.
- An average of 842 new minority women-owned firms were launched each day since 2007.
    - 327 Latina-owned firms
    - 311 African American
    - 122 Asian
    - 17 Native American and Alaska Native
    - 5 Native Hawaiian and Other Pacific Islander
- Revenue and jobs
- Minority women-owned firms employ two million workers and generate $344 billion in revenues.

Source: American Express OPEN (2016).

Ethnic Breakdown

	Latina	Black or African American	Native American	Asian	Native Hawaiian/ Pacific Islander
Number of Firms	1.9 million	1.9 million	153,400	922,700	31,100
Employed Workers	550,400	376,500	57,400	964,900	13,500
Revenue (billion)	$97	$51.4	$10.5	$170.4	$2.3
Increase Rate from 2007-2016	137%	112%	59%	76%	108%
Women-owned firms out of all in the same race	46%	46%	51%	41%	47%

Source: American Express OPEN (2016).

- Worldwide, at least 30% of women in the non-agricultural labor force are self-employed in the informal sector.
    - In Africa, this figure is 63%.

Source: American Express OPEN (2016).

Industry Trends

For comparison, women accounted for 51.4% of the 18-and-older population in the United States in 2012 and 38% of businesses.

Women Majority Industries as of 2012

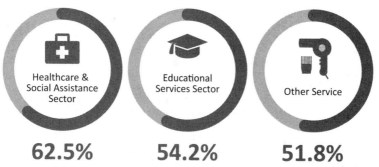

- Healthcare and social assistance sector - Women-owned firms constituted 62.5%.
- Educational services sector - 54.2%.
- Other services sector - 51.8%.

Above Average Women Industries

- Administrative support and waste management (49% women)
- Retail trade (43% women)

Source: NAWBO (2016).

Women business owners historically have had limited access to private venture capital. Therefore, equity-based capital programs, such as the SBIC, are crucial in filling that gap and need to be expanded and strengthened.

- Broad-based capital gains legislation that includes incentives to foster investment in all forms of organizations in the small business sector needs to be enacted.
- History indicates that robust entrepreneurial activity and small business ownership provide the basis for economic prosperity important to the long-term vitality and success of our nation. Therefore, government policies that foster and encourage growth and expansion of fast-growing small businesses, such as those owned by women, are crucial to the health of the U.S. economy.
- Women business owners still face greater obstacles in obtaining financing for their businesses than similarly situated men do. In addition, access to capital by women business owners is not commensurate with their business growth. Further, although the number and dollar value of venture capital and other equity investments grew rapidly in the late 1990s, women business owners continue to get a very small share of those dollars. Evidence of limitations on access include:
    - In 2000 women received only 12% of all credit provided to small firms even though, at that point, they owned close to 40% of all U.S. businesses.
    - Despite women becoming more active in the equity capital markets, in a survey conducted in late 1999, just 9% of the institutional investment deals and 2.3% of the dollars among the investors interviewed went to women-owned firms.
    - Women business owners who reported having equity investment in their firms were most likely to have investments from individuals and / or informal (73%) investors, and less likely to have corporate (25%) or venture capital (15%) investors.
    - According to Venture One, in the years 1999 – 2001 only 5% of the close to $100 billion of venture capital annually invested went to firms with women CEOs. The percentage of venture capital backed companies with women founders also remains small – 7.2% in 1999, 8.3% in 2000 and 8.2% in 2001.
    - Nearly half (47%) of all African American women business owners reported that they have encountered obstacles or difficulties when trying to obtain business financing.

Source: NAWBO (2016).

Economic Impact

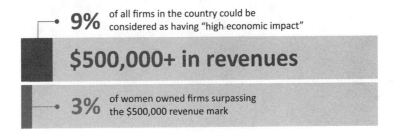

9% of all firms in the country could be considered as having "high economic impact"

$500,000+ in revenues

3% of women owned firms surpassing the $500,000 revenue mark

- Economy-wide, just 9% of all firms in the country could be considered as having "high economic impact"—meaning that they generate $500,000 or more in revenues.

- Only 3% of women owned firms likewise meet that standard.
- Relative to the overall 3% of women-owned firms surpassing the $500,000 revenue mark, women-owned firms in five industries are those most likely to be making a high economic impact.
- In most industry sectors women-owned firms are smaller than their peers.
- In two industries they stand toe-to-toe with other firms with respect to the share that achieve revenues of $500,000 or more.
- Construction - 9% of women-owned and 8% of all firms achieve revenues of $500,000 or more.
- Transportation and warehousing - 6% of women-owned and 7% of all firms achieve revenues of $500,000 or more.

Geographic Trends

The 10 states home to the greatest number of women-owned firms as of 2016 are:

- California
- Texas
- Florida
- New York
- Georgia
- Illinois
- Michigan
- Ohio
- North Carolina
- Pennsylvania

Top metropolitan areas for women-owned firms, which are found in most of these states, are:

- New York City
- Los Angeles
- Miami
- Chicago
- Atlanta
- Dallas
- Houston
- Detroit
- Washington DC
- San Francisco

The 10 fastest-growing states for women-owned firms in this regard are:

- Florida (up 67%)
- Georgia (64%)
- Texas (63%)
- Michigan (57%)
- Mississippi (56%)
- South Carolina (53%)
- Tennessee (53%)
- the District of Columbia (51%)
- South Dakota (50%)
- Louisiana (49%)

** Eight out of 10 are in the South.**
** The top five exceed the national growth rate by 10% or more.**

The top 10 metropolitan areas, ranked on growth in economic clout between 2007 and 2016, are:

- Charlotte NC/SC
- San Antonio TX
- Dallas TX, and Memphis TN/MS/AR (tied for 3rd)
- Austin TX and Indianapolis IN (tied for 5th)
- Miami FL
- Detroit MI
- Richmond VA
- Houston TX

Source: Inc. (2015).

Firm Size

Five Industries for Greatest Economic Impact

Wholesale trade	Manufacturing	Accommodation and food services	Construction	Transportation and warehousing
18%	**13%**	**12%**	**9%**	**6%**

Source: American Express OPEN (2016).

Hotbeds of Entrepreneurship

- The states with the most female-owned businesses are: Washington, D.C. (34.5%); Maryland (32.6%); New Mexico (31.7%); Hawaii (31%); and Georgia (30.9%).

Source: Forbes (2014).

- Brooklyn, New York, banks more female startups than any other single city in the United States.
- Las Vegas has the honor of the highest percentage of venture-backed companies with at least one female founder: 26%.
- Texas claims the worst record of supporting women seeking venture capital. Last year, 42 Texas startups got Series A rounds. Zero of them had female founders.
- In the United States, the frontiers of fast growth in the raw number of companies founded by women are, in order: North Dakota; Wyoming; Washington, D.C.; Arizona; Georgia; and Nevada.
- The cities in the United States where the combined economic clout of female founders is growing fastest are San Antonio; Portland, Oregon; Houston; Atlanta; and Riverside, California.

Source: Inc. (2015).

The Top 50 Women Entrepreneurs in America

1. Rebecca Shanahan   **Avella Specialty Pharmacy**
2014 revenue: $800 million   3-year growth: $469.4 million

2. Nina Vaca   **Pinnacle Group**
2014 revenue: $667.3 million   3-year growth: $455.8 million

3. Pam Evette   **Quality Business Solutions**
2014 revenue: $905.7 million   3-year growth: $298.1 million

4. Dottie Herman   **Douglas Elliman Real Estate**
2014 revenue: $543.2 million   3-year growth: $196.9 million

5. Elizabeth Elting   **TransPerfect**
2014 revenue: $471.3 million   3-year growth: $171.1 million

6. Clare Hart   **SterlingBackcheck**
2014 revenue: $297.4 million   3-year growth: $170.6 million

7. Shelly Sun — **BrightStar Care**
2014 revenue: $290.2 million   3-year growth: $133.3 million

8. Christy Wyatt — **Good Technology**
2014 revenue: $211.9 million   3-year growth: $126.5 million

9. Stella Mercado — **Mercom**
2014 revenue: $156.3 million   3-year growth: $125.7 million

10. Diane Gonzales — **Netsync Network Solutions**
2014 revenue: $191 million   3-year growth: $120.6 million

11. Susan Stone — **Blue Tech**
2014 revenue: $205.5 million   3-year growth: $99.7 million

12. Jean Moore — **Sterling Computers**
2014 revenue: $257.9 million   3-year growth: $99.6 million

13. Jennifer Maier — **WDS**
2014 revenue: $178.8 million   3-year growth: $97 million

14. June Ressler — **Cenergy International Services**
2014 revenue: $259.8 million   3-year growth: $94.3 million

15. Deb Weidenhamer — **American Auction Co.**
2014 revenue: $203.6 million   3-year growth: $84.6 million

16. Rebecca Cenni — **Atrium Staffing**
2014 revenue: $185.4 million   3-year growth: $83.5 million

17. Sharon Virts — **FCi Federal**
2014 revenue: $108 million   3-year growth: $74.1 million

18. Chris Green — **Saratoga Roofing & Construction**
2014 revenue: $81.9 million   3-year growth: $70.4 million

19. Veronica Edwards — **InGenesis**
2014 revenue: $118 million   3-year growth: $60.5 million

20. Mary Kariotis — **Merrimak Capital Co.**
2014 revenue: $96.6 million   3-year growth: $59.1 million

21. Rebecca Thomley — **Orion Associates**
2014 revenue: $107.2 million   3-year growth: $58.9 million

22. Denise Legg — **MegaCorp Logistics**
2014 revenue: $102.6 million   3-year growth: $54.8 million

23. Lauren Boyer — **Underscore Marketing**
2014 revenue: $90.2 million   3-year growth: $53.1 million

24. Jamie Rios — **Accurate Personnel**
2014 revenue: $91.5 million   3-year growth: $51.2 million

25. Tina Hodges — **Advance Financial**
2014 revenue: $74 million   3-year growth: $47.1 million

26. Vinita Gupta — **Apex Resources**
2014 revenue: $59.8 million   3-year growth: $46 million

27. Keri Wright — **Universal Asset Management**
2014 revenue: $54.8 million   3-year growth: $44.5 million

28. Lauryn Blank — **Global Facility Management & Construction**
2014 revenue: $69.9 million   3-year growth: $41.8 million

29. Therese Tucker — **BlackLine**
2014 revenue: $56.9 million   3-year growth: $41.2 million

30. Frances Pierce — **Data Systems Analysts**
2014 revenue: $106.9 million   3-year growth: $40.9 million

31. **Kristen Castillo Hall** **Logistics Planning Services**
    2014 revenue: $59.8 million   3-year growth: $40.7 million

32. **Kristen Bunnell** **RiverRoad Waste Solutions**
    2014 revenue: $68.5 million   3-year growth: $39.1 million

33. **Meredith Bronk** **Open Systems Technologies DE**
    2014 revenue: $107.9 million   3-year growth: $39.1 million

34. **Amy Kothari** **My Alarm Center**
    2014 revenue: $77 million   3-year growth: $38 million

35. **Mardi Norman** **Dynamic Systems**
    2014 revenue: $102.1 million   3-year growth: $37.6 million

36. **Cassandra Sanford** **KellyMitchell**
    2014 revenue: $92.2 million   3-year growth: $36.7 million

37. **Lauren Dixon** **Dixon Schwabl**
    2014 revenue: $53.3 million   3-year growth: $33.8 million

38. **Eva Cherry** **Silicon Mechanics**
    2014 revenue: $63.4 million   3-year growth: $33.3 million

39. **Kamakshi Sivaramakrishnan** **Drawbridge**
    2014 revenue: $32.9 million   3-year growth: $32.8 million

40. **Adriana Smith** **Taborda Solutions**
    2014 revenue: $47.5 million   3-year growth: $32.1 million

41. **Kristi Alford** **E2 Optic**
    2014 revenue: $31.6 million   3-year growth: $35.2 million

42. **Patricia Bible** **KaTom Restaurant Supply**
    2014 revenue: $65 million   3-year growth: $29.9 million

43. **Limor Fried** **Adafruit Industries**
    2014 revenue: $33.2 million   3-year growth: $29.2 million

44. **Saki Dodelson** **Achieve3000**
    2014 revenue: $67.1 million   3-year growth: $29.1 million

45. **Lisa Hufford** **Simplicity Consulting**
    2014 revenue: $43.4 million   3-year growth: $29.1 million

46. **Kathy Phillips** **Primitives by Kathy**
    2014 revenue: $47.5 million   3-year growth: $29.1 million

47. **Nancy Bray** **Shelby Mechanical**
    2014 revenue: $37.1 million   3-year growth: $28.8 million

48. **Lale White** **XIFIN**
    2014 revenue: $52.3 million   3-year growth: $28.6 million

49. **Peg Stessman** **StrategicHealthSolutions**
    2014 revenue: $40.1 million   3-year growth: $28.1 million

50. **Nellie J. Torres** **ProjectSpan Services**
    2014 revenue: $28.7 million   3-year growth: $27.4 million

Source: Inc. (2015).

Support and Resources for Women Entrepreneurship

Women-Owned Small Businesses and Federal Contracting

The SBA launched the Women-Owned Small Businesses (WOSB) Federal Contracting Program in 2011.

- The program allocates federal funds to be spent on contracts with economically disadvantaged women-owned small businesses.

Source: Small Business Administration (2016).

- As of 2016, 5% of federal contracts are now given to women owned small businesses.

Source: Forbes (2016).

About three-fourths of women-owned firms hold federal contracting certifications.
Source: WIPP (2015).

Investment Support

10 Sources for Small Business Grants
- Grants.gov
- InnovateHER Challenge
- Small Business Innovation Research and Small Business Technology Transfer programs
- Women's Business Centers
- Economic Development Agencies
- Small Business Development Centers
- Amber Grant
- Eileen Fisher Women-Owned Business Grant
- FedEx Small Business Grant
- Mission Main Street Grants

Source: Nerdwallet (2015).

Networking organizations and organizations that connect women entrepreneurs to investors.
- Astia
- Dell Women's Entrepreneur Network (DWEN)
- The Vinetta Project
- Women 2.0.

Source: Forbes (2016).

Accelerators and Training

- Accelerators, boot camps, and leadership training for women entrepreneurs.
  - Dreamit Athena
  - EY Entrepreneurial Winning
  - MergeLane
  - Million Dollar Women Workshop
  - Springboard Enterprise and Women's Startup Lab

Source: Forbes (2016).

Educational support programs.
- Hello Fearless
- Rent the Runway Project Enterprise
- Tory Burch Fellows Competition
- Women's Business Enterprise National Council (WBENC)

Source: Forbes (2016).

Networking and Advocacy Groups

Networking Groups for small- to mid-size companies
Source: Forbes (2016).

- Chic CE
- Ellevate
- The National Association of Women Business Owners
- Savor the Success
- She Owns It
- SheWorx
- The Boss Network
- Womancon

Women Presidents' Organization has more than 1,800 accomplished women entrepreneurs at the multimillion-dollar level who aim to increase their business success.
- 3% of women-owned businesses gross over a million dollars a year and qualify for WPO membership.
- 70% of WPO member do business with each other.

Source: Women Presidents Organization (2016).

Certification for Women-Owned Business, Examples

WBENC Certification (Women's Business Enterprise National Council)
The WBENC certification for women-owned businesses is one of the most widely recognized and respected certifications in the nation. Accepted by hundreds of corporations within the country and a number of federal, state, and local government agencies, WBENC certification is an important marketing tool for expanding a company's visibility among decision makers in corporate supply chain diversity and procurement organizations. WBENC is also an approved Third Party Certifier for the United States Small Business Administration (SBA) Women-Owned Small Business (WOSB) Federal Contracting Program.

- WBENC launched the Student Entrepreneur Program (SEP) to foster growth for female run businesses. The program includes one-on-one mentoring, and a pitch competition to win 10,000 in seed money for their business. The program is focused on bringing more women into the STEM field.

Source: Enterprising Women Magazine (2016) .

WBE Certification (Woman Business Enterprise)
This is the certification The National Women Business Owners Corporation (NWBOC) has provided for 20 years, and it is generally accepted by corporations and many states or local government entities.
Source: WBE Certification.

A WBENC certified WBE is a business concern, which has gone through a rigorous and stringent certification process to confirm the business is owned, managed, and controlled by a woman or women. WBENC certified WBEs use their certification credentials to gain access to WBENC corporate members, as well as a number of federal, state, and local government agencies. In addition, WBENC certified WBEs also gain access to over 10,000 other WBENC-certified WBEs in order to purchase products or services and partner on joint venture opportunities.

WOSB Certification (Woman-Owned Small Business) or EDWOSB Certification (Economically Disadvantaged Women-Owned Small Business)
These are the certifications related to the SBA procurement and federal contracting program for women business owners.
WOSB/EDWOSB certification continues to increase significantly from year to year. While still low, 8(a) certification is higher than last year. Most certifications are more prevalent for companies with higher annual revenues. Certification is least prevalent among companies with revenues under $250,000, fewer than six employees and non-WIPP members.
Source: Women in Public Policy (WIPP) Survey (2015).

VBE Certification (Veteran Business Enterprise) or VWBE (Veteran Woman Business Enterprise)
This is the newest certification offered by The National Women Business Owners Corporation (NWBOC) for veterans. We are working closely with national veteran's groups for roll-out.
Source: VBE Certification.

WEB Certification (Women's Enterprise Business)
Women's Enterprise or WEB certification, offered by The Women's Business Enterprise National Council (WBENC), verifies that the company must be at least 51% unconditionally and directly owned and controlled by one or more women who are U.S. citizens.

SDB (small disadvantaged business) certification.
For businesses that are disadvantaged but not in the 8(a) program

• DV (disabled veteran) certification.
For business owners who are veterans of the U.S. armed forces and have been disabled in action.

• MBE (minority business enterprise) certification.
For race-based minority-owned businesses.
Source: STEAM Magazine, Summer/Fall (2016).

Global Women Entrepreneurship

- In 10 economies, women are as likely as men, or more likely than men, to be entrepreneurs.
  - These economies come from three regions: El Salvador and Brazil in Latin America and the Caribbean; Vietnam, Indonesia, Malaysia, and the Philippines in Southeast Asia; and Zambia, Nigeria, Uganda, and Ghana in Africa.

Source: GEM Women's Report (2014).

- 10,000 Women.
  - In 2008, based on a growing body of research to support the economic opportunity of investing in women, Goldman Sachs launched 10,000 Women to provide women entrepreneurs around the world with business management education, mentoring, and networking, and access to capital. To date, the initiative has reached over 10,000 women from across 56 countries and resulted in immediate and sustained business growth for graduates of the program.

Source: Goldman Sachs (2016).

- The United States ranks first in the world for entrepreneurship at 82.9, eight points ahead of second ranked Australia (74.8).
- This year, the United Kingdom, Denmark, and the Netherlands climbed into the top five, displacing Sweden, France, and Germany.
- Chile outperforms the rest of Latin America and ranks #15 - among the top nations in the world for female entrepreneurship.
- Many Latin American countries experienced large declines over last year; Colombia, Peru, Venezuela, and Panama all dropped by at least five ranks.
- The percent of female entrepreneurs who are highly educated—those that have participated in some form of post-secondary education—has increased 9%.
- Overall total early-stage entrepreneurship activity (TEA) rates have increased by 7% since 2012,
- The gender gap (ratio of women to men participating in entrepreneurship) has narrowed by 6%.
- EA rates and gender gap ratios saw positive upward movement in three regions: factor- and efficiency-driven Asia; Latin America and the Caribbean; and innovation-driven Europe.
- Women ages 25-34 have the highest rates of entrepreneurship.
- 33% of women entrepreneurs in the economies studied have a secondary degree or higher level of education.
- The highest prevalence of women entrepreneurs operating in teams was in the innovation-driven Middle East (27%) and innovation-driven Asia and Oceania (24%) regions.
  - Teams were especially rare among women entrepreneurs in factor-driven Asia (7%); Africa (11%); and Latin America and the Caribbean (11%).

Global Women Entrepreneurship

33%

women entrepreneurs in the economies studied have a secondary degree or higher level of education.

25-34

years old women have the highest rates of entrepreneurship

Top 10 countries for female entrepreneurs in 2015.
1. United States
2. Australia
3. United Kingdom
4. Denmark
5. Netherlands
6. France
7. Iceland
8. Sweden
9. Finland
10. Norway
Source: Female Entrepreneurship Index (2015).

Programs and Resources for Global Women's Entrepreneurship, Examples Global Entrepreneurship Week Women

- International Women's Entrepreneurial Challenge Foundation
    - IWEC is a 501c(3) registered nonprofit organization based in New York City.
    - It is an initiative of the Barcelona Chamber of Commerce, in partnership with the Chamber of Commerce of Manhattan (New York) and FICCI/FLO (the Federation of Indian Chambers of Commerce and Industry Ladies Organization) supported by the U.S. Department of State. Soon after, The Cape Chamber of Commerce in South Africa became a vital partner.
- Dell puts Australia in the top spot for Potential Women Entrepreneur Leaders. Over half of Australian women who start businesses are college-educated, which provides them with networks and experiences that they can leverage for growth.
Source: Inc. (2015).

- GEW Women celebrates female entrepreneurs and others in the space while offering opportunities to expand their networks, identify resources, and share knowledge with women around the world.
- Focus
    - Programs around the world fostering female entrepreneurs.
    - Efforts to increase participation of young women in STEM education fields.
    - Female investors.
    - Women in leadership.
    - Women in tech.
    - Research around female owned businesses.
Source: GEW Women Global Entrepreneurship Index.

Vital Voices

- The program includes customized business skills training, technical assistance, leadership development, and access to networks to grow their businesses and increase their leadership impact.
- Through global and regional online and in-person trainings, fellows focus on strategy and long-term business value paired with action-oriented plans.
- They amplify their role as leaders in their businesses and their communities to create jobs, stimulate long-term economic growth and produce wider social benefits.
Source: Vital Voices.

Wamda

- Wamda is a platform of programs and networks that aims to accelerate entrepreneurship ecosystems across the world, with a focus in the Middle East.

Source: GEW Women (2015).

Economic Empowerment of Women (IEEW)
- The group focuses on mentoring and educating women entrepreneurs from Rwanda and Afghanistan. This is the 10th anniversary of the program in Afghanistan.

Inventions and Patents

- The number of women across the globe filing patents with the U.S. Patent and Trade Office over the past 40 years has risen fastest within academia compared to all other sectors of the innovation economy.
- From 1976 to 2013, the overall percentage of patents with women's names attached rose from an average of 2% to 3% across all areas to 10% in industry.
    - 12% in individuals and 18% in academia.
- The rate of patents with women's names was highest in Eastern Europe, Asia, and several African countries.
    - A result reflecting other research that found greater gender parity in communist and former communist countries.
- Neither academic, nor industrial, nor government patents came close to reflecting women's current representation in STEM—the fields most associated with patentable discoveries. Women make up one-third of all researchers in the STEM fields.

Source: Indiana University (2015).

- Fewer than 15% of the US based inventors listed on patents were women. At the current rate, it will take another 140 years to balance the number of female and male inventors. Changing these statistics begins by working with today's girls and women (1) to spark their interest in STEM, and (2) to promote their advancement to their maximum potential through mentorship and training. To this end, we at the USPTO launched our "All in STEM" initiative. As part of this initiative, USPTO partners with Invent Now, with whom we run an annual summer program called Camp Invention. This program reaches more than 100,000 kids every year (girls + boys including those from under privileged backgrounds) and its programs provide hands-on STEM skills, as well as basics on patents, trademarks and even entrepreneurship. The USPTO also conducts an annual National Summer Teacher Institute, designed to help middle and high school teachers better prepare our young minds for STEM careers as well as invention, innovation and entrepreneurship. And we even partnered with the Girl Scouts of America of our Nation's Capitol to create a patch on IP and innovation. If the young girls learn a little about patents, trademarks, trade secrets and copyrights, and put their innovative spirits to work on creating something, they can earn an IP patch. I was a girl scout – both a Brownie and a Junior, and the patches I remember being able to earn were on First Aid and Sewing. I think we can do better than that by giving our girls the skills they need to succeed in the 21st century innovation economy!

Source: USPTO Administrator at Million Women Mentors.

Chapter 5: Marketplace - Overview

Women have the "power of the purse" and women can use it to their advantage. When it comes to the marketplace, it all boils down to purchasing power. And women are it—not only in the United States, but worldwide. Globally, women account for $20 trillion in annual consumer spending. By 2028, women will control 75% of all discretionary spending worldwide. The income for these women is also increasing, and the spending power will continue to grow. One billion women participate in the global workforce and are enjoying the discretionary income for purchasing power.

The American context is vivid. Today, nearly half of all primary breadwinners in the home are women. This economic equality is great for business. Women's household spending in the United States is $8.2 trillion. Women in the United States make 85% of all consumer purchases. They are the decision makers in each and every sphere. For example, women purchase 94% of furnishings and make 92% of vacation decisions—from new cars to computing, women are controlling the marketplace.

What about women and wealth? Women control 51% of the total private wealth in the United States. Nine out of every 10 women eventually take charge of their family's wealth. As our population ages, this number is ever growing. Their economic power is reflected in the labor force, in education, and in women entrepreneurship. Women are absolutely key to our marketplace and economy. If a business is not marketing toward women, it's destined for failure.

Call to Action:

- Share these statistics. Few really know just how monumentally involved women are in the marketplace. Build the case for female leadership in the consumer and financial market.

- Support the banks and financial institutions that do well to promote the advancement of women by backing their endeavors.

- The number of wealthy women in the United States is growing twice as fast as wealthy men. Join the growing trend. Know how to support women with financial services and recognize the women leaders and the men who take on women as clients who care deeply.

- Tell the story of women in control as consumers and protectors of the family's financial assets. Enjoy being a consumer and family spender. Be thoughtful with how you spend your hard-earned dollars, but also realize that you have enormous power and potential to send a message to consumers with how you spend your money.

CHAPTER 5: MARKETPLACE

Overview

Women's Datapoint	Statistic
Annual Consumer Spending (Globally)	$20T
Projected Annual Income in 2017 (Globally)	$15.6T
Household Spending Annually	$8.2T
Percent of Consumer Purchases Made	85%
Earned Income From Work Annually	4.3T
Women's Control of Wealth	51% or $14T

The Global Context

Women's Global Purchasing Power

$28T — 2018
Consumer Spending

$20T — 2013
Consumer Spending

- Globally, women account for $20 trillion in annual consumer spending (U.S. dollars).
Source: Harvard Business Review (2009).

- In the next five years, consumer spending by women globally will rise to $28 trillion.
Source: Forbes (2016) and Harvard Business Review(2009).

- Women represent a growth market bigger than China and India combined—more than twice as big.
Source: Harvard Business Review (2009).

- By 2028, women will control 75% of discretionary spending worldwide.
Source: EY (2009).

- Women without children spend on average twice as much on beauty and hair-related products a month than their counterparts.
Source: New York Times.

- Women without children also spend 35% more on groceries than their counterparts.
Source: Drugstore News.

- Women without children spend 60% more days abroad.
Source: New York Times.

Market

Women and the Insurance Market Globally

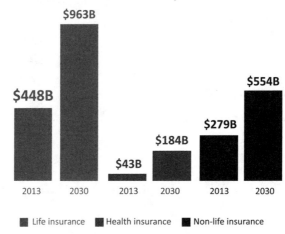

■ Life insurance   ■ Health insurance   ■ Non-life insurance

- Annual premium value of the women's global life insurance market is predicted to grow from $448 billion to approximately $963 billion in 2030.
  Source: Accenture, IFC, and AXA Group.

- Annual premium value of the women's global health insurance market is predicted to grow from $43 billion in 2013 to approximately $184 billion in 2030.
  Source: Accenture, IFC, and AXA Group.

- Annual premium value of the women's global non-life insurance market is predicted to grow from $279 billion in 2013 to approximately $554 billion in 2030.
  Source: Accenture, IFC, and AXA Group.

Earning Power

- By 2017, women's income will jump by almost $6 trillion to 15.6 trillion dollars.
  Source: EY.

Women in the Global Workforce

- One billion women participate in the global workforce—this number will likely grow to 1.2 billion in the next five years.
  Source: Boston Consulting Group.

- If women were to participate in the world of work identically to men, an additional $28 trillion or 26% of incremental global GDP, could be created.
  Source: McKinsey & Company.

Earning Power

Women's Income by 2017

$15.6T
Women's Income

Women in the Global Workforce

1B
women in the global workforce

1.2B
women in the global workforce

2013   2018

The American Context

- Today, nearly half of all primary breadwinners are women, and since 1970, women's labor has contributed $13,000 to the median family income and expanded the economy by $2 trillion dollars.

Source: FACT SHEET: Obama Administration Record for Women and Girls (2014).

- Women's economic equality is good for business. Companies greatly benefit from increasing leadership opportunities for women, which is shown to increase organizational effectiveness. It is estimated that companies with three or more women in senior management functions score higher in all dimensions of organizational effectiveness.

Source: GCC Women in Leadership Women Matter (2014) .

- It is calculated that women could increase their income globally by up to 76% if the employment participation gap and the wage gap between women and men were closed. This is calculated to have a global value of USD $17 trillion.

Source: Close the Gap! The Cost of Inequality in Women's Work (2015) .

- When more women work, economies grow. An increase in female labor force participation—or a reduction in the gap between women's and men's labor force participation—results in faster economic growth.

Source: Gender Equality in Education, Employment, and Entrepreneurship: Final Report to the MCM (2012).

- Increasing women and girls' education contributes to higher economic growth. Increased educational attainment accounts for about 50% of the economic growth in OECD countries over the past 50 years.

Source: Gender Equality in Education, Employment, and Entrepreneurship: Final Report to the MCM (2012).

- The OECD Gender Initiative examines existing barriers to gender equality in education, employment, and entrepreneurship. This website monitors the progress made by governments to promote gender equality in both OECD and non- OECD countries and provides good practices based on analytical tools and reliable data.

Source: OECD Gender Initiative.

The OECD Gender Initiative examines existing barriers to gender equality in education, employment, and entrepreneurship. This website monitors the progress made by governments to promote gender equality in both OECD and non- OECD countries and provides good practices based on analytical tools and reliable data.

Women's Purchasing Power

- Household spending by women in 2013 reached 8.2 Trillion dollars. *Source:* Catalyst.

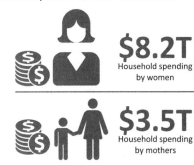

$8.2T
Household spending by women

$3.5T
Household spending by mothers

- 85% of consumer purchases in the US were made by women.
Source: FONA International.

- Mothers represent the largest consumer group with expenditures on goods and services totaling $ 3.5 Trillion-dollar in 2015.
Source: New York Times.

85%
Consumer purchases were made by women

- Women spend over $ 200 billion on new cars & mechanical servicing of vehicles each year.
Source: The Next Web.

- 75% of women identify themselves as the primary household shopper.
Source: FONA International.

- Women are already making 3 out of 4 four purchasing decisions in the home.
Source: Merrill Lynch.

Women as Decision-Makers
- Women make decisions in the purchases of 94% of home furnishings.

94%
furnishings
purchase

50%
products
marketed
to men

68%
new car
purchase

66%
personal
computer

92%
vacation
decisions

Source: Harvard Business Review.

- 50% of products typically marketed to men are purchased by women.
- 68% of new car purchase decisions are made by women.
- 66 % of personal computers are purchased by women.
- 92% of vacation decisions are made by women.
Source: FONA International.

Earning Power

- Working women in the United States generate $4.3 trillion in earned income annually.
Source: The Female Factor.

- 1.3 million women earn salaries of over $100,000.
Source: FONA International.

- By 2028, the average woman is projected to earn more than the average man in the United States.
Source: Nielsen.

- Women are the primary breadwinners in 40% of U.S. households.
Source: Business Insider.

Women and Wealth

- Women control 51% or $14 trillion of total private wealth in the United States.
Source: Harvard Business Review & Business Insider.

- 9 out of 10 women will eventually take charge of their families' wealth.
Source: Merrill Lynch.

51%
of total private wealth
were controled by women

14T
is the total private
wealth hold by women

- Women's wealth is expected to grow 7% annually.

- 27% of female respondents received their wealth through inheritance, 15% from their spouse, 9% from divorce settlements, and 5% miscellaneously.

- 30% of female respondents use family and friends as their primary source of investment advice, compared to 11% of all survey participants.
Source: NAWBO (2016).

- Private wealth controlled by women in the United States is expected to grow from $14 trillion to $22 trillion dollars by 2020.
Source: Harvard Business Review.

- The number of wealthy women in the United States is growing twice as fast as the number of wealthy men.
Source: Merrill Lynch.

- Women represent more than 40% of all Americans with gross investable assets above $600,000.
Source: BMO Financial Group.

- 45% of American millionaires are women.
Source: FONA International.

- 48% of estates worth more than $5 million are controlled by women, compared with 35% controlled by men.
- Some estimate that by 2030, women will control as much as two-thirds of the nation's wealth.
Source: Women in Leadership and Philanthropy.

Women in the Labor Force

- Women hold 48% of the jobs in the economy, almost the equivalent of 38 million more women.

- The US Economy would be 25% smaller without a high labor force participation rate for women.
Source: Boston Consulting Group.

- Women make up the majority of the workforce in 9 of the 10 occupations the BLS predicts will add the most jobs in the next eight years.
Source: Time Magazine.

Women in Education

- Women have earned nine million more college degrees than men have since 1982.

- Women now receive 57% of bachelor's degrees, 60% of master's degrees, and 52% of doctoral degrees.
Source: U.S. Department of Education.

9M
more college degrees

- Women in the US Earned 37% of the MBAs in 2010-2011.
Source: FONA International.

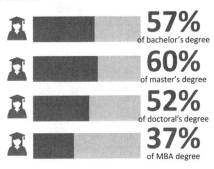

57%
of bachelor's degree

60%
of master's degree

52%
of doctoral's degree

37%
of MBA degree

Women-Owned Businesses

- Women-owned businesses comprise up to 38% (more than one-third) of all registered small businesses worldwide.
Source: Department for International Development and EY.

  - Nearly half of the businesses owned by women are in developing markets.
  - Women-owned firms have an economic impact of 3 trillion dollars that translate into the creation and maintenance of 23 million jobs, 16% of all U.S. jobs.
  - If U.S.-based women-owned businesses were their own country, they would have the 5th largest GDP in the world, trailing closely behind Germany, and ahead of countries including France, United Kingdom, and Italy.
Source: Center for Women's Business Research.

- 46% of privately held firms are now at least half-owned by women.
  - More than 10 million firms in the United States are majority-owned or equally owned by women.
Source: Women in Leadership and Philanthropy.

$3T
economic
impact

23M
jobs created

=

16%
of all U.S. jobs

Chapter 6: Finance - Overview

How about we discuss the women that live behind the numbers? In finance, women hold 54.3% of business and financial operations occupations. From accountants and editors to financial managers, that accounts for nearly four million women in total— quite an impressive number indeed. In the U.S. commercial banking industry, 57.6% are women. While the numbers are reassuring, women in those top positions are still not being promoted at the same rate as their male counterparts. The pay gap is still significant, as female financial managers make just 67.4% of what men make with the same job responsibilities.

Globally, the women's share of employment in financial and insurance activities shows a floor of 43.7% in the United Kingdom, and a ceiling of 60.9% in Finland. In the insurance industry, 1.6 million women were employed in the United States and 59.4% of all workers in the insurance industry are female. But once again, we only recognize 14% of women leaders in the insurance industry. While the opportunity is great for women in insurance, the numbers need to continue to grow.

Women in venture capital is one of the core issues requiring change. Only 4-10% of venture capital dollars go to women. It's about venture firms and venture capital distribution. While only 16% of newly launched and micro-venture firms have at least one female founder, our hope is that the number of female-led venture capital firms will grow over time, allowing for a "trickle down" effect. So, how do we support the exciting women entrepreneurs working to build growth-oriented companies, if we don't have the women we need in venture capital firms? If we can impact venture capital, then we will see the change and growth of women in finance. If the women have the wealth, then why not use these positions to support leadership in finance, insurance, and capital investment? You can play a part in this growth by taking the following steps:

Call to Action:

- Advance more women in finance and insurance industries.

- Start by advocating for more venture capital dollars to be spent on women-led businesses and support the increase of women's presence in capital venture funds. Ask for accountability on both issues.

- Recognize the top 10 female-led venture capital firms mentioned in this chapter. Learn more about them to determine where they spend their dollars, and support those companies and brands with your consumer dollars.

- Seek gender equality and equal protection within the finance industry. More than 60% of women working in U.S. hedge funds, private equity, and venture capital areas state that their gender made success more difficult.

CHAPTER 6: FINANCE

Overview

Women in S&P 500 Finance

- Women hold 54.3% of business and financial operations occupations. That is approximately 3,863,000 women in total.

  - Accountants and Auditors 63.0%
  - Financial Managers 53.4%
  - Financial Analysts 40.5%

  Source: Bureau of Labor Statistics (2015).

CEOs • 2.1%

Board seats • 18.7%

Executive/senior-level officials and managers **• 29.3%**

First/Mid-Level officials and managers **•46.1%**

Industry Labor Force **•54.3%**

Pipeline Representation

Women in the U.S. Commercial-Banking Industry	
All Employees	57.6%
First/Mid-Level Officials and Managers	48.4%
Executive/Senior Level Officials and Managers	30.9%

Women in U.S. Funds, Trusts, and Other Financial Vehicles	
All Employees	52.8%
First/Mid-Level Officials and Managers	44.7%
Executive/Senior Level Officials and Managers	27.4%

Women in U.S. Investment Banking and Securities Dealing	
All Employees	35.4%
First/Mid-Level Officials and Managers	30.9%
Executive/Senior Level Officials and Managers	16.1%

Women in U.S. Securities, Commodity, Contracts, and Other Financial Investments and Related Activities	
All Employees	40.0%
First/Mid-Level Officials and Managers	35.6%
Executive/Senior Level Officials and Managers	18.2%.

Source: Catalyst (2015).

Women Managers in U.S. Private Equity, Venture Capital, and Hedge Funds

Just 9.4% of all U.S. fund managers are women.
Source: Morningstar (2015).

- More than 60% of women working in U.S. hedge funds, private equity, and venture capital stated that their gender made success more difficult.
Source: KPMG (2014).

- Progress is slow for women managers in U.S. private equity, venture capital, and hedge funds.
Source: Catalyst (2015).

- None of the 22 largest U.S. financial firms has ever had a woman as CEO.
- Fewer than 17% of executive-level employees are women.
Source: USA Today (2016).

Gender Differences

Pay Gap:

Occupation	Median Weekly Earnings	
	Women	Men
Financial Managers	$1,127	$1,671
Financial Analysts	$1,224	$1,493
Personal Financial Advisors	$1,004	$1,637

- Financial Managers - Women make 67.4% of what men do.
- Financial Analysts -Women make 81.2% of what men do.
- Personal Financial Advisors - Women make 61.3% of what men do.
Source: Bureau of Labor Statistics (2015).

Female executives in financial services are 20-30% more likely to leave their employer than their peers in other industries.
Source: Oliver Wyman (2016).

Globally

Women's Share of Employment in Financial and Insurance Activities	
Country	% 2014
Finland	60.9%
France	57.6%
Germany	51.2%
Italy	45.4%
Japan	51.8%
Mexico	49.9%
Norway	52.5%
Portugal	45.6%
Spain	48.1%
Sweden	51.0%
Switzerland	39.8%
United Kingdom	43.7%

Source: Oliver Wyman (2016).

Women's Representation at Leadership Levels Remains Low in the Global Financial Services Industry

- The Grant Thornton International Business Report reports women hold 18% of global CFO roles.
  - Women hold 25% of senior management roles in the global financial services industry.

18%
Global CFO roles were held by women

25%
Senior management roles were held by women

Source: Grant Thornton (2015).

- At 150 of the world's major financial institutions 16% of executive committee (ExCo) members and 4% of CEOs are women.
Source: Oliver Wyman (2014).

  - Women on ExCo representation is expected to rise to 30% in 2048.
Source: Oliver Wyman (2016).

  - Over one-third of ExCos are still entirely male.
Source: Oliver Wyman (2014).

- Female representation on boards has increased by two-thirds over the last 10 years to approximately 20%.
Source: Oliver Wyman (2016).

Select Countries

Select Countries Female Representations in Finance

| **32%** | **30%** | **4%** | **2%** |
| Sweden | Norway | South Korea | Japan |

- Currently, women have the highest representation on ExCos in Norway (30%) and Sweden (32%),
- And the lowest representation in Japan (2%) and South Korea (4%).

Source: Oliver Wyman (2016).

Growth of Women's Representation Slows as It Reaches 30%

- In some countries, such as Canada, Nigeria, and Russia, female representation was relatively high in 2013 (between 20% and 30%) but has subsequently stopped growing or even gone into reverse.
- Countries where female representation on financial services boards exceeded 25% in 2013 had an average growth rate of only 0.2% between 2013-2016 compared to 2% for countries where female representation was less than 25%.

Source: Oliver Wyman (2016).

Insurance

Employment

1.6 Million
women were employed
in the insurance industry

59.4%
of all workers in the
insurance industry are women

- In 2015, there were 1.6 million women employed in the insurance sector, accounting for 59.4% of the 2.7 million workers in the insurance industry.
  - The percentage of women workers in selected insurance occupations ranges from 51% of insurance sales agents to 77% of insurance claims and policy clerks in 2015.

Source: Insurance Information Institue (2016).

Pipeline Representation		
Occupation	Total Employed	Percent of women occupation
Insurance sales agents	615	51.2%
Claims adjusters, appraisers, examiners, and investigators	321	55.3%
Insurance claims and policy processing clerks	287	77.1%
Insurance underwriters	107	58.6%
Actuaries	21	(1)

(1) Data not shown where base is less than 50,000.
Source: Insurance Information Institute (2016).

Leadership Positions:

- 14% of ExCo seats in the Insurance industry are held by women.

Women Holds

14% of ExCo seats in the Insurance industry

6% of U.S. top insurance industry executive positions

12% of insurance industry board seats.

Source: Oliver Wyman (2016).

- 6% of top insurance industry executive positions in the United States are held by women.
  - 7% in the United Kingdom.
  - Globally, women make up only 12% of insurance industry board seats.

Source: Jacobson Insurance Talent (2014).

Gender Differences in Insurance

Gender Pay Gap

• Women are currently earning only 62 cents for every dollar earned by their male counterparts in the insurance industry
Source: Jacobson Insurance Talent (2014).

Pipeline Representation in Insurance

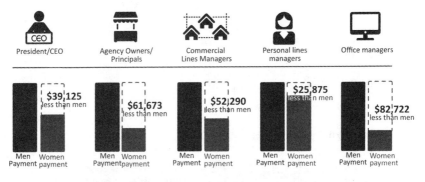

• Female president/CEO positions average $39,125 less per year than male president/CEOs.
• Female agency owners/principals earn $61,673 less on average than male owners/principals.
• Female commercial lines managers earn $52,290 less on average than male managers.
• Female personal lines managers earn $25,875 less on average than male managers.
• Female office managers earn $82,722 less on average than male office managers.
Source: Insurance Journal (2016).

Investment

Gender Differences
Women Investor

12%
higher than men's

Women investors' return

- Women investors have returns that are on average 12% higher than men's.
  - With $100,000 to invest and assuming this performance trend continued for 30 years, a woman would earn $58,000 more than a man.
- Men were also 25% more likely than women to lose money in the market.
- Men churn their portfolios 50% more than women.

Gender Differences

- In 2014, frequent traders—investors who have annual portfolio turnover of 100% or more—had median net returns of just 0.1%, compared with 4.7% for everyone else.

Source: SigFig (2015).

- In 2014, according to Vanguard, 11% of men made an exchange among mutual funds in their accounts, compared with 7% of women.

Source: Wall Street Journal (2015).

- 11% of women expected to beat the market in 2014.
  - 15% outperformed the market.
- 17% of men expected to beat the market in 2014.
  - 16% outperformed the market.
  - Men are 1.5X more confident that they will beat the market in 2015.

Source: SigFig (2015).

- 42% of women used professionally managed accounts.
  - Compared with 36% of men.
  - The others were designated "do-it-yourselfers."

Source: Wall Street Journal (2015).

Women in Venture Capital

Venture Capital

For more data on women's entrepreneurship, see Chapter 4 - Entrepreneurship

- Between 4% and 10% of venture capital funds go to women.

Source: Babson (2014) and TechCrunch (2016).

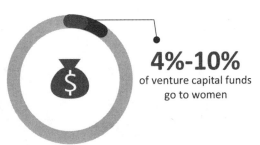

4%-10%
of venture capital funds go to women

In a survey of the top 100 venture capital firms globally:

Venture Capital Firms Globally

- 7% of the partners (54 of 755) are women.
- 38% of the top 100 firms have one or more female partner.

7%
of the partners (54 of 755) are women

14%
of the 100 top firms have 20% or more female partners

38%
of the top 100 firms have one or more female partner

3%
of the 100 top firms were founded or co-founded by women

- 14% of the 100 top firms have 20% or more female partners.
- 3% of the 100 top firms were founded or co-founded by women.

In a survey of venture capital firms of various sizes globally:

- 8% of partners are women.

In a survey of corporate venture arms and accelerator firms:

Female Partners

- Women hold just under 12% of the partner roles at both accelerators and corporate venture firms.
- Women hold 22% of the roles on the investment team at the associate, vice president and principal levels.

Source: TechCrunch (2016).

8%
of partners are women

Female-Founded Firms

- 16% of newly launched venture and micro-venture firms, 20 firms in all, had at least 1 female founder.
- Looking out over five years, the percentage drops to 12% and 29 firms.
  - This suggests that the creation of female-founded venture firms is accelerating.
- At the 29 firms founded by at least one female co-founder in the last five years, fully half of the investing partners are women.
- The percentage of funded startups with at least one female founder increased from 9% to 18% between 2009 and 2014.

Source: TechCrunch (2016).

Top 10 Female-led Venture Capital Firms

- Built by Girls [BBG]
- Aligned Partners
- Forerunner Ventures
- Illuminate Ventures
- Cowboy Ventures
- Aspect Ventures
- Belle Capital
- Golden Seeds
- The Women's Venture Capital Fund
- Monitor Ventures

Source: Female Entrepreneurs (2015).

Female Partners

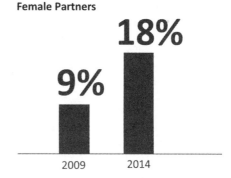

Data regarding the percentage of venture funding women-founded firms receive varies from 4%-10% depending on its source.

Chapter 7: Technology - Overview

More than ever, technology-based organizations are forging great change by becoming the industry leaders and game-changers, and by seeking tech-savvy and skilled workers. Since 80% of all jobs require some form of tech skill, every company is essentially a tech company. Technology is everywhere, and it recognizes no boundaries. But women are not moving fast enough, especially within Silicon Valley.

An example is computer science jobs. By 2020, we will see 1.4 million computer science jobs available in the United States, but women will hold only 25% of those. Currently, about 30% of all workers in the technology sector are women. While women hold 57% of all professional occupations, that number plummets to 25% when referencing computer-related jobs. It is no mystery that the tech industry is a male-dominated one, but women have an opportunity here to grow. And when women are pushed into this industry, the salary levels are coming closer to pay equity.

In the high-tech industry, the quit rate of women is more than twice as high than that of men. Almost one out of two women are quitting their jobs in the high-tech sector. The United States, as well as the global market, are both dependent on technology, and those jobs are some of the most exciting opportunities we've seen in decades, and as we continue forward, those with tech skills will dominate our economies.

One of the greatest areas of tech-related jobs opportunity is through social media. Today, 68% of all women use social media, compared to 62% of all men. As far as Facebook is concerned, 77% of women report they use it, compared to 66% of men. In terms of Pinterest and Instagram, men out use women by about 8%. In regards to LinkedIn and Twitter, the usage rates are close to equal.

As we look at women's education and technology, we learn that girls start well in technology, as females account for 56% of advanced placement test-takers. Yet, only 19% of that group participated in the advanced placement exam for computer science. We must encourage, support, and mentor those girls to move forward in this industry. Women hold 57% of undergraduate degrees, but we see a great fallout in the tech sector.

Female entrepreneurs in the tech industry have every opportunity to grow, secure contracts, and develop into some of the strongest leaders in the entrepreneurship world. This chapter discusses powerful women in tech, the best cities for women in tech, and some of the leading tech organizations and associations. Each of these nationally based organizations can prove to be indispensable for networking and employment.

Call to Action:

- Choose a tech career and work toward pay equity while remaining on the cutting edge of change.
- Get engaged by joining social media sites like Facebook, Pinterest, Instagram, and LinkedIn.
- Note the numerous associations that are tech related and growing, and get engaged in one or more and become a leader. Look for role models in both organizations and with a great employer.

CHAPTER 7: TECHNOLOGY

Jobs

- By 2020, there will be 1.4 million computer science jobs available in the United States.

Source: Bureau of Labor Statistics (2014).

While engineering and computer-related fields as some of the fastest growing fields in the United States, women only hold about **one-quarter or less** of those positions.
Source: Techrepublic (2014).

- In 2015, women held 57% of all professional occupations, yet they held only 25% of all computing occupations.
Source: NCWIT (2016).

- 30% is the average percentage of women working in the tech industry based on diversity reports published by 11 of the world's largest tech companies in 2014.
Source: CNET (2015).

Category	Female Only	Mixed-Sex Team	Male Only	Number of Matchable Patents
Communications	2.1%	8.5%	89.4%	1,163,480
Computer Hardware	1.7%	9.7%	88.5%	132,486
Computer Peripherals	1.9%	9.7%	88.4%	45,732
Information Software	2.9%	15.1%	82.0%	105,256
Semiconductors. Solid-Sate Device	2.0%	10.5%	87.5%	156,310
All Information Technology	2.1%	10.5%	87.4%	603,192

Source: NCWIT (2015).

Percent of total women employed in tech industry:
- Computer and information systems managers 27.2%
- Computer and mathematical occupations 24.7%
- Computer systems analysts 34.2 %
- Information security analysts 19.7%
- Computer programmers 21.0%
  - Software developers, applications, and systems software 17.9%
  - Web developers 34.3%
  - Computer support specialists 26.4%
  - Database administrators 38%
  - Network and computer systems administrators 15.9%
  - Computer network architects 12.1%
  - Computer occupations, all other 24.3%
  - Operations research analysts 50.7%
  - Statisticians 52.9%

Source: Department of Labor Current Population Survey (2015).

Reasons why there are so few women in tech industry:
- Why there are so few women in corporate leadership jobs.
  - Women are on average paid less than men in their first jobs.
  - Men frequently advance faster than women.
- And particularly in technology industries:
  - Women often feel like "outsiders."
  - Female role models are scarce.

Source: Fastcoexist (2015).

Women in Tech Salary

- In 2008, technical women earned an average salary of $70,370.21. Over the same time period, men's salaries averaged $80,357.

Source: NCWIT (2010).

- Among certain types of computer programmers, men made on average 28.3% more than their female counterparts.

Source: LA Times (2016).

- A U.S. female web developer makes 79 cents to the dollar men make for the same job.

Source: Deloitte (2015).

Tech Occupations

Payment as Web Developer

113

Computer and Information Technology Occupations by Selected Caracteristics: (2014 Annual Averages)				
Occupation Name	Median Weekly Earnings[1]			Women as a Percentage of Total Employed[2]
	Total	Men	Women	
All Occupations	$791	$871	$719	46.9%
Computer and Information Systems Managers	$1,730	$1,763	$1,529	26.7%
Computer Systems Analysts	$1,385	$1,460	$1,259	34.2%
Information Security Analysts	$1,419	-	-	18.1%
Computer Programmers	$1,409	$1,447	$1,253	21.4%
Software Developers, Applications, and Systems Software	$1,693	$1,736	$1,457	19.8%
Web Developers	$1,129	$1,245	$988	35.2%
Computer Support Specialists	$966	$1,049	$837	26.6%
Database Administrators	$1,517	$1,662	-	28.0%
Network and Computer Systems Administrators	$1,263	$1,286	-	19.1%
Computer Network Architects	$1,633	$1,650	-	12.4%
Computer Occupations, All Other	$1,088	$1,122	$984	23.1%

Source: Department of Labor (2014).

Women Retention in Tech

Computer and mathematical occupations fell from

27.1% to **26.5**%
women workers   women workers
2011   2014

- Trending down: Across the nation, the ratio of women in computer and mathematical occupations fell from 27.1% in 2011 to 26.5% in 2014. While the number of jobs held by women increased by about 50,000 over that time, the number of jobs held by men increased by 223,000.
Source: SmartAsset (2016).

- In the high-tech industry, the quit rate is more than twice as high for women, as it is for men: 41% for women, 17% for men.

High Tech Industry Quit Rate

41%
quit rate
for women

17%
quit rate
for men

- The percentage of computing occupations held by women has been declining since 1991, when it reached a high of 36%. In 2000, the number dropped to around 31%, and 27% in 2015.
Source: Bureau of Labor (2016).

- In the United States, which has five million information technology (IT) jobs, the ratio of female IT workers also fell from 25% to 24% from 2010 to 2014, with the proportion of women in more senior roles declining three percentage points from 30% to 27% in 2014.
Source: Deloitte (2016).

- By the end of 2016, fewer than 25% of IT jobs in developed countries will be held by women.
Source: Deloitte (2016).

- Yet 56% leave their organizations at the mid-level points (10-20 years) in their careers.
Source: Hewlett., 2008

- 41% of women leave technology companies after 10 years of experience, compared to only 17% of men.
Source: NCWIT.org (2010).

- 56% of women in technology companies leave their organizations at the mid-level point (10-20 years) in their careers. For those who leave, 24% take a non-technical job in a different company; 22% become self-employed in a tech field, 20% take time out of the workforce, and 10% go to work with a startup company.
Source: NCWIT.org (2010).

- U.S. women working in science and high-tech fields are 45% more likely than their male peers to leave the industry within a year, often due to gender bias and feelings that they are being weighed against male counterparts.
Source: The Washington Post (2014).

Gender Diversity

Gender Diversity of Computing Workforce Who Were Women: 2014					
	All Women	White Women	Asian Women	Black/ African American	Latina/Hispanic Women
% of Computer Occupations Held by Women	25%	16%	5%	3%	1%

Percentage of Jobs Held by Women by Occupation and Race: 2015					
Job Title	Black/ African American	Latina	Asian	White	Women Total
Computer & Information Research Scientists	N/A	N/A	8%	13%	19%
Computer & Information Systems Managers	2%	1%	4%	20%	27%
Computer Systems Analysts	5%	2%	8%	21%	34%
Information Security Analysts	3%	0%	N/A	14%	20%
Computer Hardware Engineers	1%	3%	4%	7%	14%
Computer Programmers	2%	1%	5%	13%	21%
Software Developers	1%	1%	7%	9%	18%
Web Developers	4%	1%	4%	25%	34%
Computer Support Specialists	4%	2%	2%	19%	26%
Database Administrators	2%	1%	4%	29%	38%
Network and Computer Systems Administrators	2%	1%	1%	13%	16%
Computer Network Architects	4%	2%	1%	8%	12%
Operations Research Analysts	10%	5%	2%	37%	51%

Source: NCWIT (2015).

Employees in Leading Tech Companies		
Top Tech Companies	Female Employee	Male Employee
Airbnb	47.5%	52.5%
eBay	41.9%	58.1%
LinkedIn	38.1%	61.9%
Hewlett-Packard	33.1%	66.9%
Facebook	28.8%	71.2%
Google	27.8%	72.2%
Cisco	26.6%	74.4%
Microsoft	24.3%	75.7%
Intel	23.8%	76.2%

Leadership in Leading Tech Companies		
Top Tech Companies	Female Leaders	Male Leaders
Airbnb	29.4%	70.6%
eBay	23.1%	76.9%
LinkedIn	27.5%	72.5%
Hewlett-Packard	20.5%	79.5%
Facebook	23.1%	76.9%
Google	16%	84%
Cisco	19%	81%
Microsoft	12.5%	87.5%
Intel	16.8%	83.2%

Source: Fortune (2015).

Social Media

Today, 68% of all women use social media, compared with 62% of all men. *Source:* Pewinternet (2015).

Social Media Usage Among Internet Users		
Social Media	Female	Male
Facebook	77%	66%
Pinterest	44%	16%
Instagram	31%	24%
Linkedin	25%	26%
Twitter	21%	25%

Facebook—72% of adult internet users/62% of entire adult population.

- 77% of female internet users are facebook users.
- 82% of online adults ages 18 to 29 use Facebook.
- 79% of those ages 30 to 49,
- 64% of those ages 50 to 64
- 48% of those 65 and older.

Source: PEW Research Center (2015).

Pinterest—31% of adult internet users/26% of entire adult population.

- Women continue to dominate Pinterest–44% of online women use the site, compared with 16% of online men.
- Those under the age of 50 are also more likely to be Pinterest users—37% do so, compared with 22% of those ages 50 and older.

Source: PEW Research Center (2015).

Instagram—28% of adult internet users/24% of entire adult population.

- Instagram continues to be popular with non-whites and young adults: 55% of online adults ages 18 to 29 use Instagram, as do 47% of African Americans and 38% of Hispanics.
  - Additionally, online women continue to be more likely than online men to be Instagram users (31% vs. 24%).

Source: PEW Research Center (2015).

LinkedIn—25% of adult internet users/22% of entire adult population.

LinkedIn is the only major social media platform for which usage rates are higher among 30- to 49-year-olds than among 18- to 29-year-olds.

- Fully 46% of online adults who have graduated from college are LinkedIn users, compared with just 9% of online adults with a high school diploma or less.
- The site continues to be popular among the employed – 32% are LinkedIn users, compared with 14% of online adults who are not employed.

Source: PEW Research Center (2015).

Twitter— 23% of all Internet users/20% of entire adult population.

- Internet users living in urban areas are more likely than their suburban or rural counterparts to use Twitter. 3 in 10 online urban residents use the site, compared with 21% of suburbanites and 15% of those living in rural areas.
- Twitter is more popular among younger adults—30% of online adults under 50 use Twitter, compared with 11% of online adults ages 50 and older.
  - Women spend nearly 10 minutes social networking through the mobile web, or through apps every day, whereas men spend a little less than 7 minutes.

Source: PEW Research Center (2015) and Nielsen (2012).

Women's Education in Tech

- Girls Comprise:
  - 56% of all Advanced Placement (AP) test-takers.
  - 46% of all AP Calculus test-takers.
  - but only 19% of all AP CS (Advanced Placement Exam for Computer Science) test-takers.

Source: NCWIT (2015).

Women with Undergraduate Degrees

57% of undergraduate degrees were held by women

40-42% of undergraduate math and physical science degrees were held by women

- Women Earn
- 57% of 2013 bachelor's degree recipients who were women
  - 18% of 2013 computer and information sciences bachelor's degree recipients who were women.
  - 14% of 2013 computer science bachelor's degree recipients at major research universities who were women.
  - 37% of 1985 computer science bachelor's degree recipients who were women.

Computer Science Bachelor's Degree Recipients

1985 — **37**% are women

2013 — **18**% are women

  - 7% decline in the number of first-year undergraduate women interested in majoring in computer science between 2000 and 2014.

Source: NCWIT (2015).

Girls and Technology

Women as percentage of total IT workforce by country for Canada, Sweden, UK and US

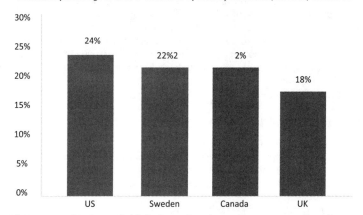

- Girls interested in STEM fields believe that they are smart enough to have a career in STEM (92% vs. 68% non-STEM girls).

- Three-quarters (71%) of STEM girls claim they are smarter than other girls their age, compared to half (51%) of non-STEM girls.

- STEM girls consider themselves hard workers (93% vs. 87% non-STEM) and feel that "obstacles make me stronger" (91% vs. 85% of non-STEM girls). STEM girls overwhelmingly feel that "whatever boys can do, girls can do" (97% vs. 91% of non-STEM girls).

- Girls who are interested in STEM have had greater exposure to STEM fields than girls who are not interested in STEM. Two-thirds (66% vs. 47% non-STEM) know someone in a STEM career, and half (53% vs. 36% non-STEM) know a woman in a STEM career. A majority of girls who are not interested in STEM (79% vs. 60% of STEM girls) know more about other careers than they do about STEM.

- 76% of STEM girls say their parents have pushed them to think about what they want to do when they grow up, compared to 67% of non-STEM girls.

- Two-thirds (65%) of mothers of STEM girls encourage their girls to pursue STEM, compared to one-third (32%) of non-STEM girls. Fathers also play a key role in STEM encouragement.

- Nearly three-quarters (71%) of STEM girls report that their fathers are very interested in STEM, compared to 52% of non-STEM girls.

- More than two-thirds (68%) of STEM girls report that their fathers encourage them to pursue STEM, compared to 35% of non-STEM girls.

- A high 81% of STEM girls express interest in pursuing a career in a STEM field—specifically, in engineering, physical/life science, math, computer science/information technology, or software development. However, only 13% say that it is their first choice.

- One-third of girls (30% STEM, 34% non-STEM) are interested in being stay-at-home moms.

- STEM girls are motivated by being in a career that requires them to think (87% STEM vs. 75% non-STEM) and a career that changes the way people do things (77% STEM vs. 66% non-STEM).

- More than half (57%) of all girls say that girls their age don't typically consider a career in STEM.
Source: GirlScouts (2012).

- Nearly half (47%) of all girls say that they would feel uncomfortable being the only girl in a group or class.

- Further, 57% of all girls say that if they went into a STEM career, they'd have to work harder than a man just to be taken seriously.

- Girls outperformed boys on a national test of technology and engineering literacy that the federal government administered for the first time in 2014.
Source: U.S. News (2016).

Women's Entrepreneurship in Tech

- Women business owners as a group are very engaged with new developments in technology. 92% report they try to stay abreast of innovations that could be incorporated into their companies.
  - When asked what else might be helpful in encouraging further innovation, most women business owners often cite incentives for partnerships between public and private companies as well as generally increased government incentives and limited government regulations.
  - Laptops, mobile devices and website management tools are nearly ubiquitous, being used by 9 companies in 10, and 4 companies in 10 report plans to add even more laptops and mobile devices in 2015.
Source: Women Impacting Public Policy (WIPP) Survey (2015).

- A study reveals that high-tech companies built by women use capital more efficiently than the norm. "More than ever before, women are influencing the face of business," it says. "They are on the cusp of becoming a leading entrepreneurial force in technology."
Source: Illuminate Ventures.

Powerful Women in Tech

The World's Most Powerful Women In Tech 2016

- Sheryl Sandberg, COO, Facebook, U.S.
- Susan Wojcicki, CEO, YouTube
- Meg Whitman, CEO, HP
- Virginia "Ginni" Rometty, CEO, IBM
- Angela Ahrendts, SVP, Apple
- Safra Catz, Co-CEO, Oracle
- Ruth Porat, CFO, Google
- Ursula Burns, CEO, Xerox
- Lucy Peng, CEO, Small & Micro Financial Services Group Alibaba
- Amy Hood, CFO, Microsoft, U.S.
- Marissa Mayer, CEO, Yahoo!
- Zhou Qunfei, Chair, Lens Technology, Hong Kong
- Gwynn Shotwell, COO, SpaceX, U.S.
- Selina Chau, Cofounder, Horizons Ventures, Hong Kong
- Mary Meeker, Partner, Kleiner Perkins Caufield& Byers, U.S.
- Jenny Lee, Managing Partner, GGV Capital, Singapore

Source: Forbes (2016).

30 Most Influential Women in 3D Printing

1. Neri Oxman, Professor at Mediated Matter Lab, MIT
2. Limor "LadyAda" Fried, Founder of Adafruit
3. Arita Mattsoff, Global Marketing Manager at Stratasys
4. Kerry Hogarth, Founder of Additive Manufacturing Show
5. Jennifer A. Lewis, Professor at Harvard & Founder of Voxel8
6. Iris Van Herpen, Fashion Designer and Artist
7. Anouk Wipprecht, Designer and Artist
8. Virginia San Fratello, Co-founder Emerging Objects, Assistant Prof. at San José State Univ.
9. Bathsheba Grossman, Sculptor and Jewelry Designer
10. Marinella Levi, +Lab, Professor at Politecnico di Milano
11. Stefanie Mueller, PhD Student at HPI Germany
12. Alice Taylor, Founder of MakieLab
13. Niki Kaufman, Founder of Normal Ears
14. Rachel Park, Journalist
15. Jemma "Jem" Redmond, Founder of Ourobotics
16. Danit Peleg, Designer and Lecturer
17. Julielynn Wong, MD, MPH, Founder of 3D4MD lecturer
18. Grace Choi, Founder of Mink
19. Bridgette Mongeon, Sculptor
20. Nora Toure, Creator of Women in 3D Printing
21. Louise "Loubie" Driggers, 3D-Designer
22. Gina Häußge, Founder of Octoprint
23. Joan Horvath, Astronomer and Autor
24. Darlene Farris-Labar, Artist
25. Nancy Liang, Design and Business Lead at Mixeelabs
26. Jessica Rosenkrantz, Co-Founder Nervous System
27. Eva Wolf, Co-Founder Airwolf3D
28. Deirdre McCormack, Chief Marketing Officer of Mcor Technologies
29. Lauren Slowik, Founder 3DIY
30. Karolina Bołądź, COO at Zortrax

Source: All3DP (2016).

10 Best American Cities for Women in Tech Jobs

SmartAsset research team used U.S. Census Bureau data and evaluated 58 metropolitan areas based on four factors: the percentage of the tech workforce that is female, the gap between men and women's earnings, women's median income after housing costs, and three-year tech employment growth.

- Washington, D.C. 40%
- Kansas City, MO 34%
- Detroit, MI 44%
- Baltimore, MD 31%
- Indianapolis, IN 29%
- Chandler, AZ 28%
- New York, NY 26%
- New Orleans, LA 38%
- Denver, CO 24%
- Fremont, CA 25%
- St. Paul. MN 26%

Percentage represents the female tech workforce.

Women Tech Associations and Organizations

Organizations and Investors Examples

- **Anita Borg Institute:** This inspiring organization works to increase the impact of women on all aspects of technology, and increase the positive impact of technology on the world's women.
- **NCWIT:** The National Center for Women & Information Technology is a coalition of over 200 prominent corporations, academic.
- **National Center for Women & Information Technology:** A nonprofit coalition of corporations, schools, government agencies, and nonprofits working together to help more women succeed in IT. Their work includes awards, programs for students, and seed funding.
- **Women In Technology International:** A network of women working in technology fields who provide support to each other through networking meetups, career services, events, and other offerings.
- **Women in Technology:** A not-for-profit organization that aims to help women advance in technology fields. They provide education in technology and leadership, networking events, mentoring, and awards. WIT membership profile consists of 95% women and 5% men.
- **Golden Seeds:** A firm that invests in early-stage companies with a female founder/CEO or executive. They also offer business training to entrepreneurs and investors.
- **NewME Accelerator:** A 12-week mentorship program in Mountain View for startups led by a minority founder (African American, Latino, or female).
- **Springboard:** Their "Forum Program" is an accelerator with two months of coaching for women-led businesses. They also offer pitch practice and educational programs to learn how to fundraise.
- **Women Innovate Mobile:** A three-month mentorship program in New York City for mobile-focused startups with at least one female founder. They offer $18,000 in funding in exchange for 6 percent equity.

- **Professional Organizations and Alliances Examples**
  - 63% have been in the technology industry for more than 10 years.
  - 19% have 6-10 years of experience.
  - 33% hold senior management position and 30% are owner, principal, or sole proprietor; 47% work for consulting/professional services companies; 12% work for software development companies, and 5% work for telecommunications companies and other industries. 30% are in sales and marketing roles; 22% in technical roles; and 42% in management.

Source: Women in Technology (2016).

Education Examples

- **Astia:** A not-for-profit organization that offers paid, week-long programs to help female entrepreneurs in technology, life sciences, and clean tech to learn skills for revenue generation, sales, and fundraising. Includes a support network of over 200 investors and 300 startup executives.

- **Girl Develop It:** Technical workshops for female programmers held around the United States, as well as in Canada and Australia. They aim to create a supportive environment where women can join the discussion and show off their skills. Courses are also available online.

- **Hackbright Academy:** A 10-week training program for women in San Francisco—half learning, half doing. Applications for the fall program are due in August, and it costs $6,000.

- **Skillcrush:** A site targeted at women to help them learn technology, including tech terms, Ask Ada (named after the first programmer), and other articles.

By Location Examples

- **Bad Girl Ventures (Ohio):** A microlending organization started by Candace Kleinthat helps women-owned startups in Ohio. Borrowers also get a nine-week course on business development.

- **C.W. Developers (Chicago):** Classes and events in Chicago for female programmers. They are in the middle of their Summer Apps Program, a series of three courses to transform your idea into a web and mobile app. They also host weekly open hack nights on Thursday, where anyone can show up and get help on coding.

- **DC Web Women (Washington, DC:** A 3,000+ member organization of women in web design and development, IT, and other digital careers (such as blogging and marketing).

- **Philly Women in Tech (Philadelphia):** A community that connects women in technology fields in Philadelphia to learn from and inspire each other. Host of the 2012 Women in Tech Summit.

- **She++ (Stanford):** A conference held at Stanford University on the opportunities, challenges, and role models for women in technology, to inspire more "femgineers"—female programmers who use their skills for positive change.

- **Web Start Women (Boston):** Courses in web design and development for women in Boston. They aim to make coding less intimidating and create a supportive environment.

- **Women in Technology (U.K.):** A network of around 7,000 individuals that helps women succeed in technology careers with networking events, job training, and recruitment services.

Initiatives, Events, and Community Examples

- **Girls in Tech:** An organization with local chapters around the world that host events. Girls in Tech University brings workshops and resources to female college students pursuing a career in technology, and they also have mentorship programs for grade-school students.
- **Webgrrls:** A global organization with local chapter events, discussion boards, and job listings. Organizers of TechSpeak for Entrepreneurs, a two-day conference in New York to teach entrepreneurs to communicate with and manage their technical employees.
- **Ada Initiative:** A nonprofit that helps more women participate in open technology, like open source software and Wikipedia. They hold conferences, do consulting for organizations, and teach workshops.
- **BlogHer:** In 2005 Elisa Camahort, Jory Des Jardins, and Lisa Stone responded to the often repeated question: "where all the women bloghers?" Blogher was their answer, the largest online community of women bloghers to date.
- **CodeEd:** A program that teaches computer science to girls in underserved communities, starting in middle school. They run classes in Boston, New York, and San Francisco.
- **Girl Geek Dinners:** A community that holds dinner events for women in STEM and helps them find inspiration and mentorship.
- **GirlGeeks:** An unassuming online community with articles for women in computing, such as career advice, technology how-tos, and inspiring stories.
- **The RAISE Project:** Created by the Society for Women's Health Research, it helps women find and apply for awards and grants in science, technology, engineering, math, and mathematics.
- **Tech Girlz:** A nonprofit that hopes to inspire and educate young girls to pursue careers in technology, through events, classes, and interviews.
- **Technovation Challenge:** A program where high school girls create a prototype for an Android app, write a business plan, and pitch to VCs, while being mentored by women in tech. Created by Iridescent Learning.
- **She's Geeky:** Organizes events with an "unconference" format—attendees create and vote on topics, like Barcamp for women. (It's unclear if they have future events planned.)
- **Women 2.0:** A media organization highlighting female entrepreneurship. Organizers of Founder Friday meetups and the PITCH conferences in Silicon Valley and New York.
- **Women in Wireless:** An organization that promotes female leaders in mobile and digital through events in D.C., New York, and San Francisco and spotlights on influential women.
- **Women Who Tech:** Organizers of the yearly Women Who Tech TeleSummit, with talks by women in technology, startups, and social media. Creators of the Women2Follow hashtag on Twitter.

Organizations and Blogs Examples

- **Advancing Women in Technology:** Advancing Women in Technology (AWT) is a nonprofit organization dedicated to the advancement of women in technology through the endowment of educational scholarships and the creation of opportunities to enhance personal and professional growth, working closely with the business community to facilitate diversity and opportunity.

- **American Association of University Women:** AAUW has been empowering women as individuals and as a community since 1881. For more than 130 years, they have worked together as a national grassroots organization to improve the lives of millions of women and their families.

- **Feminist Approach to Technology:** A not-for-profit organization based in New Delhi working toward empowering women through technology.

- **Girl Develop IT:** An organization, certified by the U.S. Board of Education, that exists to provide affordable and accessible programs to women who want to learn how to code.

- **Geek Girl Blogs:** A great blogging community for women working in IT.

- **Linuxchix:** Great network of women working in Linux.

- **National Women of Color Technology Conference:** The conference recognizes the significant accomplishments of minority women in the digital world, and attracts and leverages talent in innovative, professional, and technical positions.

- **NTEN:** A member driven organization that aspires to a world where all nonprofit organizations skillfully and confidently use technology to meet community needs and fulfill their missions. It's lead by Women Who Tech advisory committee member Holly Ross.

- **MYWIT:** For over 20 years, Women in Technology (WIT) has been striving to progress the role of women in the tech industry and to better STEM education opportunities for girls.

- **Women2.0:** A SF bay area organization that aims to increase the number of young women entrepreneurs by encouraging women to work with and in the field of technology.

- **WebChick.net:** Angela Byron's blog about working in open source.

- **WEST:** WEST is a learning community that provides women in the enterprise of science and technology with the inspiration, knowledge, and connections to reach their full potential.

- **Women & Hi Tech:** Women & Hi Tech is an organization of women and men whose goal is to attract, develop, retain, support, and promote women who are interested in technology, through networking, role modeling, education and professional development.

- **Systers:** One of the world's largest email communities of technical women in computing.

- **The Kauffman Foundation:** Provides grant making on two areas—educational achievement and entrepreneurial success. They have great studies on the positive impact women CEO's have on companies.

For more technology associations, see Chapter 9.

Chapter 8: Government - Overview

The history of women in government is about their stories. As this book is going to press, we are in the midst of the most exciting presidential campaign of our lifetimes. Whether or not you like Hillary Clinton, it is remarkable to see a female running for the president of the United States, and potentially winning. Before her, 13 other women have run for the highest office in the land. We are at a point where it is fathomable, even likely, that we will see multiple female presidents in the years to come.

We are witnessing women presidents and prime ministers in other countries, so why not in the United States? This chapter offers you the names and backgrounds of some of the women that have run for president and vice president. But there is still more work to do. The U.S. Congress is composed of only 19% women and the U.S. Senate only 20%. While there are numerous efforts pushing women to play significant roles in the Senate and U.S. House of Representatives, women comprise only 23 cabinet or sub-cabinet positions.

The third branch of government, the judicial branch, doesn't help our cause. Only 4 out of 122 U.S. Supreme Court Justices have been women. But we do have three sitting today. In the federal courts, only 35% of all sitting judges are female. As for diplomats, women comprise 44% of state department employees, but only 4.8% of foreign service officers. Yet, the exciting world of global diplomacy for women is developing.

With states like Colorado, Vermont, and Arizona leading the way, we are seeing much greater progress at the state and local level with female governors, secretaries of state, lieutenant governors, and state legislators, which are almost 25% female.

On a worldwide basis, female representation amongst global government leaders in both houses of legislatures is at 22.7%. The Nordic countries are the highest, with over 40% female representation in governing chambers. Currently, women account for 20% of the cabinet-level positions worldwide. Politics shape our lives, and impact our futures, and women are driving change in the political landscape, but we still have work to do.

Call to Action:

- There is such tremendous opportunity to change the numbers for the executive, legislative, and judicial branches. Government affords women the opportunity to serve at all levels while impacting policy.

- As we grow and mature, we should all work toward supporting women leaders at every level. Whether global, national, state, or local, we can impact policy and bring "sanity" to leadership. Run for office at the local city council, state legislatures, and delegate levels. Be a strong voice and fight for women's interests as a great public servant. There are many organizations to help along the way, as well as those willing to fund campaigns and lend real capital, as well as human capital.

- More than ever, women are serving as models for global leadership. History was made with Golda Meir in Israel and now, Theresa May in the United Kingdom, and Park Geun-hye in South Korea—all model examples that we should study, learn from, and share their message with our female friends and loved ones.

CHAPTER 8: GOVERNMENT

Federal

All domestic data is post-2015 election unless specified otherwise.

Presidential & Vice Presidential

- 14 women have run for president in the history of the United States.

The First Female Presidential Nominee of a Major Party - 2016

Hillary Rodham Clinton (2008, 2016) - A graduate of Wellesley College and Yale Law School, Hillary Clinton served on the staff of the House Judiciary Committee considering the impeachment of then-President Richard Nixon. After moving to Arkansas, she ran a legal aid clinic for the poor and was appointed by President Jimmy Carter to the board of the U.S. Legal Services Corp. She was elected to the Senate from New York in 2000 and re-elected in 2006. She served on the Health, Education, Labor, and Pensions Committee; the Environment and Public Works Committee; the Special Committee on Aging; and the Senate Armed Services Committee. She also chaired the Senate Democratic Steering and Outreach Committee, and was responsible for communicating with the public about key issues before Congress. The wife of former President Bill Clinton, she is the only First Lady of the United States ever elected to public office. Clinton was a candidate for the Democratic nomination for president in 2008, losing to then-Sen. Barack Obama.

President Barack Obama appointed Clinton to serve as U.S. Secretary of State, a position she held from 2009 - 2013. In April 2015, she announced her candidacy for the 2016 Democratic presidential nomination. In June 2016, Clinton became the first woman to be a major party's presumptive nominee for president.
Source: Rutgers (2016).

The First Female U.S. Presidential Candidate - Victoria Claflin Woodhull

In 1872, **Victoria Clafin Woodhull** became a third-party candidate, running against the incumbent Republican president, General Ulysses S. Grant and his Democratic challenger, New York publisher Horace Greeley. She would not have been able to vote for herself—that right would not be granted to American women for another 50 years—but that did not deter this pioneering feminist from making a historic bid for change.

The Female Presidential Candidates From 2000-2016

Elizabeth Hanford Dole (2000) - In January 1999, Elizabeth Hanford Dole resigned her position as president of the American Red Cross, a position she had held since 1991, to consider a run for the Republican nomination for the U.S. presidency. She dropped out of the race in October 1999.

Carol Moseley Braun (2004) - Ambassador Carol Moseley Braun was among 10 Democrats seeking the 2004 presidential nomination. An attorney and a one-term

U.S. senator (1992-1998), she was the first African-American woman to serve in the Senate.

Michele Bachmann (2012) – Michele Bachmann was a candidate for the Republican nomination for president; she won the Ames straw poll in August 2011, but withdrew from the race after a disappointing showing in the Iowa caucuses. Bachmann represented a six-county Minnesota district in the House from 2007-2015, where she was a founder of the Tea Party Caucus and a vocal, visible advocate for conservative causes. She became the first Republican woman from Minnesota elected to Congress in 2006 after serving in the State Senate from 2000-2006.

Carly Fiorina (2016) is a graduate of Stanford University, the Robert H. Smith School of Business at the University of Maryland, College Park, and the MIT Sloan School of Management. Carly Fiorina moved up in business from an entry-level employee to management trainee to, in 1999, becoming Hewlett-Packard's (HP's) CEO—the first woman to lead a Fortune 50 business. After being forced to resign her position at HP, Fiorina served in a number of advisory and policymaking positions for national and state governments and led a number of charities and nonprofits. On May 4, 2015, she announced her candidacy for the Republican nomination in the 2016 U.S. presidential election, the only woman running for the Republican nomination.
Source: Rutgers (2016).

The Female Vice Presidential Candidates From 2000-2016

Winona LaDuke (1996, 2000) - Winona LaDuke was the running mate of Green Party candidate Ralph Nader.

Sarah Palin (2008) – Sarah Palin is the second woman vice presidential nominee from a major U.S. party and the first Republican woman nominee for the vice presidency. Shortly before the Republican National Convention in September 2008, Palin was named by Sen. John McCain as his choice for the vice presidency. Born on Feb. 11, 1964, Palin was selected while serving her first term as the governor of Alaska. Palin won election as governor in 2006 by first defeating the incumbent governor in the Republican primary, then a former Democratic governor in the general election.
Source: Rutgers (2016).

Congress

Women in Congress

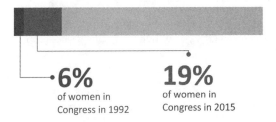

6%
of women in
Congress in 1992

19%
of women in
Congress in 2015

In the U.S. Senate

20%=20

- Overall congressional representation is approximately 19%.
- Up from 6% in 1992.

Source: The Nation (2015).

- In the Senate, women hold 20 of the 100 seats - 20%.
- In the House, women hold 84 of the 435 seats - 19.3%.

● Women in the Senate

U.S. House of Representatives

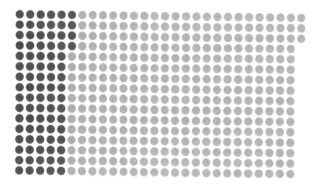

19.3%=84

● Women in the House of Representatives

Women of Color in Congress

104
women members of Congress

31.7%=33
of color women

- Of the 104 women members of Congress, 31.7% (33) are women of color.
- Total of 6.2% of congress are women of color.

Source: Rutgers (2016).

Presidential Cabinet

- 48 women have held a total of 54 cabinet or cabinet-level appointments in the history of the United States.
- Seven women currently serve in the Obama Administration in cabinet or cabinet-level positions.

Source: Rutgers (2016).

Presidential cabinet-level positions

23 Cabinet or Cabinet-level Posts Have Been Filled by Women

- Seven women have served as secretary of labor.
- Five women have served within each of these posts:
  - Secretary of health and human services.
- Four women have served within each of these posts:
  - U.S. Environmental Protection Agency administrator.
  - U.N. Ambassador.
- Three women have served within each of these posts:
  - Secretary of state.
  - Secretary of commerce.
  - Small business administrator.
  - Council of economic advisors chair.
  - U.S. (Special) Trade Representative.
- Two women have served within each of these posts:
  - Secretary of education.
  - Secretary of health.
  - Secretary of education and welfare* (health and human services).
  - Secretary of housing and urban development.
  - Secretary of the interior.
  - Secretary of transportation.
  - U.S. attorney general.
  - Office of management and budget director.
- One woman has served in each of the remaining cabinet or cabinet-level positions except three departments which have never been headed by women who were appointed and confirmed:
  - Secretary of defense.
  - Secretary of treasury.
  - Secretary of veterans affairs.

Source: Rutgers (2015).

The Supreme Court & The Judiciary

- Four of the 112 Justices to serve on the Supreme Court have been women.
    - With three women currently sitting on the bench
    - Sandra Day O'Connor (1981-2005)
    - Ruth Bader Ginsburg (1993-present)
    - Sonia Sotomayor (2009-present)
    - Elena Kagan (2010-present)
        - With the confirmation of Associate Justice Kagan, the Supreme Court had three women among its nine Justices for the first time.
        - There are currently three women among the eight Justices sitting on the court since Antonin Scalia died in February 2016.

The Supreme Court & The Judiciary:

112 Justices have served on the highest court

4 Female Justices

Federal Courts

Judges & the 13 Federal Courts of Appeal

35% =60 👤

170

- Sixty of the 170 active judges currently sitting on the 13 federal courts of appeal are female (35%).
- There are 12 women of color on the U.S. courts of appeals (7%).
    - There are seven federal courts of appeals without a single active minority woman judge.
- 33% of active U.S. district (or trial) court judges are women.
    - There are still six district courts around the country where there has never been a female judge.

Federal Judges

- There are 83 women of color serving as active federal judges across the country (10.5%).

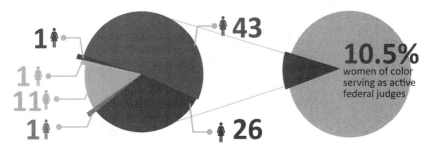

- African-American women
- Hispanic women
- Asian-American women
- Native American woman
- woman of Hispanic and Asian descent
- woman of Hispanic and African-American descent.

- 43 African-American women
- 26 Hispanic women
- 11 Asian-American women
- 1 Native American woman
- 1 woman of Hispanic and Asian descent
- 1 woman of Hispanic and African-American descent.

Source: National Women's Law Center (2016).

Diplomats

- Women make up 44% of U.S. State Department employees.
- Women make up 4.8% of U.S. Foreign Service officers.
- 4% of signatories in 31 major peace processes between 1992 and 2011 were women
  - 2.4% of chief mediators
  - 3.7% of witnesses
  - 9% of negotiators

Source: No Ceilings (2015).

Diplomats

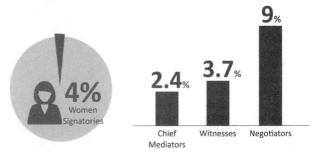

Women Ambassadors and Leaders

- 1996, 7 out of 185 women represented their countries at the United Nations (3.8%).
- 2016, 37 of 193 women represented their countries at the United Nations (19%).
- 21% of undersecretary general-level posts are held by women.
- 19% of assistant secretary general level posts are held by women.
- 11 of the 56 U.N. heads and deputy heads of mission in the field were women in 2015

Source: U.N. News Centre (2016).

- When women are involved the probability of a peace agreement lasting at least two years is increased by 20%.
    - 15 years by 35%.

Source: Women Kind (2015).

- Women make up 15.8% (40/193) of the permanent representatives and observers (commonly referred to as ambassadors) to the United Nations.

Source: Vocativ (2015).

State & Local

- On average, women are outnumbered 2 to 1 by men as state-level cabinet appointees.

Source: Center for American Progress (2014).

- In all, 77 women hold other statewide executive offices.
    - 6 governers
    - 14 secretaries of state
    - 13 lieutenant governors
    - 9 chief educational officials
    - 8 state auditors
    - 8 attorney generals
    - 7 state treasurers/CFOs
    - 3 corporation commissioners
    - 3 public service commissioners
    - 2 state controller/comptrollers
    - 1 commissioner of insurance
    - 1 commissioner of labor
    - 1 agriculture and commerce commissioner
    - 1 public utilities commissioner
    - 1 railroad commissioner

Source: Washington Post (2015).

6
Current state governors are women

2
Women of color

Governors

- Six current state governors are women (12%).
  - Only two women of color (4%).
  - 37 women have served as governor.
    - across 27 states.**

Additionally, one woman has served as governor of Puerto Rico.

Source: Rutgers (2016).

Lieutenant Governors

- There are currently 13 female lieutenant governors.

Source: Washington Post (2015).

As of 2014:

- 78 women across 36 states have served as lieutenant governor.
  - Winning 105 elections
  - Serving a collective 386 years.
- Seven states (of the 45 which have a constitutionally defined lieutenant governor position) have not had a woman appointed as lieutenant governor:
  - Arkansas
  - California**
  - Georgia
  - Idaho
  - Texas
  - Virginia
  - Washington

Source: University of Minnesota (2014).

State Legislature

15.8% 1988

24.5% 2015

1809 Female state legislators nationwide

- Midwestern states account for 40% of the cumulative female lieutenant gubernatorial service in U.S. history.
- In total, women have been elected over 110 times to the office of lieutenant governor.
  - Serving a collective 414 years in the office.

Source: Smart Politics (2016).

State Legislature

- Women make up 24.7% of all state legislators nationwide.
  - Up from 15.8% in 1988.
- Women hold 443 (22.5%) of state senate seats.
- Women hold 1,371 (25.3%) of state house seats.
- The number of women serving in state legislatures has more than quintupled since 1971.

Source: Rutgers (2015).

Statewide Elected Executive Offices

24.7% women

- Women of color make up 5% of state legislature seats.
- After the 2012 election, there are no male-only state legislatures.

Source: Center for American Progress (2014).

- In 2015, women held 24.7% of statewide elected executive offices around the country.

Source: Rutgers (2015).

Top 10 States for Female Representation in the Legislature

- Colorado (42.0%)
- Vermont (41.1%)
- Arizona (35.6%)
- Washington (34.0%)
- Minnesota (33.8%)
- Nevada (33.3%)
- Illinois (32.8%)
- Maryland (31.9%)
- Montana (31.3%)
- Oregon (31.1%)

Source: Washington Post (2015).

Mayors

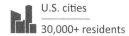
U.S. cities
30,000+ residents

18.4% of all US cities — Have a female mayor

Mayors

- 18.4% of all U.S. cities with more than 30,000 residents have a woman as a mayor.

Source: Rutgers (2015).

- 12% of the mayors of the 100 largest American cities are women.
  - Women of color are 2%

Mayors

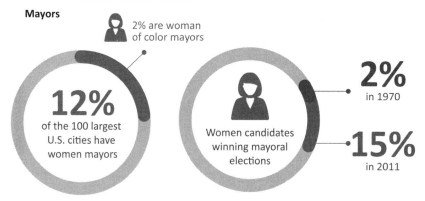

2% are woman of color mayors

12% of the 100 largest U.S. cities have women mayors

Women candidates winning mayoral elections

2% in 1970

15% in 2011

Source: Center for American Progress (2014).

- Women candidates won just 2% of mayoral elections in 1970.
  - As of 2011 they won over 15% of mayoral elections.

Source: Ferreira (2011).

Election Progress

- 40% of Americans now have at least one woman representing them in the Senate.
- New Hampshire, notably, sent an all-female delegation to Congress and elected a female governor.
- Six additional women of color were elected to the House, bringing their total number in Congress to a record 28.
- Female candidates were shown to raise as much money, and to be as successful in their election bids, as male candidates running for public office.

Source: Center for American Progress (2014).

Global

Women representation in governing chambers globally
- In the single or lower house - (22.8%).
- In the upper house - (22%).
- In both houses combined - (22.7%).
  - 13% in 1990

Source: Inter-Parliamentary Union (2016).

Women Representation in Governing Chambers by Region

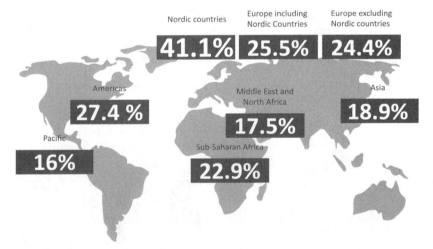

- Americas - 27.4 %.
- Europe including Nordic Countries - 25.5%
  - Europe excluding Nordic countries - 24.4%
  - Nordic countries - 41.1%
- Sub-Saharan Africa - 22.9%
- Asia - 18.9%
- Middle East and North Africa - 17.5%
- Pacific - 16%

Source: Inter-Parliamentary Union (2016).

National Parliamentarians

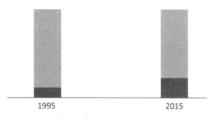

11.3%   ## 22%   ## 10
of national parliamentarians   of national parliamentarians   Women served as Head of State
were women   were women

- 22% of national parliamentarians were women.
  - A slow increase from 11.3% in 1995.
- 10 women served as Head of State.
- 14 women served as Head of Government.
- 17% of government ministers are women.
  - Many of these hold social policy portfolios such as education and family.
Source: USAID (2016).

Cabinet Positions

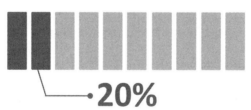

20%
of cabinet positions worldwide were held by women

- Women hold just 20% of cabinet positions worldwide.
  - They are twice as likely to hold a social portfolio as an economic one.
Source: EY (2013).

- Globally, there are 37 states in which women account for less than 10% of parliamentarians in single or lower houses.
  - Including six chambers with no women at all.
Source: USAID (2016).

Electoral Systems
- In countries with proportional electoral systems, women hold 25.2% of the seats.
- This compares with 19.6% using the plurality-majority electoral system.
- 22.7% using a mixed system.

Source: U.N. Women (2015).

- Rwanda had the highest number of women parliamentarians worldwide. Women there have won 63.8% of seats in the lower house.

Source: U.N. Women (2015).

Examples of Women Serving as Global Models

Golda Meir – Prime Minister of Israel: The first and only woman to serve as prime minister of Israel, from 1969 to 1974.

Indira Gandhi of India: Appointed prime minister of India in 1966. She was elected in 1967 and reelected twice and then returned to power.

Angela Merkel—Chancellor of Germany: Angela Merkel became German chancellor in 2005 when her Christian Democratic Union narrowly won Parliament. A chemist by training, she had held cabinet posts under Chancellor Helmut Kohl, including minister for the environment and nuclear safety. With Britain's exit from the European Union, she is now considered the senior statesman on the continent.

Ellen Johnson Sirleaf—President of of Liberia: She was elected president of Liberia in 2006. The first woman to head the government of an African nation. Johnson Sirleaf has been praised for pulling her nation out of the ashes of civil war and, more recently, out of the Ebola crisis. She won a Nobel Peace Prize in 2011, and is in the last year of her final term.

Park Geun-hye—President of South Korea: She assumed the position in Feburary 2013. Park is the first woman to be elected as president in South Korea, and is serving the 18th presidential term. Park is the first female president of a Northeast Asian nation.

Erna Solberg—Prime Minister of Norway: Assumed the position in October 2013.

Michelle Bachelet Jeria—Executive President of Chile: Assumed the position in March 2016.

Sheikh Hasina Wajed—Prime Minister of Bangladesh: Assumed the position in January 2009. She was also prime minister 1996-2001.

Beata Szydło—Prime Minister of Poland: She assumed power in November 2015. She is Poland's third female prime minister after Hanna Suchocka and Ewa Kopacz, and the first to succeed another woman (Kopacz) in office.

Margaret Thatcher—Prime Minister of Britian: She was the first woman to lead a major Western country when she became prime minister of Britain. She rose through the ranks of the Conservative Party to become prime minister in 1979, holding the position for more than 11 years. In 1990, she withdrew her bid to run again. She died in 2013.

Theresa May—Prime Minister of Britian: May, also a Conservative, became only the second female prime minister of Britain. The home secretary won the job by acclaim after other candidates dropped out of contention in the fallout from voters. May assumed the position in July 2016.

Aung San Suu Ky—State Councillor of Myanmar: Her party won 80 % of the votes in the 2015-elections, and she assumed the position in April 2016. As the Constitution is designed to prevent her from becoming president, the Parliament created the new powerful position of state councilor; a role similar to that of prime minister. She also won the 1990 elections that were annulled and was placed under house arrest for a total of 15 years over a 21-year period.

Tsai Ing-wen—President of Taiwan: A former professor and trade negotiator, Tsai Ing-wen was sworn in as president of Taiwan in May 2016.

Doris Bures—Head of the Joint Acting Presidency of Austria: She became SPÖ Member of Parliament in 1990 and party secretary general 2000-07 and again in 2008, Federal Minister without Portfolio in the Office of the Federal Chancellor in charge of Women's Affairs, Media, and Civil Service 2007-2008 and Federal Minister of Infrastructure, Trafic, Innovation, and Technology 2008-2014. She assumed office in July 2016.

Cristina Fernández de Kirchner—President of Argentina: In 2007, she became the first woman elected president of Argentina. Isabel Perón became the first female president of Argentina—and, according to some sources, the first female president in the Western Hemisphere—when she took over after the death of her husband, Juan Perón. She was deposed in a coup in 1976. Cristina Fernández de Kirchner was elected president of Argentina in 2007 and served until 2015.

Fortune's 2016 List of Game-Changing Leaders Includes 23 Women

- Angela Merkel, Chancellor of Germany
- Aung San Suu Kyi, Leader of the National League for Democracy
- Christina Figueres, Executive Secretary, U.N. Framework Convention on Climate Change
- Ruth Bader Ginsburg, Associate Justice of the U.S. Supreme Court
- Sheikh Hasina, Prime Minister of Bangladesh
- Nikki Haley, Governor of South Carolina
- Reshma Saujani, Founder and CEO of Girls Who Code
- Anna Maria Chavez, CEO of Girl Scouts USA
- Carla Hayden, Librarian of Congress nominee
- Alicia Garza, Patricia Cullors, and Opal Tometi, co-Founders of Black Lives Matter
- Chai Jing, Freelance journalist in China
- Rosie Batty, Founder of the Luke Batty Foundation
- Kristen Griest and Shaye Haver, U.S. Army Rangers
- Christine Lagarde, Managing Director of the IMF
- Gina Raimondo, Governor of Rhode Island
- Amina Mohammed, Minister of Environment, Nigeria
- Melinda Gates and Susan Desmond-Hellmann, co-Chair and CEO of the Gates Foundation
- Mina Guli, CEO of Thirst
- Clare Rewcastle Brown, Editor and Founder of the Sarawak Report

Source: Fortune (2016).

Historical Timeline

2016: Theresa May became the 2nd female prime minister of the United Kingdom.

Carla Hayden became first woman nominated for librarian of Congress. She would be the first African American to hold the position.

Former First Lady, senator of New York, and secretary of state, Hillary Clinton clinches the nomination for the Democratic Party, becoming the first female candidate for president on the ballot of a major party.

2015: The Senate confirmed Michelle K. Lee as the undersecretary of commerce for Intellectual Property and director of the U.S. Patent and Trademark Office (USPTO). Lee is the first woman and the first person of color to lead the USPTO.

2014: In January, the Senate confirms Janet Yellen as the chairwoman of the Federal Reserve Board. She is the first woman to hold the position.

Megan Smith was named as the first female CTO of the United States.

Megan Brennan was named as the first female U.S. postmaster general.

2013: The ban against women in military combat positions is removed; this overturned a 1994 Pentagon decision restricting women from combat roles.

2012: Elizabeth MacDonough was the first female appointed as Parliamentarian of the Senate.

New Hampshire elects the first all-woman congressional delegation in U.S. history, with Sens. Jeanne Shaheen and Kelly Ayotte and Reps. Carol Shea-Porter and Ann McLane Kuster.

2010: Elena Kagan is confirmed to the Supreme Court of the United States; Kagan is the fourth female to serve on the Supreme Court.

2009: Hillary Rodham Clinton becomes the third woman to hold the post of secretary of state.

Sonia Sotomayor becomes the third female and first Hispanic Supreme Court Justice.

2008: Hillary Clinton wins the New Hampshire Democratic presidential primary, becoming the first woman in U.S. history to win a presidential primary contest.

Sarah Palin, governor of Alaska, becomes the first woman to run for vice president on the Republican ticket.

2007: Nancy Pelos becomes the first woman Speaker of the House of Representatives.

2005: Condoleezza Rice becomes the first African-American female secretary of state.

Angela Merkel becomes the chancellor of Germany.

1997: Madeleine Albright is sworn in as secretary of state. She is the first woman in this position as well as the highest ranking woman in the U.S. government.

1993: Shiela Widnall becomes the first secretary of a branch of the U.S. military when she is appointed to head the Air Force.

Janet Reno becomes the first woman U.S. attorney general.

1992: Carol Moseley-Braun, of Illinois, becomes the first African-American woman elected to the Senate.

1991: On January 2, Sharon Pratt Dixon is sworn in as mayor of Washington, D.C., becoming the first black woman to serve as mayor of a major city.

1990: Dr. Antonia Novello is sworn in as U.S. surgeon general, becoming the first woman (and first Hispanic) to hold that job.

1989: Ileana Ros-Lehtinen, of Florida, becomes the first Hispanic woman elected to Congress.

1981: Sandra Day O'Connor is appointed by President Ronald Reagan to the Supreme Court, making her its first woman Justice.

1972: Juanita Kreps becomes the first woman director of the New York Stock Exchange. She later becomes the first woman appointed secretary of commerce.

1969: Shirley Chisholm, of New York, becomes the first African-American woman in Congress and the first female black U.S. representative. Her motto is: "Unbought and unbossed." She served in the House for 14 years.

1965: Patsy Takemoto Mink, of Hawaii, is the first Asian-American woman elected to Congress. She served in the House for 24 years.

1964: Margaret Chase Smith, of Maine, becomes the first woman nominated for president of the United States by a major political party, at the Republican National Convention in San Francisco.

1960: Oveta Culp Hobby becomes the first woman to serve as secretary of health, education, and welfare. She is also the first director of the Women's Army Auxiliary Corps (WAAC), and the first woman to receive the U.S. Army Distinguished Service Medal.

1933: Frances Perkins is appointed secretary of labor by President Franklin D. Roosevelt, making her the first woman member of a presidential cabinet.

1932: Hattie Wyatt Caraway, of Arkansas, becomes the first woman elected to the Senate.

1925: Nellie Tayloe Ross becomes the first woman to serve as governor of a state, in Wyoming. In the fall of 1924, she was elected to succeed her deceased husband, William Bradford Ross. (Miriam Amanda "Ma" Ferguson is inaugurated governor of Texas days later.)

1922: Rebecca Felton, of Georgia, is appointed to the Senate to fill a temporary vacancy. The first woman senator, she serves for only two days.

1916: Jeannette Rankin, of Montana, is the first woman to be elected to the House.

1887: Susanna Medora Salter becomes the first woman elected mayor of an American town, in Argonia, Kansas.

1879: Belva Ann Lockwood becomes the first woman admitted to practice before the Supreme Court.

1872: Victoria Claflin Woodhull becomes the first woman presidential candidate in the United States when she is nominated by the National Radical Reformers.
Source: World Library (2016).

Chapter 9: Associations - Overview

There are thousands and thousands of women's associations and nonprofit groups responsible for networking and advancement. In fact, women enjoy more than 1.5 million nonprofit organizations. There is an extraordinary opportunity to join in, lead, and build through one of these organizations. This chapter provides examples of business associations, nonprofits, girl's organizations, STEM organizations, and diversity associations that you can join. Leadership skills are built and relationships are made through engagement with organizations and associations.

Out of the 1.5 million nonprofit organizations, about 1 million of them are public charities, about 100,000 are private foundations, and almost 370,000 consist of other types of nonprofit organizations, including chambers of commerce, fraternal organizations, and civic leagues. Regarding business associations, this chapter offers detailed descriptions of some of the most impactful and useful ones. For example, there is Advertising Women in NY (AWNY), whose mission is to empower women in the advertising industry to achieve personal and professional fulfillment at each stage of their careers and the Association for Women in Communications (AWC), that champions the advancement of women across all communications disciplines by recognizing excellence, promoting leadership, and positioning its members at the forefront of the evolving communications era.

These organizations, which span numerous industry sectors, provide supportive and caring opportunities to women across the business arena. If you are a business owner, the National Association of Women Business Owners (NAWBO) is there to help you. If you want to get certified as a woman-owned business, Women's Business Enterprise National Council (WBENC) is there to support billions of dollars in contract opportunities. If you care deeply about public policy, then joining Women Impacting Public Policy (WIPP) may be a great fit for you. If you are leading a small business, Bringing Out Successful Sisters (BOSS) should offer you fantastic resources. The point is that no matter where you come from or what you are doing, you are not alone in the journey to develop female-led businesses.

We share many types of organizations, from technology to education. Engage at the local, state, or national level or on a global basis. Be involved—"what you give, you will reap." With that said, the following tools will help you develop and grow with millions of women by your side:

Call to Action:

- Join at least one nonprofit or female led organization. Become an active member, attending local meetings, voting, and networking with the other members in the organization. There is a tremendous amount to learn and these nonprofits offer you a fast track to obtain valuable information. The networking is significant as is the opportunity to use resources.

- Familiarize yourself with both the national and local associations. Keep a running list, and remain willing to share this list with your fellow female professionals. There is no doubt that we all need as many resources as possible to support our success. Lead and help your colleagues to ensure we all flourish.

CHAPTER 9: ASSOCIATIONS

Overview

- There are thousands of women's associations and nonprofits worldwide.
  - Global associations/nonprofits.
    - These nonprofit organizations focus on issues of global concern. Many offer professional exchange and/or volunteer opportunities abroad.

Source: ASHA (2016).

- National and domestic associations/nonprofits.
  - 1.5 million nonprofit organizations are registered in the United States. This number includes public charities, private foundations, and other types of nonprofit organizations, including chambers of commerce, fraternal organizations, and civic leagues.

Source: National Center for Charitable Statistics (NCCS) (2016).

Nonprofit Organization

1.5M
nonprofit
organizations

Tax-Exempt Organizations Breakdown

70%
1,097,689
public charities

1.5 M
tax-exempt
organizations

6.68%
105,030
private foundations

23.4%
368,337 other types

- 1,571,056 tax-exempt organizations in the United States, including:
  - 1,097,689 public charities.
  - 105,030 private foundations.
  - 368,337 other types of nonprofit organizations, including chambers of commerce, fraternal organizations, and civic leagues.

Source: NCCS Business Master File (2016).

- Community associations/nonprofits.

  - The National Council of Nonprofits is a trusted resource and advocate for America's charitable nonprofits. Through a powerful network of state associations and 25,000-plus members—the nation's largest network of nonprofits—they serve as a central coordinator and mobilizer to help nonprofits achieve greater collective impact in local communities across the country.

Congregations

312,373

congregations in the United States

Source: Council of Nonprofits (2016).

  - There were an estimated 312,373 congregations in the United States in May 2016.

Source: American Church Lists (2016).

Business Associations and Nonprofits Examples

Advertising Women in NY (AWNY): AWNY's mission is to empower women in the advertising industry to achieve personal and professional fulfillment at each stage of their careers. Membership now stands at around 1,700 and ranges from senior level executives to those just beginning their careers.

- AWNY members are professionals active in the advertising, marketing, media, digital, promotion, and public relations industries.
- Most members live and work in the tri-state area of New York, New Jersey, and Connecticut, and the organization is also open to those who live outside of this area.

Association for Women in Communications (AWC): The AWC is a professional organization that champions the advancement of women across all communications disciplines by recognizing excellence, promoting leadership, and positioning its members at the forefront of the evolving communications era.

- AWC has more than 2,000 active members, ranging in age from 18-91+. The average age is 41; most members are females from urban or suburban settings.
- Response from the AWC member survey indicates 94% are college graduates; 47% hold graduate study or degrees; just over half work in for-profit businesses and most work in companies with fewer than 100 employees; most are salaried, full-time employees; and approximately 40% are in the executive or management roles.
- Of those who responded, about half work in public relations, marketing, or communications management; the others work in fields including journalism, graphic design, photography, website development, and publishing.

Commercial Real Estate Women Network (CREW Network): CREW Network is a networking organization dedicated to advancing the achievements of women in commercial real estate. With nearly 9,000 members in more than 70 markets across North America, it focuses on business development, leadership development, industry research, and career outreach.

Enterprising Women Magazine: *Enterprising Women* is a magazine whose goal is to help women achieve the success they want through empowerment, professional networks, education, inspiration, promotion, celebration, and support.

- Members are women business owners—a community more than 10 million strong.

eWomenNetwork: eWomenNetwork adds hundreds of new members monthly and produces over 2,000 women's business events annually through 118 U.S. and Canadian chapters. It is the largest women's business event company in the world. The chapters are led by talented and caring managing directors who are not volunteers, but skilled professionals who are financially rewarded for growing the chapters and coordinating all monthly networking activities. eWomenNetwork provides thousands of speaking opportunities showcasing the best and brightest thought leaders and experts. There is no organization that features more women speakers than eWomenNetwork.

Financial Women's Association (FWA): FWA is a nonprofit professional organization established in 1956 by a group of Wall Street women. Its goals are: to advance professionalism in finance and in the financial services industry with special emphasis on the role and development of women; to attain greater recognition for women's achievements in business; and to encourage women to seek career opportunities in finance and business.

- Nearly 90% of FWA members are employed either with an outside firm or are self-employed.
- 85% hold senior positions of power and influence within their companies.
- Members are employed by companies ranging in size from very large (64%) and medium-size firms (23%) to small firms (12%).
- About 57% have completed some graduate school and post-graduate studies. About 14% hold multiple graduate degrees and 4% are at the PhD level; 99% have earned a college degree.
- Most members are long-term FWA members.

National Association for Female Executives (NAFE): Founded in 1972, NAFE provides education, networking, and public advocacy to empower its members to achieve career success and financial security. Members are women executives, business owners, entrepreneurs, and others who are committed to NAFE's mission: the advancement of women in the workplace.

- Through the annual NAFE Top Companies for Executive Women list and NAFE Women of Excellence Awards programs, it recognizes the outstanding work done on behalf of the advancement of women.

The Center for Women's Business Research: The Center provides knowledge about women business owners and their enterprises worldwide. It provides original, ground-breaking research to document the economic and social contributions of women-owned firms, and consulting and public relations services to maximize the benefits of this knowledge.

- The Center's first major piece of research was to document the existence of—and thereby legitimize—larger businesses owned and run by women (previously the U.S. Census Bureau did not collect "C Corp" data by gender).
- Most of the legislation, programming, and women-business-owner advocacy organizations use the work of the Center for women's business research to provide the rationale for recommendations for programs and policies that support women-owned businesses.

Entrepreneurial Associations and Nonprofits Examples

National Association of Women Business Owners (NAWBO): NAWBO propels women entrepreneurs into economic, social, and political spheres of power worldwide by: strengthening the wealth-creating capacity of our members and promoting economic development within the entrepreneurial community; creating innovative and effective change in the business culture; building strategic alliances, coalitions, and affiliations; and transforming public policy and influencing opinion makers.

- Business size: 68% of businesses have employees; of which 17% have 10 or more employees.
- Revenue: 25% of NAWBO members make more than $1 million in annual sales; and 34% make more than $500,000.
- Years in business: NAWBO members have owned their businesses for an average of 10 years.
- Age: 75% of NAWBO members are over the age of 45; 25% are in the 35-44 age group.

Women Impacting Public Policy (WIPP): WIPP is a national nonpartisan public policy organization that advocates for and on behalf of women and minorities in business in the legislative processes of our nation, creating economic opportunities and building bridges and alliances to other small business organizations.

- As an organization which represents over 4.7 million businesswomen, they have within their ranks Republicans, Democrats, Independents, liberals, conservatives, and every variety of opinion. They urge and encourage their members to become involved and politically active as their consciences dictate, but these members do not speak for the organization or for its positions.

Women Presidents' Association (WPO): The organization was formed to improve business conditions for women entrepreneurs, and to promote the acceptance and advancement of women entrepreneurs in all industries. The WPO is the premier membership organization for women presidents, CEOs, and managing directors of privately held multimillion-dollar companies. Through global, confidential, and collaborative peer-learning groups, the WPO accelerates business growth, enhances competitiveness, and promotes economic security. It is the ultimate destination for successful women entrepreneurs.

Bringing Out Successful Sisters (BOSS) Network: BOSS Network's mission is to promote and encourage the small business spirit and career development of women. They support women to become independent and successful in their endeavors, aiming to provide growth through professional development, resources, marketing, and promotional opportunities to members.

Women's Business Enterprise National Council (WBENC): The WBENC, founded in 1997, is the largest third-party certifier of businesses owned, controlled, and operated by women in the United States. WBENC, a national 501(c)(3) nonprofit, partners with 14 regional partner organizations to provide its world-class standard of certification to women-owned businesses throughout the country. Outside of the United States, certification is provided by our alliance partner, WEConnect International.

National Women's Business Council (NWBC): The NWBC is a bipartisan federal advisory council created to serve as an independent source of advice and policy recommendations to the president, Congress, and the U.S. Small Business Administration on economic issues of importance to women business owners. The Council's mission is to promote bold initiatives, policies, and programs designed to support women's business enterprises at all stages of development in the public and private-sector marketplaces, from startup to success to significance.

- NWBC is composed of 15 members who are appointed to three-year terms:
  - A presidentially appointed chair.
  - Eight women business owners or chief executives, half in the political party of the U.S. president and half who are not.
  - Six representatives of national women's business organizations.

Center for Women and Enterprise (CWE): CWE is a U.S. nonprofit organization dedicated to helping females start and grow their businesses. They provide opportunities for women entrepreneurs and women in business to increase professional success, personal growth, and financial Independence.

- CWE has worked with more than 30,200 Massachusetts and Rhode Island entrepreneurs since 1995.

International Women's Entrepreneurial Challenge Foundation (IWEC): IWEC is an initiative of the Barcelona Chamber of Commerce, in partnership with the Chamber of Commerce of Manhattan (New York) and FICCI/FLO (the Federation of Indian Chambers of Commerce and Industry Ladies Organization) supported by the U.S. Department of State. IWEC's goal is to develop a global business network for successful women business owners, helping them gain and expand access to international markets. IWEC also presents a platform for the exchange of knowledge, experience, and connectivity among women business owners worldwide; setting the stage for new business opportunities and joint ventures; and promoting social dialogue among women entrepreneurs and business leaders.

Savor the Success: Savor the Success is a virtual business school, community center, and wellness lifestyle hub for women entrepreneurs, makers, and creators. They offer high-impact schools, support circles, a lively community, ground-breaking events, *SAVOR LIFE* magazine, and a bookstore with its best-selling Daily Action Planner.

- Chosen as Forbes' Best 100 Websites for Women where accomplished founders, creators, connectors, and movers, and shakers "push each other to achieve through meeting benchmarks - together."

Women's Rural Entrepreneurial Network (WREN): WREN is a membership-driven organization. These members benefit from and support WREN's many initiatives and resources, including Local Works, its retail store featuring the products of nearly 300 vendors; the Gallery at WREN, the Local Works Farmers Market and Outdoor Marketplace; its WINGS program for girls and boys 8-14; its incubator office program; and its public access technology center. Members work on their businesses and projects while learning new, creative skills through workshops, mentorship, networking, events, and a peer-learning environment.

- 1,400 members living in New England and beyond.

For more entrepreneurial associations, see Chapter 7.

Education Associations and Nonprofits Examples

American Association of University Women (AAUW): The AAUW advances equity for women and girls through advocacy, education, philanthropy, and research.

- AAUW (formerly known as the American Association of University Women) is a nationwide network of more than 100,000 members and donors; 1,000 branches; and 500 college and university institution partners.

General Federation of Women's Clubs (GFWC): The GFWC is a nonpartisan, nondenominational women's volunteer service organization founded in 1890. More than 100,000 members in affiliated clubs in every state and more than a dozen countries work in their own communities to support the arts, preserve natural resources, advance education, promote healthy lifestyles, encourage civic involvement, and work toward world peace and understanding.

Women's Sports Foundation: The Women's Sports Foundation is a national charitable educational organization dedicated to advancing the lives of girls and women of all ages and skills levels through physical activity. The Women's Sports Foundation was established in 1974 to advance the lives of women and girls through sports and physical activity. They provide financial fuel to aspiring champion athletes.

Healthcare Associations and Nonprofits Examples

American Medical Women's Association (AMWA): The AMWA is an organization which functions at the local, national, and international level to advance women in medicine and improve women's health. They achieve this by providing and developing leadership, advocacy, education, expertise, mentoring, and through building strategic alliances.

- With approximately 5,000 members in the United States, Canada, and 30 other countries, AMWA members work on staff or as freelancers for a wide range of businesses and organizations.

Girls Organizations Examples

National Girls Collaborative Project (NGCP): The vision of the NGCP is to bring together organizations throughout the United States that are committed to informing and encouraging girls to pursue careers in STEM.

- The goals of NGCP are to:
  - Maximize access to shared resources within projects, and with public and private-sector organizations and institutions interested in expanding girls' participation in STEM.
  - Strengthen capacity of existing and evolving projects by sharing exemplary practice research and program models, outcomes, and products.
  - Use the leverage of a network and the collaboration of individual girl-serving STEM programs to create the tipping point for gender equity in STEM.

Currently, 32 collaboratives, serving 40 states, facilitate collaboration between 22,800 organizations who serve 16.35 million girls and 8.5 million boys.

Black Girls CODE: Black Girls CODE works to provide young and pre-teen girls of color opportunities to learn in-demand skills in technology and computer programming at a time when they are naturally thinking about what they want to be when they grow up. Trying to introduce programming and technology to a new generation of coders, coders who will become builders of technological innovation and of their own futures.

- As of 2013, Black Girls CODE has seven established institutions, and has operated in seven states in the United States, as well as Johannesburg, South Africa. They have reached over 3,000 students, and plan to expand to eight more cities in the United States.

Girls Inc: Girls Inc. provides more than 140,000 girls across the United States and Canada with life-changing experiences and solutions to the unique challenges girls face. The Girls Inc. experience consists of people, an environment, and programming that together empower girls to succeed. Trained staff and volunteers build lasting, mentoring relationships in girls-only spaces that are physically and emotionally safe and where girls find a sisterhood of support with shared drive, mutual respect, and high expectations. Hands-on, research-based programs provide girls with the skills and knowledge to set goals, overcome obstacles, and improve academic performance. Informed by girls and their families, Girls Inc. also works with policymakers to advocate for legislation and initiatives that increase opportunities for girls.

Girl Scouts of the USA: Girl Scouts of the USA is an organization dedicated solely to girls, where, in an accepting and nurturing environment, girls build character and skills for success in the real world. Girl Scouts' membership has reached 3.4 million members throughout the United States, including U.S. territories, and in more than 90 countries through USA Girl Scouts Overseas.

Girls Who Code: Girls Who Code has gone from 20 girls in New York to 10,000 girls in 42 states. That's the same number of girls who graduate each year with a degree in computer science. When girls learn to code, they become change agents in their communities. Whether it's a game to illustrate the experience of an undocumented immigrant or a website to provide free college prep, their girls create technology that makes the world a better place.

- A national nonprofit organization working to close the gender gap in the technology and engineering sectors. Has over 10,000 alumni of their program.
- 65% of clubs participants say they are considering a major or minor in computer science because of Girls Who Code.
- 90% of Girls Who Code Summer Immersion Program participants said they were planning to major or minor in computer science or a closely related field.

Girlstart: Girlstart's mission is to increase girls' interest and engagement in STEM through innovative, nationally recognized informal STEM education programs. Girlstart aspires to be the national leader in designing and implementing innovative, high-quality informal STEM education programs that inspire girls to transform their world.

- Girlstart After School 2015 reached 1,441 girls across 54 programs.
- Girlstart Summer Camps 2015 reached 719 girls with 47% participating at no cost through scholarships.
- Girls in STEM 2015 reached 532 girls with 33% participating at no cost through scholarships.
- Teacher Professional Development 2015 reached 1,727 educators.
- Public STEM Programming 2015 reached 19,642 community members through 66 community STEM events.

Political Associations Nonprofits Examples

League of Women Voters of the United States (LWV): The LWV of the United States, a nonpartisan political organization, has fought since 1920 to improve systems of government and impact public policies through citizen education and advocacy. The League's enduring vitality and resonance comes from its unique decentralized structure. The LWV is a grass-roots organization, working at the national, state, and local levels.

National Organization for Women (NOW): The largest organization of feminist activists in the United States, NOW has 500,000 contributing members and 550 chapters in all 50 states and the District of Columbia. Since its founding in 1966, NOW's goal has been to take action to bring about equality for all women.

Science and Technology Associations and Nonprofits Examples

Association for Women in Science (AWIS): Founded in 1971, the Association for Women in Science (AWIS) is the largest multi-disciplinary organization for women in science, technology, engineering, and mathematics (STEM). We are dedicated to driving excellence in STEM by achieving equity and full participation of women in all disciplines and across all employment sectors. AWIS reaches more than 20,000 professionals in STEM with members, chapters, and affiliates worldwide. Membership is open to any individual who supports the vision and mission of AWIS.

Society of Women Engineers (SWE): For more than six decades, SWE has given female engineers a place and voice in the engineering industry. SWE is a not-for-profit educational and service organization that empowers women to succeed and advance in the engineering field, and to be recognized for their life-changing contributions as engineers and leaders.

Women in Technology (WIT): WIT has an exceptional mentor-protégé program which includes one-on-one mentoring sessions and great speaking programs. It also has several special interest groups, including Diversity Outreach, Executive Women, Sales & Marketing, Technology, and Women Business Owners. In addition, it has a Girls in Technology Program and a Workforce Development Program.

- Also worth mentioning is its tremendous commitment to philanthropic causes through galas, golf tournaments, and other events. WIT has many committees that offer everyone involvement at some level if they choose to get involved. They include advocacy, communications, membership, mentorship, programs, special events, strategic alliances, women in government, and many more.

Women in Technology International (WITI): WITI is a trade association for tech-savvy women that empowers women in business and technology to achieve unimagined possibilities. WITI has programs and partnerships that provide connections, resources, opportunities, and a supportive environment of women committed to helping each other.

- With 167,000+ registered users, WITI is the premier global organization helping tech-savvy women attain their professional goals.

Diversity Associations and Nonprofits Examples

Diversity Woman Magazine: The business-focused editorial content is designed for women business leaders, executives, and entrepreneurs of all races, cultures, and backgrounds, who have unique interests and concerns. *Diversity Woman* is the only magazine on the market designed exclusively to help smart, savvy, diverse, and multicultural women leaders achieve their career and business goals. Each issue is brimming with insights from women business leaders and other experts who speak from real-world experience, offering sage advice, information, and inspiration.

Diversity Woman also plays a mentorship role. Both the magazine and website serve as a forum and membership directory to connect aspiring businesswomen directly with other women in leadership roles.

Asian American Business Women Association: The Asian American Business Women Association works to highlight women in every area of expertise, at all different levels and business industries. In its network, you will have access to business and professional women, corporate executives, healthcare professionals, and financial consultants who specialize in the areas of small- to medium-size businesses, education, and nonprofit organizations.

LATINA*Style* Magazine: LATINA*Style* broke new ground in 1994 by launching the first national magazine dedicated to the needs and concerns of the contemporary Latina professional working woman and the Latina business owner in the United States. With a national circulation of 150,000 and a readership of nearly 600,000, LATINA*Style* reaches both the seasoned professional and the young Latina entering the workforce. The culturally sensitive editorial environment it provides showcases Latina achievements in all areas, including business, science, civic affairs, education, entertainment, sports, and the arts.

National Council of Jewish Women (NCJW): The NCJW is a volunteer organization that has been at the forefront of social change through championing the needs of women, children, and families—while taking a progressive stance on such issues as child welfare, women's rights, and reproductive freedom.

National Council of Negro Women (NCNW): The NCNW is a council of national African-American women's organizations and community-based sections. NCNW's mission is to lead, develop, and advocate for women of African descent as they support their families and communities. NCNW fulfills this purpose through research, advocacy, and national- and community-based services and programs.

- Today, the NCNW is a council of 39 affiliated national African-American women's organizations and over 240 sections—connecting nearly 4 million women worldwide.

National Coalition of 100 Black Women: The purpose of the National Coalition of 100 Black Women is to:

- Foster principles of equal rights and opportunities.
- Promote awareness of the black culture.
- Develop the potential of membership for effective leadership and participation in civic affairs.
- Take action on specific issues of national and international importance.
- Cooperate with other persons and organizations to achieve mutual goals.

National Hispanic Business Women Association (NHBWA): The benefits of joining the NHBWA are:

- Access to conference room facilities.
- Quarterly free business seminars.
- Annual business conference through affiliate organization.
- Business to business referrals.
  - Mentoring opportunities throughThe U.S. Small Business Administration's SCORE Program.
  - Annual awards and scholarship gala reduced fee.
  - Website marketing opportunities.
  - Scholarship opportunities.
  - Shipping discounts.

The Asian American Women's Alliance (AAWA): The mission of the AAWA is to establish an alliance of members dedicated to building support among Asian American women in all walks of life through professional and personal growth. The AAWA seeks to create opportunities for mutual learning and nurturing; mentor relationships; career and leadership development; personal and group support; and engagement in community services.

U.S. Pan Asian American Chamber of Commerce (USPAACC): As a thought leader with 30-year of track record in business matchmaking accomplishments, strong partnerships with corporations, government, and Asian American businesses, the USPAACC is poised to raise the bar to yet another level.

Global Associations and Nonprofits Examples

Astia: Astia provides capital, connections, and guidance that fuel the growth of highly innovative, women-led ventures around the globe. It is dedicated to the success of women high-growth entrepreneurs, their teams, and their ventures.

- Astia Access: Programs including the Venture Lunch Series that ensure success by increasing investment opportunity and providing access to expertise and networks. Thought leadership around inclusive innovation.
- Astia-Angels: Founded in 2013, Astia Angels is comprised of a global network of women and men investors who consider investments in the Astia-qualified companies that are progressing through Astia Expert Sift™ and receiving full

visibility into a pipeline of high-quality deals from the earliest stages.
- Astia-Fund: The Astia Fund will invest in exceptional, inclusive team ventures that have proven themselves throughout the Astia system review process.

Catalyst: Catalyst is a nonprofit organization that expands opportunities for women in business. It is a resource for research, information, and advice about women at work.
- More than 400 organizations are members.

International Federation of Business and Professional Women (BPW International): BPW International is a network of professional women with affiliates in over 95 countries. Their members include women leaders, entrepreneurs, business owners, executives, and young career women.

Vital Voices: Their mission is to identify, invest in, and bring visibility to extraordinary women around the world by unleashing their leadership potential to transform lives and accelerate peace and prosperity in their communities. Vital Voices Global Partnership is the preeminent nongovernmental organization (NGO) that identifies, trains, and empowers emerging women leaders and social entrepreneurs around the globe, enabling them to create a better world for us all.

- Their international staff and team of more than 1,000 partners, pro bono experts and leaders, including senior government, corporate, and NGO executives, have trained and mentored more than 15,000 emerging women leaders from over 144 countries in Africa, Asia, Eurasia, Latin America and the Caribbean, and the Middle East since 1997. These women have returned home to train and mentor more than 500,000 additional women and girls in their communities.

Zonta International: Zonta International is a global organization of executives and professionals working together to advance the status of women worldwide through service and advocacy. With more than 31,000 members in 66 countries and geographic areas, members volunteer their time, talents, and support to local and international service projects, as well as scholarship programs.

Venture Nonprofit Example

Women's Venture Fund (WVF): WVF helps women establish thriving businesses in urban communities by providing funding and business development programs. Their services include entrepreneurial training, technical assistance, advisory services, and loans for women entrepreneurs.

For more information on venture capital, see Chapter 4.

Chapter 10: Education - Overview

Education is extraordinarily important to our growth and success. We are realizing that the job market is as competitive as it has ever been. A collegiate education is now just a starting point. More than ever, men and women are flocking to obtain graduate degrees, further progressing their educational endeavors. As women, we have to keep up with the rapidly moving times. The exciting news is that women are soaring in the world of education. There are 12.7 million women enrolled in undergraduate and graduate schools across the country. There are many significant resources and we cite them. For example, My College Options provides statistics in all areas of education, as well as other STEM data.

Women comprise the majority of undergraduate and graduate degrees. If we just look at master's degrees alone, women are enrolling and securing 60% of those coveted and valuable degrees. If we look at PhDs, women make up 42% of science and engineering (S&E) doctorates, but 57% of non-S&E doctorates. We have equity, and we should continue to really push our women all the way up the educational system. Yet, when we look at education amongst the labor force, the numbers are not as strong. But the pipeline of associate degrees, master's degrees, and PhDs are all trending toward women. With education, the pathway to jobs opens.

This chapter breaks down the data by industry from engineering, computer science, math, and statistics to economics and accounting. The STEM degrees show that women demonstrate some passion for these areas, as 25% of women are interested in STEM careers. Nevertheless, we still see low participation numbers for women in engineering, computer sciences, mathematics, statistics, and physics. These number are not growing, but seem to remain relatively stagnant. Regardless, we know the impact of mentoring in education.

One out of four female students report the greatest challenge in college is finding the mentorship they so desperately crave. The numbers are reassuring, but we can do even better if we consciously work to support one another and look for opportunities to lift one another up.

Call to Action:

- Use the data of women in education to encourage others. Note the degree levels conferred. See the college planning profile and other useful resources.

- If you are still enrolled in a learning institution, take the time to find a younger student and mentor her. She needs the resources and experience you have gained through your years of education.

- If you are a professional in the workforce, look for local opportunities to speak to high school or college students, sharing your journey with them and offering to act as a mentor along the way.

CHAPTER 10: EDUCATION

Overview

Data Point	Women's Statistic
High school graduation rate	94%
College enrollment rate (among high school graduates)	73%
Possess a bachelor's degree or more	30.2%
Percent of overall undergraduate degrees earned	60%
Percent of master's degrees	60%
Percent of master's degrees in business and management	44%
Percent of master of business administration degrees (MBAs)	37%
Percent of law degrees	47%
Percent of medical degrees	48%
Percent of the college-educated entry-level workforce	59%
Percent of S&E doctorates (PhDs)	42%
Percent of doctorates excluding S&E	57%

Source: U.S. Bureau of Labor Statistics (2015).

Participation in Education

K-12 Primary Education

Participation in Middle/High School

Participation in Education

- Women ages 25-64 - 6% did not graduate from high school in 2014
- Among 2014 high school graduates, young women (73%) were more likely than young men (64%) to be enrolled in college.

Source: U.S. Bureau of Labor Statistics (2015).

Undergraduate

Participation in Secondary Education

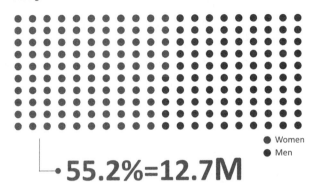

Undergraduate

● Women
● Men

55.2%=12.7M

- **12.7 million:** Number of women enrolled in undergraduate college and graduate school in 2014. Women comprised 55.2% of all college students (undergraduate and graduate).

Source: American Community Survey (2014).

Undergraduate

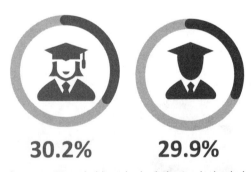

30.2%   29.9%

- **30.2%** - age of women 25 and older who had obtained a bachelor's degree or more as of 2014. The percentage of men 25 and older who had obtained a bachelor's degree or more as of 2014 was 29.9%.

Source: American Community Survey (2014).

- Women earn almost 60% of undergraduate degrees.

Source: American Center of Progress (2014).

- Women ages 25-64 - 40% held college degrees in 2014.

Source: U.S. Bureau of Labor Statistics (2015).

Graduate

Participation in Graduate Education

Graduate Degree

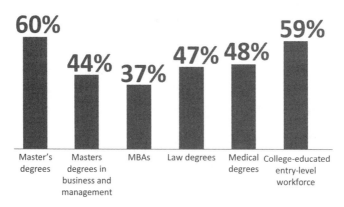

- 60% of all master's degrees.
- 44% of master's degrees in business and management.
  - 37% of MBAs.
  - 47% of all law degrees.
  - 48% of all medical degrees.
  - 59% of college-educated entry-level workforce.

Source: American Center of Progress (2014).

PhD

- Women make up 42% S&E doctorates.
- Women make up 57% non-S&E doctorates.

Source: National Science Foundation (2014).

Phds

S&E doctorates   Non-S&E doctorates

42%   **57%**

General Educational Outlook

- Women ages 25 and older median usual weekly earnings in 2014.

Source: U.S. Bureau of Labor Statistics (2015).

- High school diploma ($578).
- Associate's degree ($701).
- Bachelor's degree or higher ($1,049).

Weekly Earnings

$701
Associate's degree

$578
High school diploma

$1,049
Bachelor's degree or higher

Labor Force
Source: U.S. Bureau of Labor Statistics (2015).

- Young women 16 to 24 years old who were high school dropouts between October 2013 and 2014 had a labor force participation rate of 41.9%.
- Those who had graduated from high school between January and October 2014 but were not enrolled in college had a rate of 68.0%.
- In October 2014, 41.3% of women ages 16 to 24 who were enrolled in either high school or college were in the labor force.
- Among those not enrolled in school, women were less likely to be in the labor force than men (74.4% compared with 83.1%).

The Percent of Men and Women Who Have Completed Selected Levels of Education from 2005 to 2015

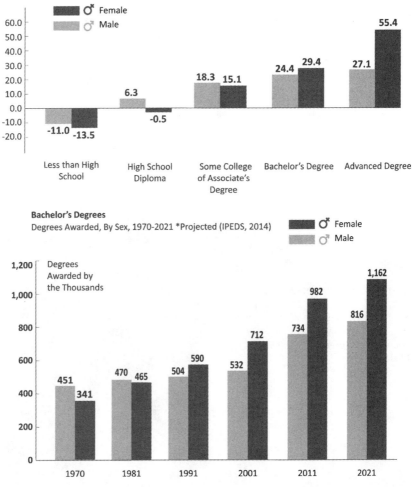

Bachelor's Degrees
Degrees Awarded, By Sex, 1970-2021 *Projected (IPEDS, 2014)

Associate Degrees
Associate Degrees Awarded, by Sex, 1970-2021
*Projected (IPED 2014)

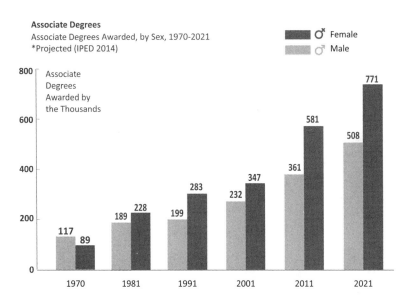

Master's Degrees
Degrees Awarded, By Sex, 1970-2021 *Projected (IPEDS, 2014)

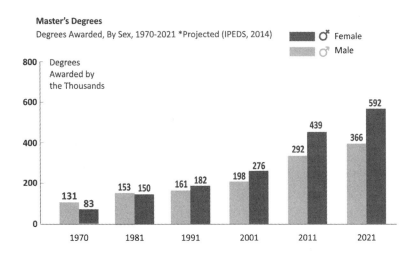

Source: My College Options (2016).

Doctoral Degrees
Degrees Awarded, By Sex, 1970-2021 *Projected (IPEDS, 2014)

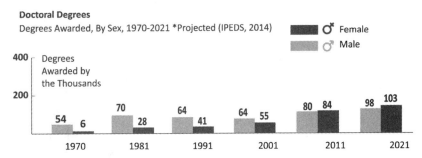

Female
Male

Source: U.S. Department of Education, National Center for Education Statistics, Earned Degrees Conferred, 1869–70 through 1964–65; Higher Education General Information Survey (HEGIS), "Degrees and Other Formal Awards Conferred" surveys, 1965–66 through 1985–86; Integrated Postsecondary Education Data System (IPEDS), "Completions Survey" (IPEDS-C:87–99); IPEDS Fall 2000 to Fall 2012, Completions Component; and Degrees Conferred Projection Model, 1980–81 to 2023–24. (This table was prepared March 2014.)

Data - S&E Degrees

Women have earned 57% of all bachelor's degrees and about half of all S&E bachelor's degrees since the late 1990s. Women's level of participation, however, in S&E fields varies, and within fields, it tends to be consistent over every degree level. In most fields, the proportion of degrees awarded to women has risen since 1993. The proportion of women is lowest in engineering, computer sciences, and physics. Women earn about one-third of the doctorates in economics and slightly more than one-fourth of doctorates in mathematics and statistics.
Source: National Science Foundation (2015).

At University of Illinois Urbana-Champaign (UIUC), the trend with an incoming class of computer science majors that is nearly half women. The percentage of freshmen 2016 who plan to pursue a computer science degree has almost doubled in a year, from 24 percent in 2015 to 46 percent thisi fall. And the average freshman entering the program scored in the 99th percentile on the ACT college entrance exam. The increase comes at a time when tech companies such as Facebook often blame the "pipeline", or number of women and minorities entering the industry, for the lack of a diverse talent pool. Women in technical roles comprise 17 percent of the social media giant's workforce, according to The Wall Street Journal. Growth among racial and ethnic minorities in the incoming class of the College of Engineering increased from 19 percent to 25 percent.
Source: Chicago Business Journal.

Science & Engineering

"Women's participation in the S&E workforce varies greatly by occupation. Women are more likely than men to be employed as psychologists or as technologists and technicians in the life sciences. Although women are more likely than men to work in a health-related occupation, they are less likely to work as a diagnosing health practitioner, such as a physician, surgeon, or dentist."
Source: National Science Foundation (2015).

| Employed Women Within the S&E Workforce as a Percentage of Selected Occupations: 2013 ||
Occupation	Percent
All occupations	46.1
All S&E occupations	29.0
Computer and math scientists	25.4
Economists	47.2
Engineers	14.8
Life scientists	48.5
Physicists and astronomers	11.8
Psychologists	73.8
Social and related scientists	61.5
S&E-related occupations	56.3
Diagnosing health practitioners	36.6
Health-related occupations	68.6
S&E precollege teachers	55.8
Technologists and technicians in life sciences	62.6
Non-S&E occupations	48.1

Science

White men constitute about one-half of the S&E workforce. In all racial and ethnic groups, more men than women work in S&E occupations. Together, Asian and underrepresented minority women represent about 1 in 10 persons employed in S&E occupations.

Source: National Science Foundation (2015).

| Scientists and Engineers Working in S&E Occupations: 2013 |||
Race, Ethnicity, and Sex	Number	Percent
White Men	2,860,000	51
White Women	1,102,000	20
Asian Men	680,000	12
Asian Women	286,000	5
Black Men	159,000	3
Black Women	108,000	2
Hispanic Men	227,000	4
Hispanic Women	114,000	2
Other Men	77,000	1
Other Women	29,000	1

Note: Hispanic may be any race. Other includes American Indian or Alaska Native/Native Hawaiian or Other Pacific Islander, and multiple race.

- These five most influential women are pioneers in the field of science and medicine.

Source: TIME100 (2015).

  - Dr. Joanne Liu, President, Médecins Sans Frontières (MSF).

  - Emmanuelle Charpentier and Jennifer Doudna, Creators of gene-editing technology-CRISPR-Cas.

  - Dr. Pardis Sabeti, geneticist who sequenced the Ebola genome from the most recent outbreak.

  - Elizabeth Holmes, health technology entrepreneur, CEO, Theranos.

- Differences between Caucasian women and men: In contrast to underrepresented minorities, among whites, women earn a lower proportion of S&E degrees than do men at all degree levels. The gap is largest at the doctoral level. In 2012, white women earned 19% and white men earned 24% of all S&E doctorates.

S&E Degrees Earned by Caucasian Women and Men: 1993–2012					
Year	Bachelor's, Women	Bachelor's, Men	Master's, Women	Master's, Men	Doctorate, Women	Doctorate, Men
1993	33.8	42.8	22.7	36.2	20.2	34.9
2003	32.3	33.4	21.8	24.5	22.0	27.8
2012	29.0	31.1	21.2	24.3	19.2	24.0

Underrepresented minority women earn a higher share of S&E degrees than do underrepresented minority men at all degree levels, especially at the bachelor's level. In the past 20 years, the proportion of women nearly doubled at the bachelor's degree level.

S&E Degrees Earned by Underrepresented Minority Women and Men: 1993–2012					
Year	Bachelor's, Women	Bachelor's, Men	Master's, Women	Master's, Men	Doctorate, Women	Doctorate, Men
1993	6.3	5.2	2.8	3.2	1.7	2.0
2003	9.8	6.6	6.3	4.6	3.6	2.9
2012	11.2	7.6	8.2	5.5	4.1	3.2

Differences between women and men in S&E degrees.

- Asians: Among Asians, women and men earn similar proportions of S&E degrees. At the doctoral level, the proportion of S&E degrees earned by Asian women has more than doubled since 1993, reaching the same level as the proportion earned by Asian men in 2012.

S&E Degrees Earned by Asian Women and Men: 1993–2012						
Year	Bachelor's, Women	Bachelor's, Men	Master's, Women	Master's, Men	Doctorate, Women	
1993	2.7	3.6	2.0	4.0	1.3	3.2
2003	4.3	4.7	3.1	3.9	2.5	3.2
2012	4.5	4.7	2.9	3.8	3.1	3.1

- More than doubled at the master's and doctoral degree levels. The proportion of underrepresented minority women earning S&E degrees grew faster in the 1990s than in the past decade.

Engineering

Although the number of women earning degrees in engineering has increased in the past 20 years, women's participation remains well below that of men at all degree levels and in all fine fields of engineering. Since 1993, the proportion of women in engineering has increased at all degree levels, but mostly at the master's and doctoral levels. In general, women earn larger proportions of degrees in chemical, materials, industrial, and civil engineering than in aerospace, electrical, and mechanical engineering.

Low Participation Field for Women in Engineering: 1993, 2002, 2012			
Year	Bachelor's	Master's	Doctorate
	Number of Women		
1993	9,981	4,094	558
2002	12,682	5,563	896
2012	15,981	9,896	2,006
	Percent Women		
1993	15.9	14.8	9.6
2002	20.9	21.2	17.2
2012	19.2	22.9	22.6

Source: National Science Foundation, National Center for Science and Engineering Statistics, special tabulations of U.S. Department of Education, National Center for Education Statistics, Integrated Postsecondary Education Data System, Completions Survey.

25 Of The Most Powerful Female Engineers In 2016

1. Diane Greene — Engineer And Tech Entrepreneur, Google
2. Peggy Johnson — Executive Vice President of Business Development, Microsoft
3. Tara Bunch — Vice President, Applecare
4. Jessica Mckellar — Director Of Engineering, Dropbox
5. Sharon Frinks Chiarella — Vice President, Amazon
6. Anna Patterson — Vice President of Engineering, Google.
7. Denise Dumas — Vice President of Operating-System Engineering, Red Hat
8. Helen Grenier — Ceo, Cyphy
9. Noramay Cadena — Cofounder, Make In La
10. Juliette Mccoy — Global Chief Engineer, Ford
11. Lakecia Gunter — Test Engineering Leader, Intel's R&D Labs
12. Michal Segalov — Software Engineer and Manager, Google Play; Cofounder, Mind the Gap
13. Daniela Raijman — First Female Engineer, Google's R&D Center In Tel Aviv, Israel
14. Vinita Paunikar — Vice President, Oracle Corp.
15. Emily Ratliff — Senior Director Of Security, Linux Foundation
16. Ayah Bdeir — Founder & CEO, Littlebits
17. Kimberly Bryant — Founder & CEO, Black Girls Code
18. Cynthia Breazeal — Founder & CEO, Jibo
19. Trisha Kothari — First Female Engineer, Affirm
20. Jessica Rannow — Senior Industrial Engineer & Engineering Project Manager, Amerisourcebergen
21. Rosalind Fox — Deere's Director of Global Diversity, John Deere
22. Eva Saravia — Vice President of Global Programs, Bohemia Interactive Simulations
23. Jennifer Braganza — Business-Strategy Manager, Bank of America
24. Heidi Ellis — Professor of Computer Science & Information Technology, Western New England University
25. Sumita Basu — Strategist & Technical Assistant, Intel Corp.

Source: Business Insider (2016).

Computer Science

The proportion of women in computer sciences is highest at the master's level. Since 1993, the number of women in computer sciences has risen at all degree levels. Although the proportion of women with degrees in computer sciences has increased considerably at the doctoral level, it has declined at the bachelor's level

Low Participation Field for Women in **Computer Sciences**: 1993, 2002, 2012			
Year	Bachelor's	Master's	Doctorate
	Number of Women		
1993	6,951	2,795	116
2002	13,690	5,640	171
2012	8,730	5,840	361
	Percent Women		
1993	28.3	27.0	14.4
2002	27.5	33.2	22.8
2012	18.2	27.8	21.4

Source: National Science Foundation, National Center for Science and Engineering Statistics, special tabulations of U.S. Department of Education, National Center for Education Statistics, Integrated Postsecondary Education Data System, Completions Survey.

Mathematics and Statistics

Women's share of degrees in mathematics and statistics remains below that of men, particularly at the doctoral level. Women's representation in mathematics and statistics is higher at the bachelor's and master's levels, reaching approximately 40%— about double that of women in engineering and computer sciences at all degree levels. Despite increases in the numbers of women earning degrees in mathematics and statistics since 2002, the proportion of women has declined, particularly at the bachelor's level.

Low Participation Field for Women in Mathematics and Statistics: 1993, 2002, 2012			
Year	Bachelor's	Master's	Doctorate
	Number of Women		
1993	6,999	1,532	274
2002	5,752	1,475	268
2012	8,536	2,707	471
	Percent Women		
1993	47.1	40.8	23.8
2002	46.9	43.1	28.9
2012	43.1	40.6	28.2

Source: National Science Foundation, National Center for Science and Engineering Statistics, special tabulations of US Department of Education, National Center for Education Statistics, Integrated Postsecondary Education Data System, Completions Survey.

Physics

Despite increases in the number of women earning degrees in physics, the proportion of women in this field, averaging about 20% across all degree levels, is the lowest of all the physical sciences. In the past 20 years, the proportion of women earning degrees in physics increased more at the doctoral level than at the bachelor's and master's levels, but the numbers of women in this field remain very small.

Low Participation Field for Women in Physics: 1993, 2002, 2012			
Year	Bachelor's	Master's	Doctorate
Number of Women			
1993	677	318	170
2002	824	286	170
2012	1,062	409	350
Percent Women			
1993	16.6	17.9	13.3
2002	22.6	21.1	15.5
2012	19.1	21.8	20.0

Economics

Within the social sciences, women's participation is lowest in economics. In the past two decades, the number of women earning degrees in economics has increased at all degree levels. Despite the increase in numbers, over the past decade the proportion of degrees in economics awarded to women declined at the bachelor's level and remained flat at the master's level. Women's share of degrees in economics increased at the doctoral level.

Year	Bachelor's	Master's	Doctorate
Number of Women			
1993	6,812	816	239
2002	7,387	1,050	271
2012	8,780	1,735	421
Percent Women			
1993	29.8	29.9	23.4
2002	33.8	39.6	28.2
2012	29.7	40.1	33.1

Accounting
Women of color are earning a much smaller percentage of college degrees in accounting.
- Bachelor's degrees earned in accounting and related services in 2013–14.
  - 7.5% African-American women.
  - 8.1% Asian women.
  - 8.2% Hispanic/Latina women.

- Master's degrees earned in accounting and related services 2013–2014.
  - 2.8% African-American women.
  - 4.6% Asian women.
  - 3.1% Hispanic women.

More than half of all accountants and auditors are women.
- 63% of all accountants and auditors in the United States are women.
- In one survey, women are 47% of all professional staff at CPA firms, but make up just 22% of partners and principals.
- The percentage of women on management committees is growing: 23% in 2015 compared to 17% in 2011.
  - Women make up 47% of senior managers (compared to 38% in 2011).

Women of color are underrepresented in accounting.
- 85% of all professional staff at CPA firms are white according to AICPA.
- 31% of new hires in 2013-14 were people of color.
  - Women of color make up 16% of those employed in accounting, tax preparation, bookkeeping, and payroll services.

- Half of people of color surveyed do not feel obligated to stay at their current firm.
  - Women of color are more likely than men of color to leave for the same money, to do similar tasks.

Global: the proportion of women studying accounting worldwide has remained constant the past four years
- The overall percentage of women studying accounting worldwide is approximately 50%.

The Gender Pay Gap Persists in Accounting

- Women working as accountants or auditors earn a weekly median salary of $999, compared to the weekly median salary of $1,236 earned by men in the same fields.
- 47% of the firms participating in MOVE (an annual survey that monitors women's career track in accounting) now review and confirm an equitable pay starting point for all employees.
Source: Catalyst (2016).

- Women hold 25% of senior management roles in the global financial services industry.
Source: Grant Thornton (2015).

STEM

Graduate

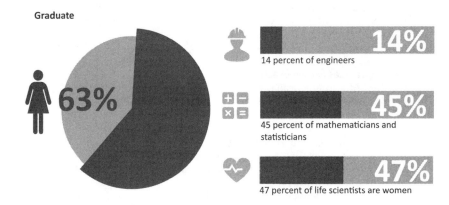

14 percent of engineers

45 percent of mathematicians and statisticians

47 percent of life scientists are women

- 63% - The percentage of social scientists who were women, the heaviest representation of women among all STEM fields.
- Among other STEM fields, approximately:
  - 14% of engineers.
  - 45% of mathematicians and statisticians.
  - 47% of life scientists were women.

Source: 2012 American Community Survey.

Profile of Female Students

College Planning Profile for the Class of 2016 Female Students

- Female students in the class of 2016 report taking advanced courses such as:
  - Honors programs (28%).
  - Advanced placement (22%).
  - College/dual credit courses (19%).
  - Gifted/accelerated programs (8%).
  - International Baccalaureate (2%).
  - Other advanced programs (9%).

Source: My College Options (2016).

Profile of Female Students

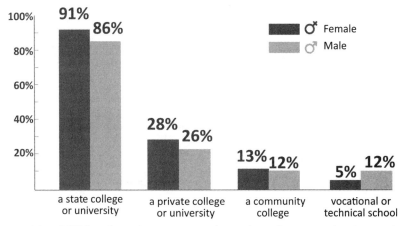

- More 2016 female graduates compared to male graduates are planning to attend a state college or university (91% vs. 86% respectively).
  - A private college or university (28% vs. 26% respectively).
  - Community college (13% vs. 12% respectively).

Top Six Majors

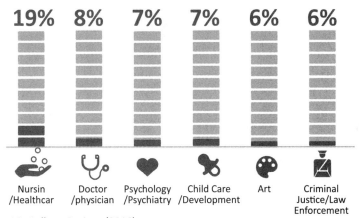

Source: My College Options (2016).

Significantly more 2016 male graduates compared to female graduates are planning to attend a vocational or technical school (12% vs. 5% respectively).

- The top six major and career interest areas reported by class of 2016 female students are:
  - Nursing/Healthcare (19%).
  - Doctor/Physician (8%).
  - Psychology/Psychiatry (7%).
  - Child care/Development (7%).
  - Art (6%).
  - Criminal justice/Law enforcement (6%).

  Source: My College Options (2016).

College Plans of Female Students Interested in a STEM Career

- About 30% of female high school students interested in a STEM major or career will be the first in their families to attend college.
- More female students compared to male students are planning to attend a state college or university (88% vs. 80% respectively), as well as a private college or university (31% vs. 25% respectively).
- Significantly more female students interested in a STEM major or career compared to male students are planning to participate in an academic/honors club in college (31% vs. 15% respectively) and more female students are planning to participate in community service and volunteering in college than male students (25% vs. 8% respectively).

Source: My College Options (2016).

STEM Interest and Extracurricular Program Participation

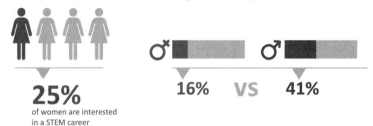

25%
of women are interested
in a STEM career

16% VS **41%**

One in four high school students
interested in a STEM career are female.

In 2016 female students are reported to be significantly less likely
than their male counterparts to pursue a college major or career
in STEM (16% vs. 41% respectively).

- One in four high school students interested in a STEM career is female.
- Female students in the class of 2016 are significantly less likely than their male counterparts to report plans to pursue a college major or career in STEM (16% vs. 41% respectively).
- Male high school students are about 8.5 times more likely to say they plan to pursue a career in engineering or technology compared to female students.
- Two-thirds of female students interested in a STEM major or career plan to specifically pursue the sciences, compared to only 20% of male students interested in STEM.
- Female students interested in STEM are most interested in pursuing:
  - Biology (25%).
  - Science (14%).
  - Marine biology (14%).
  - Chemistry (9%).
  - Mathematics/Statistics (7%).

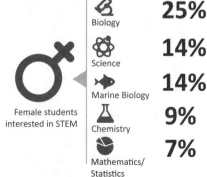

Female students
interested in STEM

Biology **25%**

Science **14%**

Marine Biology **14%**

Chemistry **9%**

Mathematics/
Statistics **7%**

- Three in 10 female students report participating in clubs or extracurricular programs that encourage STEM.
- Female students who participate in STEM clubs, competitions, or other extracurricular programs report:
  - That they feel more motivated to do better in their STEM-related classes (40%).
  - That participation has helped them in their other academic courses (23%).
  - That participation has increased their understanding about STEM (23%).
- Nearly four in 10 female students report a lack of awareness of STEM competitions.
- About 23% of female students report participation in STEM competitions.
- Of the female students that have not participated in STEM competitions, slightly more than half have reported a desire to do so in the future.
- Two in three female students who report past participation in STEM competitions are planning to do so again in the future.

Source: My College Options (2016).

Mathematics Courses and Competitions

- Six in 10 female students report their enjoyment in learning mathematics.
- The top three reasons female students report a lack of enjoyment in mathematics learning are that they believe they are not good at it (27%), they think it is boring or uninteresting (22%), or they believe learning mathematics is too difficult.
- More female students than male students report taking lower to mid-level mathematics courses including geometry, algebra I and II, trigonometry, and pre-calculus, while male students are more likely to have taken higher level mathematics courses like calculus I and II and advanced placement calculus.
- Female students are more likely than male students to have participated in math study groups and advanced math tutoring, as well as serving as a math tutor.
- Male students are more likely to have participated in a math honor society and math research class.
- Only 13% of female students and 16% of male students report having participated in a math competition.
- About 21% of male and female students are interested in participating in a math competition in the future.
- While lack of interest and lack of awareness are the top two reasons both male and female students report not having participated in math competitions, female students are more likely than male students to report a lack of confidence (16% vs. 9% respectively) and a lack of enjoyment in completing (12% vs. 9% respectively).

Source: My College Options (2016).

Computer Science Courses

- Significantly more female than male seniors studying computer science report having started their studies before 9th grade (30% vs. 18% respectively); an equal number of both female and male seniors report taking computer science in 9th grade (29%), while male seniors are more likely to have taken computer science in grades 10, 11 and 12.
- Four in 10 female students studying computer science, compared to 55% of male students, are interested in taking computer science courses but are unable to do so.
- The top two reasons female students studying computer science report being

unable to take more computer science courses are limited room in class schedules (57%) and lack of desired courses available to them (27%).
- Six in 10 female students studying computer science, compared to 45% of male students, are not interested in taking additional computer science courses.
- Significantly fewer female students report taking computer science courses because of a personal interest compared male students (38% vs. 66%).
- Significantly more female students than male students report taking computer science to fulfill a high school graduation requirement (37% vs. 19%), and male students report taking computer science to broaden their career choices (41% vs. 36%).
- Nearly 22% of female students and 20% of male students taking computer science report plans to work in a field where computer science skills will be useful.
- About 15% of male students and 11% of female students taking computer science report plans to take computer science courses in college.
- More male than female students studying computer science believe the knowledge and skills they learn in class will be very useful to their careers (53% vs. 36% respectively).

Source: My College Options (2016).

Career and Technical Education (CTE)

- Significantly more female students than male students taking CTE courses are planning to attend a four-year college or university (74% vs. 53% respectively).
- Female students taking CTE courses are significantly more likely than male students to report plans to pursue a career related to their CTE coursework (65% vs. 54% respectively).
- Nearly 42% of female students report taking CTE courses to help them learn more about a specific career and 34% say they want to explore different careers.
- Female students taking CTE courses are significantly more likely than male students to report gaining multiple benefits from their CTE coursework.
- Female students taking CTE courses report gaining:
  - skills that will help them get a job in the future (65%).
  - a better understanding of their academic courses through real-world examples (51%).
  - the ability to work as part of a team (43%).
  - the ability to be creative and innovative (35%).

Source: My College Options (2016).

Mentoring Relationships

1/4
female students were
motivated and supported.

- One out of four female students reports the greatest challenges in attending college are confidence, motivation, and support.
- Only 6% of female students interested in pursuing STEM are encouraged to do so by a mentor.
- Twenty percent of current female high school students interested in a STEM dis-

Mentoring Encouragement

|||||||||||| 6%

cipline say they want to learn more about mentoring and motivational programs to help prepare them for the future.
- Four in 10 female students interested in a STEM career report having a mentor in their lives.
- More than three in four female students interested in a STEM career, who also have a mentor, feel they will be successful in pursuing a career in STEM.
- Nearly 61% of female students consider themselves a mentor.
- Half of female students who do not consider themselves a mentor believe that they could be someday.
- While 31% of female students prefer a mentor of the same gender, 63% are open to a mentor of any gender.

Source: My College Options (2016).

Internship Experiences

- Nearly one in four female students reports having a family member who is a STEM professional.
- About half of female students report having spent a day at a professional job or worksite where they learned what it was like to have a career.

25%
Female students have STEM professional relatives

- Seven in 10 female students believe an internship is very important to getting into college or for their future careers, however, only one in 10 female students has actually participated in an internship.
- Lack of awareness is the number one reason female students have not participated in internships.
- Female students with a family member who is a professional in a STEM field are two-thirds more likely to report an interest in pursuing a career in STEM compared to those who do not have a family member in a STEM field.

Source: My College Options (2016).

Business and Entrepreneurship Interest

- About 53% of female students have considered starting their own businesses, compared to 62% of male students.
- Female students are significantly less likely than male students to say they have considered a technology-based business (17% vs. 38% respectively).
- The top three reasons female students report a lack of interest in starting their own businesses are a lack of interest (27%), not sure how to get started (23%) and not enough money (21%).
- About 5% of female students in the class of 2016 are interested in a business career, 3% are interested in being a business owner or entrepreneur, and 1% are interested in a career in international business.

Source: My College Options (2016).

Business and Entrepreneurship Interest

Students who have considered starting a business

Foreign Language Studies

- The top five languages studied by female students are:
  - Spanish (65%)
  - French (20%)

Top Five Language Studies

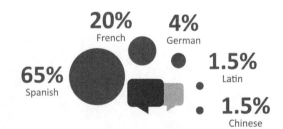

- German (4%)
- Latin (1.5%)
- Chinese (1.5%)

Source: My College Options (2016).

- More female students than male students say they wish they could have started to learn a foreign language earlier in school (57% vs. 48% respectively).
- Only 4% of female students are planning to pursue a major in foreign language in college.
- Female students are significantly more likely than male students to have future plans related to foreign language (77% vs. 67% respectively).
- Nearly half of female students in foreign language classes report plans to continue foreign language study in high school.
- More than 38% of female students studying foreign language believe they will use their language skills in their future careers and 31% are planning to study a foreign language in college.
- Female students are significantly more likely than male students to believe that their foreign language studies will be extremely important in the future (24% vs. 17% respectively).

Source: My College Options (2016).

Education/Teaching Career Interest

- Nearly 41% of female students report that they have considered becoming a teacher compared to 27% of male students.
- More female students indicate that a teacher has inspired them to consider teaching as a career compared to male students (30% vs. 19% respectively).
- Only 5% of female students are encouraged by a mentor to pursue a career in teaching.

Source: My College Options (2016).

Chapter 11: Military & Veterans - Overview

There are few professional careers we celebrate and respect more than those brave souls that enroll in our armed forces, fighting to protect our freedom. In regard to public service and a love for our beautiful country, there's no better story than women currently in the military, as well as those that have served in the past. Today, women comprise 15.13% of the enlisted active duty force. One in 11 veterans are female. Women make up 18% of the reserve guard forces. The highest percentage of active duty servicewomen is in the U.S. Air Force with 18.91%.

We are working to change public policy and advance women in the armed forces to ensure women veterans get jobs after their service. For the breakout of female veterans, 67% are white, followed by 18.4% black, and 8.2% Hispanic. Women are getting the attention to move into leadership positions in the military and obtain great jobs after their service is over.

The top industries for women veterans are of great interest, and healthcare and social assistance lead the way with 18.2% of the jobs. We still lack pay equity, as female veterans are making less than their male counterparts, even though there is a major focus to get women into the open jobs. In this chapter, we provide the story of women and male veterans as entrepreneurs.

As of 2012, veterans made up 9.1% of all business owners. Out of those, 383,302 were veteran women-owned businesses. That number is growing. Those businesses generated some $18 billion in receipts. As of 2016, California, Texas, Florida, New York, and Georgia lead the way in terms of female veteran-owned businesses. Diving even deeper, Virginia serves as a model, as they have over 100,000 female veterans, and over 14% of their total veteran population is female—the highest rate in the nation. An astounding 90% of the female veterans are in the working-age population, so the female power is there.

Virginia is a exemplary state and the V3 program is profiled in the following pages. In addition, there are numerous programs that help employers provide the precise pathway to great jobs for female veterans. Once again, these organizations serve as pathways, networking organizations, job referrals, training facilities, and mediums to engage and advocate for more civil work for women veterans—what a salute to women in military and women as veterans. But they need our help. Some of the steps we can take are:

Call to Action:

- Get engaged to support our women in the military and join the effort to support the jobs pathway for women veterans.

- Support female veteran-owned small businesses by using your consumer dollars in their stores and on their websites. Use their products and support our country in the process.

- Enroll in the armed forces and serve our country. This may not be an option for many readers of this book, but our armed forces are starving for dedicated, determined, and driven professionals.

CHAPTER 11:
MILITARY & VETERANS

Statistical Overview

- Women make up 15.13% of the enlisted active duty force.
- About 1 in 11 veterans is female.
- Women make up 18% of reserve guard forces.
- Female veterans are 11% more likely than their male counterparts to hold a college degree.
- About 9% of female veterans served in officer positions, compared to 6% for their male counterparts.
- Veteran women business ownership has increased by almost 300% over the last decade.

Number of Active Duty Persons Enlisted by Gender and Service Branch

As of 2014*	Army	Navy	Marine Corps	Air Force	DoD* Total

Number of Active Duty Persons

DoD Total 200,692 **15.13**% 1,125,581

13.89% Female 70,058 | **17.83**% 57,327 | **7.56**% 14,207 | **18.91**% 59,100

Army | Navy | Marine Corps | Air Force

Male 434,272 | 264,272 | 173,684 | 253,353

	Army	Navy	Marine Corps	Air Force	DoD Total
Male	434,272	264,272	173,684	253,353	1,125,581
Female	70,058	57,327	14,207	59,100	200,692
Percent Female	13.89%	17.83%	7.56%	18.91%	15.13%

2014 is the latest demographics report on active duty enlisted members by service branch and gender.

DoD = Department of Defense.

Source: Military OneSource (2015).

Veterans Population

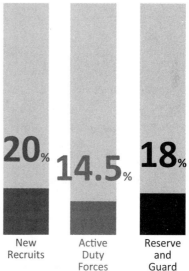

- 1 in 11 veterans is female - 9%
- 1 in 63 women is a veteran - 1.59%

Source: U.S. Department of Veterans Affairs (2016).

Women constitute approximately:

- 20% of new recruits.
- 14.5% of the 1.4 million active duty forces.
- 18% of the 850,000 reserve and guard forces.

Source: Disabled American Veterans (2015).

- The percentage of women veterans is expected to increase to almost 18% of the total veteran population by 2040.

Source: U.S. Department of Veterans Affairs (2015).

- In 2011, nearly 9% of women veterans had served as officers during their military service.
  - Compared to 6% of male veterans.

Source: U.S. Department of Veterans Affairs (2014).

Female Military Composition

20% — New Recruits

14.5% — Active Duty Forces

18% — Reserve and Guard Forces

Education & Labor Force Participation

	College Graduates	Labor Force Participation Rate	Unemployment Rate
Male Veterans	31%	50%	N/A
Male Non-Veterans	34%	75%	N/A
Female Veterans	42%	62%	5.4%
Female Non-Veterans	38%	58%	5%

Source: U.S. Bureau of Labor Statistics (2016).

- 1 in 8 veterans in the labor force is female - 12%.
- Among women in the labor force, 1 in 58 is a veteran - 1.71%.
- Among men in the labor force, 1 in 9 is a veteran - 11%.

Source: U.S. Department of Veterans Affairs (2016).

- Nearly 84% of female veterans are of working age (17–64 years).
  - Compared to 55% of male veterans.

Source: Easter Seals Dixon Center (2015).

- 13% (1.4 million of the 10.7 million) of veterans in the labor force were women in 2014.

Source: U.S. Bureau of Labor Statistics (2016).

- In 2013 and 2014, 14% of employed women Veterans worked for the government.
  - Compared with 2% of employed women non-Veterans.

Source: U.S. Department of Veterans Affairs (2015).

Median Age:

- Male Veteran - 64
- Female Veteran - 49
- Male Non-Veteran - 41
- Female Non-Veteran - 47

Source: U.S. Department of Veterans Affairs (2014).

Ethnic Breakdown of Female Veterans in 2014

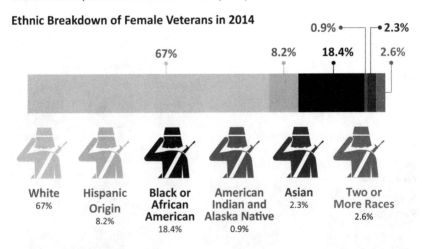

- White - 67%
- Hispanic - 8.2%
- Black or African American - 18.4%
- American Indian and Alaska Native - 0.9%
- Asian - 2.3%
- Two or More Races - 2.6%
- Other - 0.2%

Source: U.S. Department of Veterans Affairs (2016).

- In 2009, the average age of women veterans was 48 years, compared to 63 years for their male counterparts.
Source: U.S. Department of Veterans Affairs (2015).

- Women make up 20% of post-9/11 veterans.
  - Compared to 4% of the World War II, Korean War, and Vietnam-era veterans.
Source: Disabled American Veterans (2015).

- Women make up nearly 11.6% of OEF/OIF/OND Veterans.
OEF - Operation Enduring Freedom; OIF - Operation Iraqi Freedom; OND - Operation New Dawn.
Source: U.S. Department of Veterans Affairs (2016).

Professions of Women Veterans

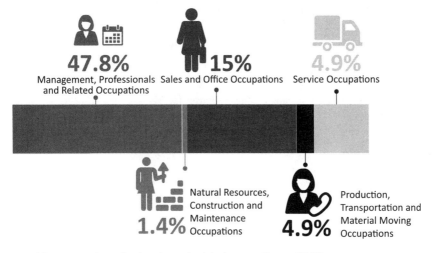

- Management, professionals, and related occupations - 47.8%.
- Sales and office occupations - 30.8%.
- Service occupations - 15.2%.
- Production, transportation, and material moving occupations - 4.9%.
- Natural rsources, construction, and maintenance occupations - 1.4%.
Source: National Business Women's Council (2012).

Top Industries for Women Veterans:

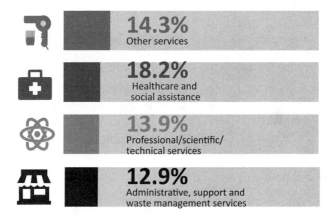

Top Industries for Women Veterans

- Healthcare and social assistance (18.2%).
- Other services (14.3%).
- Professional, scientific, and technical services (13.9%).
- Retail and trade (12.9%).

Source: National Business Women's Council (2012).

Median Incomes

- Male Veteran - $36,672.
- Female Veteran - $30,929.
- Male Non-Veteran - $31,586.
- Female Non-Veteran - $21,071.

Source: U.S. Department of Veterans Affairs (2014).

Female Veteran Entrepreneurs

383,302

97,114

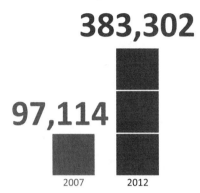

2007   2012

Women Veterans in Business

Female Veteran Entrepreneurs:

- All veterans made up 9.1% of all business owners in 2012.
- As of 2012, there are 383,302 veteran women-owned businesses in the United States.
    - This reflects an increase from 2007 of nearly 300%.
        - An additional 286,188 businesses.

Source: U.S. Small Business Administration (2016).

Female-Owned Veterans Businesses

Female Veteran Business

- In 2012, 4.4% of veteran business owners were women.
- Up from 2.5% in 2008.
    - From 1984 to 2004 ventures by women represented 1.8% of all veteran ventures.

Source: U.S. Small Business Administration (2013).

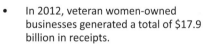
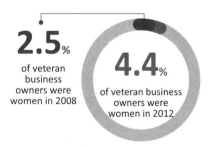

2.5% of veteran business owners were women in 2008

4.4% of veteran business owners were women in 2012

- In 2012, veteran women-owned businesses generated a total of $17.9 billion in receipts.
    - Businesses with no employees generated a total of $7.1 billion in receipts.
    - Businesses with employees generated a total of $10.9 billion.
- In 2015, the Small Business Administration's programs provided 239 loans to veteran women-owned firms totaling $87 million.

Source: U.S. Small Business Administration (2016).

Top States for Female Veteran Entrepreneurs

- California (45,846 firms, or 12% of VWOBs).
- Texas (37,822 firms or 9.9% of VWOBs).
- Florida (34,990 firms or 9.1% of VWOBs).
- New York (24,587 firms or 6.4% of VWOBs).
- Georgia (20,808 firms or 5.4% of VWOBs).

VWOB = Veteran Women-Owned Business.
Source: U.S. Small Business Administration (2016).

Occupational Trends of Female Veterans

	Management	Computer and Mathematical	Protective Services
Male Veterans	14%	4%	7.01%
Male Non-Veterans	13%	4.2%	2.68%
Female Veterans	12%	3.8%	3.49%
Female Non-Veterans	10%	1.5%	0.9%

Source: U.S. Bureau of Labor Statistics (2016).

Virginia: A Model State for Veterans

- Virginia has over 100,000 female veterans, and over 14% of their total veteran population is female – the highest rate in the nation.
- An astounding 90% of their female veterans are in the working-age population.

V3 Program

- The V3 program helps employers develop and implement long-term strategies and nationally recognized best practices in recruiting, hiring, and retaining veterans.
- The V3 program not only aims to educate and train companies on why it is a good business decision to recruit, hire, train, and retain veterans, but also to help those committed companies meet their hiring goals.
- Since the execution of the initial concept, the V3 program has grown to reach hundreds of companies, who have pledged over 13,000 jobs to veterans, resulting in over 10,000 actual hires reported so far.

Source: Virginia Department of Veterans Services (2015).

Women Veterans Organizations Examples

AcademyWomen: AcademyWomen is a global leadership and professional development organization that empowers aspiring, current and past women military leaders through mentoring, training, and growth opportunities to impact positive change locally, nationally, and globally. This mission is achieved by serving a broader community of all military women, families, and veterans.

National Association of Black Military Women: The National Association of Black Military Women is an association of women located throughout the country who are veterans or current members of the armed forces. It was founded under the former name of "The Black WAAC, WAC, Women in Service."

National Women Veterans United: The National Women Veterans United is a 501(c)(3) nonprofit organization in which membership is composed of women who are military veterans or currently enlisted in the armed forces including the national guards and reserves regardless of race, color, age, religion, or sexual orientation.

Women as Veteran Entrepreneurs (WAVE): The purpose of WAVE is to provide a forum for veteran woman-owned small businesses to promote success through: creating the opportunity to meet prime contractors to discuss business teaming; sub-contracting and mentoring opportunities; providing information detailing success strategies for doing business with the government; networking; and creating a sense of civic responsibility to give back to support our women veterans. WAVE is a recognized 501(c)(3) nonprofit organization.

American Women Veterans: American Women Veterans is the nation's preeminent, nonpartisan, 501(c)3 nonprofit organization dedicated to preserving and promoting the legacy of servicewomen, veterans, and their families. It welcomes veterans and supporters from all eras and branches of service.

- Engaging and advocating for new or improved policies that improve the lives of women veterans and its families.

- Sponsoring retreats, conferences, and symposiums focused on empowering its members and communities.

- Conducting outreach campaigns to raise awareness among service women and veterans of its benefits, entitlements, and services.

- Promoting positive images and public awareness of women's contributions from all branches and eras of service.

- Embracing continued service to its communities and the nation through philanthropic projects.

- Cultivating leadership and professionalism within the military ranks and its communities.

Chapter 12: Mentoring - Overview

There is nothing more important to our continued growth and development than encouragement, engagement, networking, and supporting one another. When it comes to mentors, one of the most influential players is the Million Women Mentors (MWM). The organization supports the engagement of one million STEM mentor relationships (male and female) to increase the interest and confidence of girls and women to persist and succeed in STEM programs and careers. MWM set a goal of one million mentor relationships effective 2020. As of October 2016, there have been over 750,000 mentoring pledges made. That number is quickly growing. There have been over 450,000 completed mentoring relationships to date, stemming from some 37 states. There have been many governors, lieutenant governors, and committees in these states, as well as 67 partner organizations representing the engagement of 30 million women and girls and corporate and entrepreneurial leaders engaged. The mentoring movement moves swiftly and offers other pathways such as sponsorship, internships, and apprenticeships.

In 2014, My College Options surveyed 368,000 girls who plan to pursue a STEM career and 4% of them indicated they were encouraged to pursue one, but just two years later, an updated study showed an increase to only 6%. Even worse, one out of three young people have never had a mentor. These numbers need to change for us to have a chance at bridging the gender disparity.

One out of four women report that the greatest challenges in attending college are confidence, motivation, and support. We need to change this. The goal is to create a mentor mindset, and we are already seeing that 61% of female students consider themselves to be a mentor. A mentor's influence is significant: 65% of women who have been mentored go on to be mentors themselves

The results of a great mentor are phenomenal. About 72% of mentees cite increased job satisfaction and 72% cite increased organizational commitment. The same is true of mentors: 79% of mentors cite increased job satisfaction and 74% cite increased organizational commitment. Mentorship is extraordinarily important, yet 67% of women said they've never been a mentor for no other reason than because they've not been asked. We must seize the opportunities that we have to be mentors, supporters, advocates, sponsors, and champions for girls and women in the system. If we do so now then pay equity and equity in general are ever closer.

The business community is stepping up with 71% of Fortune companies offering mentoring programs. The same is true for higher education, organizations, and government. Join the mentoring movement if you have not, and take the following steps:

Call to Action:

- Become a mentor and a sponsor. Offer internships and related opportunities. There are mentoring programs everywhere, and the most important thing is to get involved and help.

- Get a program running and set great metrics. Follow the success of the mentors and mentees, and communicate the data.

CHAPTER 12: MENTORING

2016 MWM HIGHLIGHTS

MWM supports the engagement of one million STEM mentors (male and female) to increase the interest and confidence of girls and women to persist and succeed in STEM programs and careers.

MWM is an initiative of STEMconnector in collaboration with 60+ partners reaching more than 30 million girls and women; 45+ corporate sponsors; and 35+ state leadership teams.
Source: MWM, Advancing Girls and Women Through Mentoring (2016).

Pledges

- Over 768,000 mentor pledges made to date.
- Goal of 800,000 mentor pledges for 2016.

Mentor Pledges

Results

Be Counted! Campaign Results

- BE COUNTED!: There have been over 450,000 completed mentoring relationships as of July 2016 through our Be Counted! Campaign.

Pledge Goal from Education Sector

States

STATES Leadership

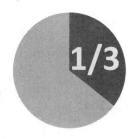

Million Women Mentors has leadership teams in over

36
States

- MWM has leadership teams in over 36 states and marching forward to all 50.
- MWM – IA has nearly completed their 5000 pledge, with initiatives like the Mayors Project, Coaches Mentoring Challenge, and a Fellowship Program for recent STEM grads.
- MWM – TN surpassed their pledge goal with corporate partnerships with Cisco, Deloitte, Eastman Chemical Co., and several higher education institutions.
- MWM – IN has completed one-third of its pledge goal through strong support in the education sector.

- MWM-VA worked with Gov. Terry McAuliffe to send out a letter to all businesses throughout the state to support MWM. They also have a strong focus on veterans for their initiative.
- State of the States Report updated on www.MillionWomenMentors.org.
- WBENC is working with MWM states to add entrepreneurship members to each state committee.

Governors and Lieutenant Governors

Two governors and 16 lieutenant governors engaged as honorary state chairs with 20 mayors Involved.

- Iowa – Lt. Gov. Kim Reynolds, national honorary chair for MWM
- Virginia – Gov. Terry McAuliffe
- Rhode Island – Gov. Gina Raimondo
- Alabama – Lt. Gov. Kay Ivey
- Arkansas – Gov. Tim Griffin
- Idaho – Lt. Gov. Brad Little
- Illinois – Rep. Tammy Duckworth
- Indiana – Lt. Gov. Sue Ellspermann
- Kansas – Lt. Gov. Joe Colyer
- Kentucky – Lt. Gov. Jenean M. Hampton
- Maryland – Lt. Gov. Boyd Rutherford
- Montana – Lt. Gov. Mike Cooney
- Missouri – Lt. Gov. Peter Kinder
- New Jersey – Lt. Gov. Kim Guadagno
- New York – Lt. Gov. Kathy Hochul
- Ohio – Lt. Gov. Mary Taylor
- Pennsylvania – Lt. Gov. Mike Stack
- Tennessee - Lt. Gov. Ron Ramsey
- Utah – Lt. Gov. Spencer J. Cox

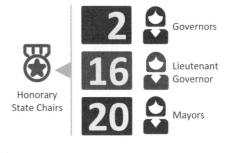

Honorary State Chairs

2 Governors

16 Lieutenant Governor

20 Mayors

Sponsors and Corporate Management

- So many companies are stepping up. Example in MWM Leaders of many companies is global BP. Note that BP recognizes and values the breadth of knowledge and talent of its employees, and the company is proud to back initiatives that inspire them to make a difference. For these

Sponsors at Platinum Level

60 Sponsors

8 Committed

reasons, BP is proud to support Million Women Mentors (MWM) and has produced a model Women's Mentoring Guide. BP set a global goal to have women in 25 percent of group leadership roles and 30 percent of senior level leadership roles by 2020. By fostering girls' interest and confidence in STEM education, BP aims to increase the number of women in these fields.

Source: BP.

195

- Top corporate chairs actively engaged with MWM committees.
- 60 sponsors with 8 committed at the platinum level examples.

Platimun Leadership

- TATA Consultancy Services – Developed the MWM website and worked with MWM to develop a way to easily examine the variety of mentoring activities within their company (job shadowing, internships, etc.).
- BP – Created special webpage using MWM-provided custom link to engage employees as MWM mentors.
- Deloitte – MWM developed metrics recording user types for retirees and current employees to support Deloitte corporate-wide push.
- PepsiCo Inc. – Creating a strategy to engage mentors with strategic MWM partner organizations.
- Walmart – Utilized MWM platform to connect with thousands of girls through high school mentoring events, career accelerator days, and national launch event.

Partner Examples

- Engaged with over 65 partners serving girls and women across the country.
- Science Olympiad – Currently has pledged 57,000 for 2016 and completed 108,000 mentoring relationships for girls between 2014 and 2015.
- AAUW – Has a 2016 pledge of 1600, with 13,469 completed mentoring relationship so far.
- FIRST – Has completed 80,000 mentoring relationships through their robotics competitions.
- Mind Research – Pledged 100,000 to engage corporate partners.
- 4-H Council – Major pledge with MWM.

Technology

- Tata Consultancy Services has created millionwomenmentors.org in partnership with the STEMconnector/MWM team.
- New MWM portal being released in September 2016 with new communities and mentor relationship logging features.
- Training for the members, sponsors, and partners on using the portal is available.

Best Practices

- MWM employee resource group town hall Mar. 30, 2016 with panelists from Cigna, Corning, GM, and Lockheed Martin.
- Corporate mentoring workshop in Minnesota with 20+ MWM sponsors and partners.
- Guidebooks and handouts.
- Creating best practice models for corporate, state, and partner efforts.

Higher Education

- Working with higher education institutions to support STEM mentoring relationships with MWM.
- Workshop geared toward broadening participation of women in advanced technological education.

Events

- National MWM summit and gala annual event for 2016. Oct. 4-5, 2016 (2015 attendance over 500).
- State events in 2016 in the following states: Arkansas, Arizona, California, Florida, Iowa, Idaho, Illinois, Kansas, Missouri, Pennsylvania, South Carolina, Tennessee, and Virginia with lieutenant governor, state chairs, and/or governor participation.
- Resolutions passed in five state legislatures and presented in capitols.
- Monthly state leaders calls allow for discussion of best practices.
- Women's mentoring events in January 2016 during National Mentoring Month.
- Special Senate Salute on Mar. 15, 2016 with 160 attendees, 20 senators, and 22 congressional and Obama Administration leaders as speakers.
- Corporate sponsors best practices event June 21, 2016 in Minneapolis, featuring TATA Consultancy Services, BP, and PepsiCo Inc.
- MWM staff and sponsors attending and supporting 50 conferences with keynotes, panels, and outreach.

Communication and Resource Examples

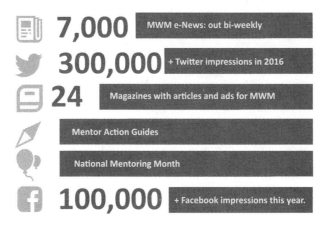

7,000 MWM e-News: out bi-weekly

300,000 + Twitter impressions in 2016

24 Magazines with articles and ads for MWM

Mentor Action Guides

National Mentoring Month

100,000 + Facebook impressions this year.

- MWM e-News: out to 7,000 bi-weekly.
- TWITTER: Over 300,000 Twitter impressions in 2016.
- 24 magazines with articles and ads for MWM.
- Mentor Action Guides for different age groups in development, Middle School Mentor Action Guide released on website.
- National Mentoring Month: gained over 210 new Twitter followers, increased impressions by 198%, average of 1,900 impressions per day.
- Over 100,000 Facebook impressions this year.

Global

- Six countries to date including Mexico and Poland.
- Mexico has mentorship program, which pairs female STEM students on scholarships with mentors from PepsiCo Inc. STEM.
- Pakistan, United Arab Emirates, and others planning state MWMs.

Entrepreneurs

- Strong entrepreneurship committee composed of top STEM women entrepreneurs.
- WEBNC is working to assist entrepreneurs.
- Enterprising Women Special Edition with STEMpreneurs and MWM Entrepreneurship Committee.
- Camp Invention, a partnership with the nonprofit Invent Now. Each year, more than 100,000 elementary school-aged kids in all 50 states participate in the week-long, summer enrichment program called "Camp Invention," where they get hands-on experience on how to design, prototype, build, test, and refine a specific device.

Source: MWM (2016).

- USPTO has partnered with Urban Alliance, a program that provides internship and mentorship opportunities for high school students. The USPTO must hire many people with STEM backgrounds. A number of bright and enthusiastic students brought their talents to the USPTO this past school year. USPTO was the federal agency with the largest number of Urban Alliance interns.

Source: USPTO (2016).

- Fewer than 15% of the US based inventors listed on patents were women. At the current rate, it will take another 140 years to balance the number of female and male inventors. Changing these statistics begins by working with today's girls and women (1) to spark their interest in STEM, and (2) to promote their advancement to their maximum potential through mentorship and training. To this end, we at the USPTO launched our "All in STEM" initiative. As part of this initiative, USPTO partners with Invent Now, with whom we run an annual summer program called Camp Invention. This program reaches more than 100,000 kids every year (girls + boys including those from under privileged backgrounds) and its programs provide hands-on STEM skills, as well as basics on patents, trademarks and even entrepreneurship. The USPTO also conducts an annual National Summer Teacher Institute, designed to help middle and high school teachers better prepare our young minds for STEM careers as well as invention, innovation and entrepreneurship. And we even partnered with the Girl Scouts of America of our Nation's Capitol to create a patch on IP and innovation. If the young girls learn a little about patents, trademarks, trade secrets and copyrights, and put their innovative spirits to work on creating something, they can earn an IP patch. I was a girl scout – both a Brownie and a Junior –, and the patches I remember being able to earn were on First Aid and Sewing. I think we can do better than that by giving our girls the skills they need to succeed in the 21st century innovation economy!

Source: USPTO Administrator at Million Women Mentors (2016).

Veterans

- Engaging with state teams and the national level to create pathways to jobs for women veterans.
- Collaboration with companies and organizations with women veterans' commitments.
- Virginia, Iowa, Tennessee MWM teams are planning engagement with state veterans.

For more information, see Chapter 11.

- Together, MWM and PepsiCo Inc. had a vision for a STEM revolution—one mentor, and one girl, at a time. We've already seen some amazing progress, but imagine what could happen if every STEM professional made a commitment to mentoring one-on-one for just two hours a month. We could truly change the game.
- Maya Angelou once said: "In order to be a mentor, and an effective one, one must care." We all care about the phones in our hands, the computers on our desks, and the cars that we drive. But we must care even more about the girls who want to invent, explore, and discover the next generation of amazing STEM breakthroughs, but who just need a little encouragement to do so.
- We can be the catalyst, and these girls can—and will—build the future.

Students and Mentoring

STEM Mentor Encouragement

4%
of 368,000
2014
2016
6%

- 4% of 368,000 girls who plan to pursue STEM said a mentor encouraged them has increased to 6% of female students who interested in pursuing STEM and encouraged to do so by a mentor.
- 1 out of 3 young people have never had a mentor.
- 1 out of 4 female students reports the greatest challenges in attending college are confidence, motivation, or support.
- 20% of current female high school students interested in a STEM discipline say they would like to learn more about mentoring and motivational programs to help prepare them for the future.
- 4 in 10 female students interested in a STEM career report having mentors in their lives.
- Female students with family members who are professionals in a STEM field are two-thirds more likely to report an interest in pursuing a career in STEM com-

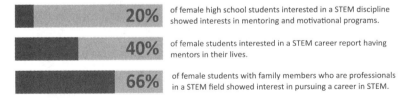

20%	of female high school students interested in a STEM discipline showed interests in mentoring and motivational programs.
40%	of female students interested in a STEM career report having mentors in their lives.
66%	of female students with family members who are professionals in a STEM field showed interest in pursuing a career in STEM.

pared to those who do not have family members in a STEM field.
- More than 3 in 4 female students interested in a STEM career who also have mentors feel they will be successful in pursuing a career in STEM.
- Nearly 61% of female students consider themselves a mentor.

Mentor Mindset

61%

of female students
consider themselves
a mentor.

- Half of female students who do not consider themselves a mentor believe that they could be someday.
- While 31% of female students prefer a mentor of the same gender, 63% are open to a mentor of any gender.
- Seven in 10 female students believe an internship is very important to getting into college or for their future careers, however, only one in 10 female students has actually participated in an internship.
- Lack of awareness is the number one reason female students have not participated in internships.

Source: My College Options.

Influence of Mentors

of women who have been
mentored will be mentors
themselves

of women who have received
support are developing
others

of high potential women who
were sponsored, were
developing others

- 65% of women who have been mentored go on to be mentors themselves.
- Being developed matters: a higher percentage of high potentials who had received developmental support in the past two years were more likely to be offering similar support to a protégé.
- 59% of those who received developmental support were now, in turn, developing others.
- 47% of those who hadn't received this type of support were developing others.
- The type of development received matters: if high potentials had received sponsorship, they were more likely to be paying it forward.
  - 66% of high potentials who were sponsored were developing others.
  - 42% who hadn't been sponsored were developing others.
- Developing a protégé predicted high potentials' compensation growth as well as their advancement.

- Women and men benefitted equally from developing others. There was no difference in compensation growth or career advancement between women and men who were developing others.
- Women are more likely to develop others when compared to men.
  - Among high potentials who reported they had someone developing them over the course of their careers, women were more likely than men to now be paying it forward and offering similar support to someone else.
  - 65% of women who had been developed were paying it forward, compared to 56% of men.
- Women were more likely than men to be developing women.
  - 73% of women who were developing others were developing female talent compared to only 30% of men who were developing female talent.

Source: Catalyst.

Formal Mentoring Programs

- Formal mentoring overall.
  - Out of the women who have had a formal mentor, only 50% of them stated that the organization has a formal program for mentoring.
  - 26% of women who have had a formal mentor stated that there was no formal mentoring program available.
  - Along with mentoring not being a common practice for women, we also discovered that mentoring is unchartered territory for most organizations. This makes it even more challenging for women to connect with mentors.
  - Only 56% of organizations have a formal program for mentoring.

- Formal programs encourage informal mentoring.
  - 61% of women who are frequently asked to be an informal mentor work for an organization that has a formal program for mentoring.
  - 48% of those women who are frequently asked to be an informal mentor work for an organization with no formal mentoring program available.
  - 34% of women who are frequently asked to be a formal mentor work for an organization that has a formal program for mentoring.
  - 18% of women who are frequently asked to be a formal mentor work for an organization that has no formal mentoring program available.

Source: DDIWorld.

Formal Mentoring Plan

26% of women who have had a formal mentor stated that there was no formal mentoring program available

61% of women who are frequently asked to be an informal mentor work for an organization that has a formal program for mentoring

56% of organizations have a formal program for mentoring

Corporate Mentoring

- 71% of Fortune 500 companies offer mentoring programs to their employees.
- 78% of women in senior roles have served as formal mentors at one time.
- 54% of women reported that they have only been asked to be a mentor a few times in their career or less.
- 20% of women% reported they have never been asked to be a mentor.
- 74% of women indicated that they mentor because they have benefited from their own mentorship experiences.
- 55% of non-millennial women said women-specific corporate mentorship programs could better help female employees succeed in business.
- 52 % of non-millennial women said that women-specific networking could help female workers thrive.

Source: Chronus.

Corporate Mentoring

71% of Fortune 500 companies offer mentoring.

78% women in senior roles have served as mentors.

54% of women have been asked to be a mentor.

Mentor Facts

34%	43%	51%	66%
of women Baby Boomers had a mentor	women in Generation X had a mentor	women in Generation Y have a mentor	of women connect with their mentors in person

- 72% of mentees cited increased job satisfaction (in terms of tangible benefits).
- 79 % of mentors cited increased job satisfaction (in terms of tangible benefits).
- 74% of mentors cited increased organizational commitment.
- 72% of mentees cited increased organizational commitment.
- 52% of mentors cited increased diversity awareness.
- 54% of mentees cited increased diversity awareness.

Source: Diversity Inc.

- 67% of women who said that they have never been a mentor said it's because no one ever asked.
- 52% of women said that they had never had a mentor said it's because they never encountered someone appropriate.
- Nearly 1 out of every 5 women in the United States does not have a mentor.

- Only 34% of women Baby Boomers had a mentor.
- 43% of women in Generation X had a mentor.
- 51% of women in Generation Y have a mentor.
- The top five reasons women rely on their professional networks other than for job hunting is for professional guidance, recommendations, career advancement, collaboration, and keeping current with industry news and trends.
- 66% of women connect with their mentors in person rather than through email, IM, or phone.

Source: LinkedIn survey of 1,000 female professionals in the United States.

- So many companies are stepping up. Example in MWM Leaders of many companies is global BP. Note that BP recognizes and values the breadth of knowledge and talent of its employees, and the company is proud to back initiatives that inspire them to make a difference. For these reasons, BP is proud to support Million Women Mentors (MWM) and has produced a model Women's Mentoring Guide. BP set a global goal to have women in 25 percent of group leadership roles and 30 percent of senior level leadership roles by 2020. By fostering girls' interest and confidence in STEM education, BP aims to increase the number of women in these fields.

Source: BP.

Organization Examples

- Mentor Net
- US2020

US 2020: Explore mentoring opportunities by ZIP code or keywords. When you have found your perfect match, simply click "Count Me In!" and you'll be connected directly to the program's volunteer liaison. After selecting "Count Me In!", the volunteer liaison from the hosting organization will email you to say hello and provide additional guidance on their programs. They will help you complete your enrollment process to become a mentor in their program. The program partners start their programs with a volunteer training and will support you throughout the entire mentoring experience. The program partners start their programs with a volunteer training and will support you throughout the entire mentoring experience US2020.

Chapter 13: STEM - Overview

Remember, STEM refers to those jobs in science, technology, engineering, and math. By 2018, 71% (or higher) of jobs will require STEM skills. But as of the publishing of this book, women only represent 24% of the STEM workforce. This chapter outlines not only the opportunity, but also the importance of growth in STEM occupations. While women make up almost 50% of the entire workforce, we see that number plummet in STEM-related jobs. As we crunch the numbers, we further learn that there is only 22% female faculty in information sciences, 19% in math, 18% in physical sciences, and 12% in engineering. These numbers all need to improve. In life sciences, women account for 34% of the workforce, still almost 15% lower than non-STEM job sectors. With women making exceptional strides in education, it is somewhat of a surprise that more faculty leaders are not encouraging an influx into STEM jobs. Why so few? Of 100 female bachelor students, 12 graduate within STEM fields—yet only 3 continue in STEM fields after 10 years. When shining the light on minorities, the numbers are even more concerning. Minority women comprise fewer than 1 in 10 employed scientist and engineers. The gender disparity persists in the workforce in a glaring way. The women of color are interested, but far too often are left out. But it is not all bad news. The small group of women that do work in STEM sectors actually recognize 33% more income than comparable women in non-STEM jobs, which is considerably higher than the STEM premium for men. That comes out to enjoying 92 cents of every dollar a male makes in STEM jobs. That number is even higher in the technology sector, where women find 96 cents for every dollar their male counterparts realize. As every data set shows, there is a great opportunity to gain pay equity in STEM jobs. This chapter shows the data, the number of STEM degrees, the diversity, and STEM-related higher education. The path to STEM starts as early as grade school. We learn that girls who take calculus in grade school are three times more likely to major in a science or engineering field than those that do not. About 74% of high school girls across the country are interested in the fields and subjects of STEM. So much so that high school girls earn more math and science credits than do boys. And girls' GPA, aggregated across math and science classes, are higher than boys; however, boys tend to do better on standardized tests, such as the SAT or ACT. The numbers don't lie. Girls are destined for STEM, and show remarkable progress and engagement at an early age. Somewhere along the way that passion and desire is lost when they get older. If we are to celebrate STEM jobs and show young women the value in choosing them, we must work to recognize the following:

Call to Action:

- If only one in four female high school students are interested in STEM, let's work to excite and engage to improve that number to at least two in four students. This will help grow our equity, raise salaries, and bridge the gap.

- We see the gross imbalance in access and quality of STEM education in primary school must be addressed systematically if the nation is to fulfill its mission of developing a diverse workforce of innovative and world-class STEMs.

- Engaging our daughters in STEM will help them to remain interested and develop the valuable tools and skillsets to thrive in the rapidly growing STEM job markets and gain career satisfaction and pay equity.

CHAPTER 13: STEM

Overview of Chapter Data

Datapoint	Statistic
Jobs in 2018 That Will Require STEM Skills	71%
Women's Representation in the STEM Workforce	24%
Women's Representation in the S&E Workforce	28%
Percent of S&E Degrees Held by Minority Women	11.2%
STEM Wage Gap (compared to men)	92%
Technology Wage Gap (compared to men)	96%
Women's Representation in STEM Teaching Faculty	29%
Percent of STEM Degrees Held by Women	20%
Percent of High School Girls That Are Interested in the Subjects of STEM	74%

STEM Occupations

71% of jobs in 2018 will require STEM skills.
Source: Solving the Equation - Quick Facts Sheet (2015).

Women in STEM Jobs

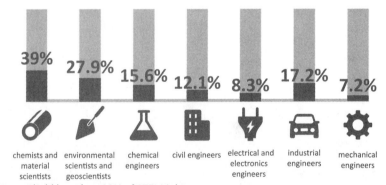

Women hold less than 25% of STEM jobs.
Source: STEMconnector® (2016).
Women make up 47% of the total U.S. workforce, but are much less represented in particular S&E occupations.
- 39% of chemists and material scientists are women.
- 27.9% of environmental scientists and geoscientists are women.
- 15.6% of chemical engineers are women.
- 12.1% of civil engineers are women.
- 8.3% of electrical and electronics engineers are women.
- 17.2% of industrial engineers are women.
- 7.2% of mechanical engineers are women.

Source: National Girls Collaborative Project - Statistics (2016).

Female Faculty

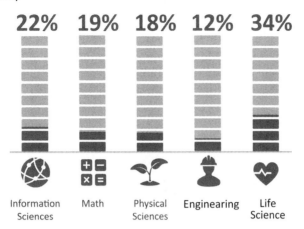

22%	19%	18%	12%	34%
Information Sciences	Math	Physical Sciences	Engineering	Life Science

- Women fill close to 50% of all jobs in the United States, but they hold less than 25% of STEM jobs.
- Of 100 female bachelor students, 12 graduate within STEM fields – yet only 3 continue in STEM fields after 10 years.
- In the United States, 75% of all students are women and students of color, but only represent 45% of STEM degrees.

Source: PepsiCo Inc. (2016).

- Women made up less than one-quarter of the faculty in computer and information sciences (22%), math (19%), the physical sciences (18%), and engineering (12%). In the life sciences, women made up only one-third (34%) of the faculty. In all cases, women were better represented in lower faculty ranks than in higher ranks among STEM faculty in four-year colleges and universities.
- More than half (52%), however, quit their jobs by mid-career (about 10 years into their careers). High-tech companies in particular lost 41% of their female employees, compared with only 17% of their male employees. In engineering, women have higher attrition rates than their male peers have, despite similar levels of stated satisfaction and education.

Source: AAUW: Why So Few?: Women in STEM (2013)

- Women have seen no employment growth in STEM jobs since 2000.

Source: Forbes: Where Are The Women? (2012). STEM Fields and the Gender Gap

- About 40% of the full-time faculty in degree-granting colleges and universities in the United States in 2005 were women; however, women's representation in STEM disciplines was significantly lower.

Source: AAUW: Solving the Equation - Quick Facts Sheet (2015)

- In 2013, only 12% of engineers and 26% of computing professionals were women.

Source: AAUW: Solving the Equation - Quick Facts Sheet (2015).

- Women remain underrepresented in the science and engineering workforce, although to a lesser degree than in the past, with the greatest disparities occurring in engineering, computer science, and the physical sciences.
Source: National Girls Collaborative Project - Statistics (2016).

- One study found that the women who leave engineering are just like the women who stay. The difference is the workplace culture.
Source: AAUW: Solving The Equation, Print Publication (2015).

- Women made up 1% of engineers in 1960 and about 11% of engineers by 2000.

Percentage of Women in Engineering

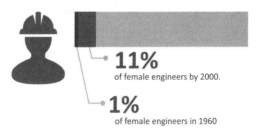

11%
of female engineers by 2000.

1%
of female engineers in 1960

Source: AAUW: Why So Few?: Women in STEM (2013).

- Studies show that stereotypes and biases often lead employers—both men and women—to select male candidates, regardless of qualifications.
Source: AAUW: Solving the Equation - Quick Facts Sheet (2015).

- Another recent study found that potential employers systematically underestimated the mathematical performance of women compared with men, resulting in the hiring of lower performing men over higher performing women for mathematical work.
- Women who left engineering were less likely to have opportunities for training and development, support from co-workers or supervisors, and support for balancing work and non-work roles than were women who stayed in the profession.
Source: AAUW: Solving the Equation - Executive Summary (2015).

- Gender diversity (technical workers only) - top Silcon Valley tech companies: From most diverse to least: Indiegogo (67% male, 33% female); eBay (76% male, 24% female); Pinterest (79% male, 21% female); Apple (80% male, 20% female); Pandora (82.1% male, 17.9% female); LinkedIn (83% male, 17% female); Google (83% male, 17% female); Yahoo (85% male, 15% female, 1% other/undisclosed);Facebook (85% male, 15% female); and Twitter (90% male, 10% female).
Source: Fortune: How Tech Companies Compare in Employee Diversity (2014).

- Female attrition rates are also higher in technology than they are in other non-STEM fields.
- Only about 20% of women working in other non-STEM professional occupations left their fields during the 30-year span covered by the study. Women in STEM

also were more likely to leave in the first few years of their career than women in non-STEM professions.

- Depending on the subcategory, male-only teams account for 82-90% of all information technology patents (Ashcraft & Breitzman, 2012). Female-only teams account for approximately 2% while mixed-sex teams count for 8-15%. As a result, women are even more underrepresented in technology patenting than they are in the technology workforce overall.
- The most recent study by the Center for Talent Innovation found that 32%— roughly 1 in 3 SET women—report that they feel "stalled" in their careers and are likely to quit their jobs in one year.

Source: NCWIT: Women in Tech: The Facts (2016).

Diversity in Stem Occupations

< 1 in 10

- Minority women comprise fewer than 1 in 10 employed scientists and engineers.

Source: NGCP: The State of Girls and Women in STEM (2015).

- Women, minorities, and persons with disabilities remain underrepresented in STEM higher education professions, while they are increasing percentages of the overall workforce and population at large.
- Gender disparities persist in the workforce, where women made up only 29% of tenure-track faculty in STEM fields in 2008 and accounted for less than one-third of all S&E employment in 2010.

Source: University of Pennsylvania: Realizing STEM Equity and Diversity Through Higher Education-Community Engagement (2015).

- Once they graduate, the differences between men and women with PhDs continue. While industry tends to pay the largest salaries, women are more likely than men to work in government and academic settings. In fact, women in the study were 13 percentage points less likely than men to work outside of academia and government.

Source: Ohio State University: Young Women in STEM Fields Earn up to One-Third Less Than Men (2016).

- A recent estimate indicates that 28 % of S&E workers in the United States are women, even though they comprise almost half of the U.S. workforce. Similarly, while underrepresented racial and ethnic groups comprise 26% of the general population, only 10% of U.S. workers are in S&E.

Source: Huffington Post: Increasing Diversity in the STEM Pipeline (2014).

- When women and minorities do complete in undergraduate STEM programs, they face still more disparity. The STEM wage gap between men and women in the United States is almost $16,000 per year, and £17,000 in the United Kingdom. Today's median wage for blacks employed in U.S. STEM jobs is $75,000 and around $77,000 for Hispanics, while whites earn a little over $88,000 annually.
Source: WIRED: 5 Numbers That Explain Why STEM Diversity Matters to All of Us (2015).

- The empirical research is clear: A more diverse STEM population portends huge benefits to tech innovation at large. And some would also argue, provides a much-needed moral compass.
Source: WIRED: 5 Numbers That Explain Why STEM Diversity Matters to All of Us (2015).

- According to a University of Maryland and Columbia Business School joint study, gender diversity at the management level leads to a $42 million increase in value of S&P 500 firms.
Source: WIRED: 5 Numbers That Explain Why STEM Diversity Matters to All of Us (2015).

- The U.S. S&E workforce is composed of 55% white men and just 1% Hispanic women.
Source: Huffington Post: Lack of Diversity in STEM Is Dangerous for Our Students (2013).

- In 2015, women made up 25% of computing-related occupations. Levels of participation are even more concerning when it comes to women of color.
Source: Bureau of Labor (2016).

- Women's experience of feeling stalled in their careers also varies by race/ethnicity. African-American women experience the highest perceived stall rates at 48%. Thirty-four percent of white women feel stalled, and 32% Asian and Hispanic women feel stalled.
Source: Hewlett (2014) and Women in Tech: The Facts (2016).

- Industries outside of technology employ more women software engineers than do the tech industry. Women accounted for about 32% of software engineers in healthcare and 25% in banking, compared to only 20% in the tech industry.
Source: Women in Tech: The Facts (2016).

Diversity in the STEM Workforce

In 2014, women were:
- 12% of the engineering workforce.
- 26% of the computing workforce.

Within the 2014 computing workforce:
- 5% were Asian women.
- 3% were African-American women.
- 2% were Hispanic/Latina women.

U.S. workforce shortages:
- The United States expects 1.4 million computing-related job openings from 2010-22.
- Only 32% of these jobs can be filled by U.S. computing graduates.
Source: Chevron (2016).

In the technology chapter, under STEM Education - Diversity in STEM Education.
- Diversity in STEM Education.
- Women earn only 18% of bachelor's degrees awarded in engineering and computer science, and 19% in physics.

Underrepresented minority women make up 16% of the population, but only earn:
- 3% of bachelor's degrees in engineering.
- 5% of bachelor's degrees in computer sciences.
- 6% of bachelor's degrees in physical sciences.

Percentage of computer science majors who are women is declining:
- 37% in 1985.
- 18% in 2013.

Source: Chevron (2016).

STEM Wage Gap

- Women with STEM jobs earned 33% more than comparable women in non-STEM jobs, considerably higher than the STEM premium for men.

Source: U.S. Department of Commerce (2014).

Stem Wage Gap Among Women

33%

more was earned by women in STEM jobs.

- Funneling more women into STEM fields is just one part of a much larger economic priority for Americans to gain higher paying jobs. About 92 cents on dollar for pay equity and up to 96 cents on a dollar for tech jobs.

Source: STEMconnector® (2016).

- Our latest research shows that among full-time, year-round workers in 2013, women were paid 78% of what men were paid. A gender pay gap persists in nearly every industry—even the high-paying STEM careers.
- In engineering and architecture, women were typically paid 82% of what their male counterparts were paid, or about $65,000 annually, compared to $79,000 for men. It seems that entering a high-paying field like engineering or computing still does not protect women against the pay gap.
- In addition, the pay gap only gets worse as women dedicate more time to their careers. According to one study, today's women are even more achievement-oriented than men are, yet women's paychecks tell a different story.

Source: AAUW: Even in High-Paying STEM Fields, Women Are Shortchanged (2015).

"Both men and women earn the most in industry, but the pay gap between the sexes is even larger there than it is in academics and government," Weinburg said.

Source: Ohio State University: Young Women in STEM Fields Earn up to One-Third Less Than Men (2016).

- Gender differences in salaries for academic jobs in S&E could lead women to leave the sector. A pay gap is not present throughout academic science, however. In 2010, in only 6 of 24 fields were salaries of males significantly greater than those of females: assistant and full professors in economics; life science assistant professors; associate and full professors in engineering and the physical sciences; and full professors in geoscience.

Stem Wage Gap

Source: Scientific American: Do Women Earn Less Than Men in STEM Fields? (2015).

- Claudia Goldin analyses suggest that women's status in science may be the result of personal choices and time-flexibility preferences as opposed to gender differences in human capital and sex-based salary discrimination.

Source: Scientific American: Do Women Earn Less Than Men in STEM Fields? (2015).

Nationalities of STEM Women

| Asian Women | African-American Women | Hispanic/Latina Women |

Within the 2014 computing workforce:
- 5% were Asian women.
- 3% were African-American women.
- 2% were Hispanic/Latina women.

Source: TechBridge: Changing the Game for Girls in STEM (2013).

STEM Degrees

- In the mid-1980s women earned slightly more than one-third (36%) of the bachelor's degrees in computer science; by 2006 that number had dropped to 20%.

Source: AAUW: Why So Few?: Women in STEM - AAUW (2013).

- GoldieBlox introduced the world's first girl engineer character, Goldie Blox, when it launched in 2012. Its mission was to close the gender gap in STEM by making toys for girls that inspire an early interest in science, technology, engineering and math.
- GoldieBlox recently launched "GoldieBlox: Adventures in Coding – The Rocket Cupcake Co.," an iOS app designed to teach young inventors (ages 4+) the fundamentals of coding and get girls interested in coding at an early age.
- In early 2017, GoldieBlox will debut children's books based on Goldie Blox, the world's first girl engineer character. GoldieBlox announced its licensing agreement with Random House in June 2016.

- Since its founding, GoldieBlox has been recognized as a leader in children's entertainment and has reached billions of consumers through TV, radio and digital as the first start-up with a Super Bowl commercial and a float in the Macy's Thanksgiving Day Parade.

Source: GoldieBlox.

GoldieBlox is the award-winning children's multimedia company disrupting the pink aisle in toy stores globally and challenging gender stereotypes with the world's first girl engineer character. Through the integration of storytelling and STEM (Science, Technology, Engineering and Math) principles, GoldieBlox creates toys, books, apps, videos, animation and merchandise; the tools that empower girls to build their confidence, dreams and ultimately, their futures. Since its founding in 2012, GoldieBlox has been recognized as a leader in children's entertainment and has reached billions of consumers.

Female Minority

- In 2014, women accounted for 57.3% to men's 42.7% of all degrees granted— and the gender disparity in STEM degrees and what that means for both individuals and the country cannot be ignored.

Source: Higher Education Today: Where Are the Women in STEM? (2015) .

Degrees in STEM Per Gender

Diversity In STEM Higher Education

- African-American women earned 57% of physical science degrees awarded to African Americans in 2007; still, the overall number of African-American women earning physical science bachelor's degrees was less than 600.

Source: AAUW: Why So Few?: Women in STEM (2013).

- The rates of S&E course taking for girls/women shift at the undergraduate level and gender disparities begin to emerge, especially for minority women.
- In 2012, 11.2% of bachelor's degrees in S&E, 8.2% of master's degrees in S&E, and 4.1% of doctorate degrees in S&E were awarded to minority women.
- In 2012, 3.1% of bachelor's degrees in engineering, 6.5% of bachelor's degrees in physical sciences, 5.4% of bachelor's degrees in mathematics and statistics, 4.8% of bachelor's degrees in computer sciences, 9.7% of bachelor's degrees in biological sciences, and 14.2% of bachelor's degrees in social sciences were awarded to minority women.

Source: National Girls Collaborative Project - Statistics (2016).

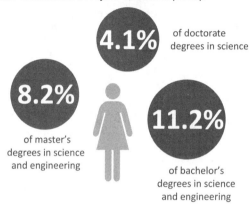

Fewest STEM Degrees

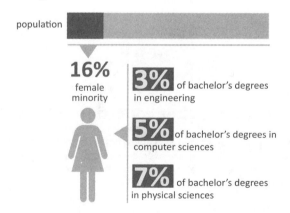

- Underrepresented minority women make up 16% of the population, but only earn:
  - 3% of bachelor's degrees in engineering.

- 5% of bachelor's degrees in computer sciences.
- 7% of bachelor's degrees in physical sciences.

Source: The State of Girls and Women in STEM (2015).

- Women have earned about half of all S&E bachelor's degrees since the late 1990s, and the proportion of women earning doctoral degrees grew from 42% to 47% over the last decade, but major gender disparities persist among certain fields.

Source: Realizing STEM Equity and Diversity Through Higher Education-Community Engagement (2015).

- African Americans make up only 5% of undergraduate engineering degrees, as compared with 13% of overall undergraduate enrollment. Latinos fare similarly, and many schools wrestle with gross imbalances from a gender perspective.

Source: A More "Diverse" Approach to Diversity in STEM Education (2015).

- In the United States, less than half of the students who enter into STEM undergraduate curricula as freshmen will actually graduate with a STEM degree. There is even greater disparity in the national STEM graduation rates of students from underrepresented groups with approximately three-fourths of minority students leaving STEM disciplines at the undergraduate level.

Source: Hierarchical Mentoring: A Transformative Strategy for Improving Diversity and Retention in Undergraduate STEM Disciplines (2012).

- Linking girls with mentors and exposing them to STEM in the early years can provide an edge, but these are also among the things that too many girls are missing—and what many women say could have made a difference in their STEM pursuits.

Source: Bias and Stereotypes Sideline Girls in STEM (2015).

- A recent analysis of international differences in the composition of engineering and computing fields makes clear that the surrounding culture makes a difference in the gender makeup of these fields. Women in the United States earn approximately one-fifth of all computing degrees, whereas in Malaysia women earn about half of all computing degrees. Similarly, in the United States women earn fewer than one-fifth of engineering degrees. In Indonesia, however, women earn almost half of engineering degrees, and in a diverse group of countries women account for about one-third of recent engineering graduates.

Source: AAUW: Solving The Equation - Executive Summary (2015).

Harvey Mudd Engineer Leader

Source: Harvey Mudd.

- Among underrepresented students, Latinas continue to express the least interest in STEM careers.

Source: Techbridge: Changing the Game for Girls in STEM (2013).

Girls in STEM—Grade School

- Calculus can make a difference. Girls who take calculus in high school are three times more likely to major in an S&E field than those who do not.
Source: AAUW: Why So Few?: Women in STEM, Executive Summary (2013).

- Nationally representative surveys show that the number of girls who say they are very interested in a STEM career remains less than 25%. It turns out, though, that girls' self-reported lack of interest is often due to lack of exposure to STEM.

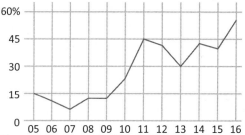

Source: Techbrige: Changing the Game for Girls in STEM (2013).

- A difference in average math performance between girls and boys no longer exists in the general school population.
Source: AAUW: Why So Few?: Women in STEM (2013).

- Seventy-four percent of high school girls across the country are interested in the fields and subjects of STEM.
- African-American and Hispanic girls have high interest in STEM, high confidence, and a strong work ethic, but have fewer supports, less exposure, and lower academic achievement than Caucasian girls.
- Specifically, high school girls earn more math and science credits than do boys; and girls' GPAs, aggregated across math and science classes, are higher than boys. Boys, however, tend to do better on standardized tests, such as the SAT or ACT.
- A high 81% of STEM girls express interest in pursuing a career in a STEM field—specifically, in engineering, physical/life science, math, computer science/information technology, or software development. Nevertheless, only 13% say that it is their first choice

High School Student in STEM

74%
high school girls interested in STEM

Source: Girl Scouts: Generation STEM (2012).

- Such gross imbalance in access and quality of STEM education in primary school must be addressed systemically if the nation is to fulfill its mission of developing a diverse workforce of innovative and world-class scientists, technologists, engineers, and mathematicians.

Source: University of Pennsylvania: Realizing STEM Equity and Diversity Through Higher Education-Community Engagement (2015).

- Some studies have shown that beginning at age 12, girls begin to like math and science less, expect not to do as well in these subjects, and attribute their failures to lack of ability. These findings among 9- to 12-year-old girls have longer term effects and, by high school, girls self-select out of higher level math and science courses, such as chemistry, physics, and calculus, thus reducing their chances to pursue STEM majors in college and pursue STEM-related careers.
- Girls report having lower levels of confidence in their math abilities and experience higher levels of anxiety when performing math-related tasks than boys.

Source: Techcrunch: Why STEM's Future Rests in the Hands of 12-Year-Old Girls (2016) .

- The percentage of females taking precalculus/analysis (37%) was higher than that of males (34%), as was the percentage of females taking algebra II (78% compared to 74%). An equal percentage of males and females (17%) took calculus.
- More females than males took advanced biology (50% versus 39%), while males took physics at higher rates than females (42% versus 36%).
- Males were 6 times more likely to have taken engineering (6% versus 1%).

Source: Techcrunch: National Girls Collaborative Project - Statistics (2016).

- Over 25% of girls having had access to higher levels of education and achieving greater equality in the number of years spent in education between men and women contribute to higher economic growth.

Source: MCM: Gender Equality in Education, Employment, and Entrepreneurship: Final Report to the MCM (2012) and Women in STEM Research - Findings From Recent MyCollegeOptions® College Planning Study (2014).

- Girls are twice as likely as boys to look to their parents for college and career advice over any other resource. Parents are also girls' primary roles models. Encouragement from family, regardless of their technical expertise, can foster and reinforce girls' interest in STEM.

Source: Techbrige: Changing the Game for Girls in STEM (2013).

- Compared to the other groups, AfricanAmerican girls were more likely to cite friends and community programs outside of school as helping them explore career interests, including IT. In addition, this group was more likely to value being able to work independently in their future job or career.

Source: Changing Futures Foundation: Survey of Teen Views on Tech Careers (2015).

College plans of female students interested in a STEM career.:
- 30% of female high school students interested in a STEM major or career will be the first in their families to attend college.
- More female students compared to male students are planning to attend a state college or university (88% vs. 80% respectively), as well as a private college or university (31% vs. 25% respectively).
- Significantly more female students interested in a STEM major or career compared to male students are planning to participate in an academic/honors club in college (31% vs. 15% respectively) and more female students are planning

to participate in community service and volunteering in college than male students (25% vs. 8% respectively).
- Harvey Mudd College, in Claremont, California, has been an outlier in producing female programmers for a decade. This year, for the first time, more women than men graduated with a degree in computer science. Nationally, about 16% of undergraduate computer- cience majors are women. At Harvey Mudd, that figure is 55%.

Source: Quartz (2016).

STEM Interest and Extracurricular Program Participation

- One in four high school students interested in a STEM career is female..
- Female students in the class of 2016 are significantly less likely than their male counterparts to report plans to pursue a college major or career in STEM (16% vs. 41% respectively).
- Male high school students are about 8.5 times more likely to say they plan to pursue a career in engineering or technology compared to female students.
- Two-thirds of female students interested in a STEM major or career plan to specifically pursue the sciences, compared to only 20% of male students interested in STEM.
- Female students interested in STEM are most interested in pursuing:
  - biology (25%)
  - science (14%)
  - marine biology (14%)
  - chemistry (9%)
  - mathematics/statistics (7%).
- Three in 10 female students report participating in clubs or extracurricular programs that encourage STEM.
- Female students who participate in STEM clubs, competitions or other extracurricular programs report:
  - That they feel more motivated to do better in their STEM-related classes (40%).
  - That participation has helped them in their other academic courses (23%).
  - That participation has increased their understanding about STEM (23%).
- Nearly 4 in 10 female students report a lack of awareness of STEM competitions.
- Twenty-three percent of female students report participation in STEM competitions.
- Of the female students that have not participated in STEM competitions, slightly more than half have reported a desire to do so in the future.
- Two in three female students who report past participation in STEM competitions are planning to do so again in the future.

Source: My College Options (2016).

For more information on the plans of high school girls, see Chapter 10 - Education.

High School Student in STEM

1 in 4
high school students
interested in a STEM
career is female

Chapter 14: Gender Equality - Overview

This chapter focuses on the issues of gender equality and pay equity. The U.S. statistical overview indicates that as of 2015, the gross national income per capita reflects men receiving about $63,000 and women far behind them, at $43,000. What makes this even more concerning is that women are recognizing this disparity after attending more schooling and obtaining higher education than their male counterparts. Only 56.3% of women ages 15 and older participate in the labor force, 12% less than men. In addition, when women enter the workforce, they are working on average 5-6 more hours per week than men. But it all really boils down to one important statistic: 65% of women say their gender faces at least some discrimination in society today, compared with only 48% of men who believe the same about these women. We know it, and the numbers support our position.

White females see 78-79 cents on the dollar when compared to male pay scales, and that number drops considerably to 64 cents for African Americans and 54 cents for Hispanics. The challenge here is to reduce that pay gap, and enjoy pay wage equality. There was a time when the majority of women remained at home with the family, but that time is no more. In 2014, couples in which only the husband worked represented 19% of married-couple families. That means that amongst married families, over 80% of women are playing a pivotal role in the workforce, and those women accounted for 37% of their families' incomes. In 2014, 29% of wives earned more than their husbands. This isn't necessarily progress, but it shows that women are entering the workforce, and contributing mightily when they do.

Note that the new McKinsey Global Institute report shows that if every U.S. state matched the state with the greatest improvement in gender parity, some $2.1 trillion could be added to the economy by 2025.

This chapter shows wage gaps by industry. In terms of wage equality, we are seeing varying degrees of success in each of these industries; however, one common thread is that men still make more money than women while fulfilling the same or similar job responsibilities. Within this chapter is the research demonstrating the global contribution of women at work and the global wage gaps that exist outside of the United States.

A goal to gain pay equity is needed and you can help achieve it. Throughout this book, we have worked to demonstrate to you that we can elevate women through education, advocacy skills, leadership from corporations, entrepreneurs, etc. A couple important steps you can take include:

Call to Action:

- Share the statistical data this book has provided and inform those around you (including men) of the pay gap and gender inequality.

- Economic empowerment for women is a critical aspect of gender equality. Get engaged and equalize the playing field by collaborating with those that work for pay equity.

- Join the growing number of women who are excited about the potential to enter the STEM job market.

CHAPTER 14: GENDER EQUALITY

U.S. Statistical Overview

In 2015	Men	Women
Gross National Income Per Capita	$63,157.50	$43,053.90
Pay Gap	N/A	78%
Expected Years of Schooling	15.7	17.2
Mean Years of Schooling	12.9	13
Labor Force Participation Rate (ages 15 and older)	68.9%	56.3%
Life Expectancy at Birth	76.7	81.4
Population With at Least Some Secondary Education	94.8%	95.1%
Average Hours Worked per Week*	35.9	41.0

Source: U.N. Development Programme (2015).

**Bureau of Labor Statistics (2015).

For more info on women's demographics, see Chapter 1: Demographics.

- 65% of women say their gender faces at least some discrimination in society today.
  - Compared with 48% of men who believe women face some discrimination.

Source: Pew Research Center (2015).

- Gender equity in STEM means that females account for 50 percent of the individuals involved in STEM fields. When we look at the percentage of STEM bachelor's degrees awarded to female students for the last two decades, based on NSF statistics, we find that there is no gender difference in the biosciences, the social sciences, or mathematics, and not much of a difference in the physical sciences. The only STEM fields in which men genuinely outnumber women are computer science and engineering.

Source: PBS NewsHour Women STEM Careers.

Legal Gender Differences

- Women representation in governing chambers globally - 22.7%.
Source: Inter-Parliamentary Union (2016).

- In a study of 173 countries, 155 have at least one legal difference restricting women's economic opportunities.
  - 100 of them have laws that restrict the types of jobs that women can do.
  - 18 of them have laws allowing husbands to prevent their wives from accepting jobs.
  - Women are disadvantaged by five or more legal differences in 54 of these countries.

Restricting Opportunities

173 countries

155 countries have at least one legal difference restricting women's economic opportunities.

- 11 countries still allow customary or religious law to supersede some or all constitutional provisions, which can compromise women's rights.
- 32 constitutions do not explicitly guarantee protection of equal rights for men and women.
- 9 countries legally restrict women's freedom of movement.
- 27% treat women's ability to pass citizenship to a child or spouse differently from men's.
Source: No Ceilings (2015).

- Women's Equality Day is a day proclaimed each year by the United States President to commemorate the granting of the vote to women throughout the country. Women in the United States were granted the right to vote on August 26, 1920, when the 19th Amendment to the United States Constitution was certified as law. The amendment was first introduced many years earlier in 1878. Every president has published a proclamation for Women's Equality Day since 1972, the year after legislation was first introduced in Congress by Bella Abzug. This resolution was passed in 1971 designating August 26 of each year as Women's Equality Day.
Source: Wikipedia.

- The observance of Women's Equality Day not only commemorates the passage of the 19th Amendment, but also calls attention to women's continuing efforts toward full equality. Workplaces, libraries, organizations, and public facilities now participate with Women's Equality Day programs, displays, video showings, or other activities.
Source: National Women's History Project.

Pay Gap

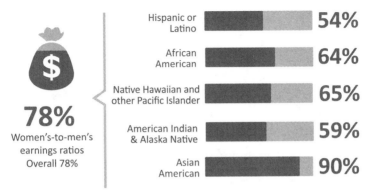

78%
Women's-to-men's
earnings ratios
Overall 78%

Hispanic or Latino	**54%**
African American	**64%**
Native Hawaiian and other Pacific Islander	**65%**
American Indian & Alaska Native	**59%**
Asian American	**90%**

- Women's-to-men's earnings ratios - overall 78%
  - Hispanic or Latino - 54%*
  - African American - 64%*
  - Native Hawaiian and Other Pacific Islander - 65%*
  - American Indian and Alaska Native - 59%*
  - Asian American - 90%*

When compared to white non-hispanic males.
Source: Center for American Progress (2015).

- Bringing women's wages into line with men's would add $28 trillion to global GDP.
Source: Women Kind (2015).

- Bringing women's wages into line with men's would add $4.3 trillion to the U.S. GDP.
Source: McKinsey Global Institute (2016).

Higher education's impact on the adjusted* difference in earnings:

- GED/High School - 2.3%
- PhDs - 5.15%
- MBAs - 4.7%
- MDs - 4.6%

Source: Fast Company (2015).

Using a proprietary compensation algorithm, PayScale is able to estimate a controlled median pay for females by adjusting for outside compensable factors across gender (years of experience, education, company size, management responsibilities, skills, and more), and calculate the difference in pay between similar men and women working the same jobs.

- If every U.S. state matched the state with the greatest improvement in gender parity, some $2.1 trillion could be added to the economy by 2025. These numbers are compelling which is why advocates and leaders can impact structural barriers.

Source: McKinsey Global Institute Report.

Wage Gap by Industry

Natural Resources, Construction, and Maintenance  **67¢**

Computer and Mathematical **82¢**

Production and Transportation  **73¢**

Architecture and Engineering  **81¢**

Professional and Related  **74¢**

Business, Management, and Financial  **75¢**

Service  **79¢**

Sales and Office related  **81¢**

- Natural resources, construction, and maintenance - 67 cents to man's dollar.
- Production and transportation - 73 cents.
- Professional and related - 74 cents.
- Computer & Mathematical - 82 cents.
  - Architecture and engineering - 81 cents.
  - Community and social service - 88 cents.
  - Education, training, and library - 79 cents.
- Business, management, and financial - 75 cents.
- Service - 79 cents.
  - Police and sheriff's patrol officers - 71 cents.
  - Bailiffs, correctional officers, and jailers - 91 cents.
  - Food preparation and serving workers, fast food - 97 cents.
  - Maids and housekeeping cleaners - 99 cents.
- Sales and office related - 81 cents.

Source: U.S. Department of Labor (2014).

- A study on the gender pay gap using salary data from more than 1.4 million full-time employees from PayScale, an online crowdsourced salary database, reveals that men aren't just outearning women in male-dominated fields, they make more money in every industry. According to the PayScale data, "There is no industry where women earn equal to or more than men overall, even when controlling for all measured compensable factors." Men dominate mining, quarrying, and oil and gas extraction, so it's no surprise that these industries have the largest controlled gender pay gap at 5.4%. But taken together, the male-dominated farming, fishing, and forestry occupations have the largest controlled gender pay gap, at nearly 10%.

Source: Fast Company (2015).

- Salesforce named in the top 50 companies changing the world as the tech trail-blazer says no to the gender pay gap. When Salesforce found that 6.6% of its staff needed salary adjustments to ensure gender equity in pay, it took the results public and put up money to close the gap. Its CEO spoke out and Salesforce launched a leadership program to help women rise through the ranks.
Source: Fortune Magazine (2016).

Leadership Representation Gap

- Women hold almost 52% of all professional-level jobs, but lag behind men when it comes to their representation in leadership positions.
  - 14.6% of executive officers.
  - 4.6% of Fortune 500 CEOs.
  - They hold 16.9% of Fortune 500 board seats.
Source: Center for American Progress (2014).

Select Industries' Leadership Gaps

- Financial services
  - Women are 54.2% of the labor force.
  - 12.4% of executive officers.
  - 18.3% of board directors.
  - None are CEOs.
  - Gender pay gap in 2014.
Source: Bureau of Labor Statistics (2015).
    - Financial managers - Women make 67.4% of what a man does.
    - Financial analysts -Women make 81.2%.
    - Personal financial advisors - Women make 61.3%.
- Healthcare and social assistance
  - 78.4% of the labor force.
  - 14.6% of executive officers.
  - 12.4% of board directors.
  - None are CEOs.
- Legal Profession
  - 5.4% of associates.
  - 25% of nonequity partners.
  - 15% of equity partners.
- Medicine
  - 34.3% of all physicians and surgeons.
  - 15.9% of medical school deans.
- Information technology (at Silicon Valley startups)
  - 9% of management positions.
  - 14% of senior management positions.
- Media
  - 3% of creative directors in advertising.
  - 16% of all the directors, executive producers, producers, writers, cinematographers, and editors who worked on the top-grossing 250 domestic films of 2013.

- And were 28% of all off-screen talent on broadcast television programs during the 2012-13 prime time season.
Source: Center for American Progress (2014).

Global Diplomacy

- Only 4% of signatories in 31 major peace processes between 1992 and 2011 were women.
    - 2.4% of chief mediators.
    - 3.7% of witnesses.
    - 9% of negotiators.
- When women are involved the probability of a peace agreement lasting at least 2 years is increased by 20%.
    - 15 years by 35%.
Source: Women Kind (2015).

- A recent UN survey of women's participation in peace processes from 1992 to 2011 found that women make up:
    - 9% of negotiating delegations.
    - 4% of signatories.
    - 2% of chief mediators.
Source: No Ceilings (2015).

For more information on corporate women, see Chapter 2 - Women and Corporations.

Capital Access

- 4% of venture capital funds go to women.**
Source: Babson (2014).

- Between 2010 and 2015, 10% of venture dollars globally funded startups that reported at least one female founder.**
- During the same time period, 17% of seed/angel rounds globally funded startups that reported at least one female founder.

Data regarding the percentage of venture funding women-founded firms receive varies from 4%-10% depending on its source.
Source: TechCrunch (2016).

Home and Family

- Among married-couple families, 53% had earnings from both the wife and the husband in 2013 in 2014.
- Couples in which only the husband worked represented 19% of married-couple families in 2014.
- In 2013, working wives contributed 37% of their families' incomes in 2014.
- 29% of wives earned more than their husbands in 2014.
Source: U.S. Bureau of Labor Statistics (2015).

Global

Contribution of Global Work

- In 2015, the global labor force participation rate was 50% for women.
  - Compared with 77% for men.
- Worldwide in 2015, 47% of women were employed.
  - Compared with 72% of working-age men.
- Analyses of total hours worked in time-use surveys, shows that women contribute 52% of global work.
  - Compared to men's 48%.*

In a sample representing 69% of the global adult population regarding both paid and unpaid work hours.

Source: U.N. Development Programme (2015).

- Women farmers control less land than men. Less than 20% of landholders are women.

Source: Women Kind (2015).

For more information on women globally, see Chapter 15 - Global Women.

11 Gender Equality Initiatives

- Implicit Bias Workshops
- Diversity Guidelines to Search Committees
- Processes and Pathways to Advancement and Promotion
- Salary Equity Studies
- Professional and Leadership Development Programs
- Family Friendly Programming and Policies
- Inclusive and Open Processes for Appointments
- Reporting System Awareness – Increase awareness of in-person and anonymous reporting channels for experiences of bias, including gender bias.
- Success Story Promotion – Regularly promote the success stories and achievements of women through internal and external communication channels.
- Event Promotion – Promote events on campus that feature and celebrate women, such as the Eighth Annual Diversity Symposium's focus on gender equity.
- Gender Equity Data – Analyze data on faculty attrition and compile reports that provide employee data and trends.

Source: Georgia Tech Gender Equity Initiatives.

Wage Gaps by Industry

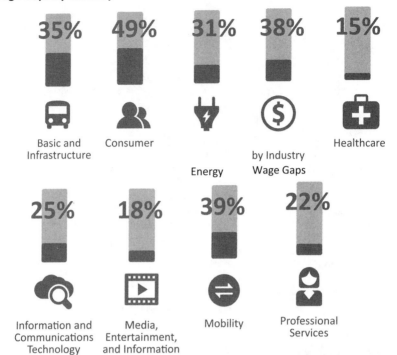

Industry	Wage Gap
Basic and Infrastructure	35%
Consumer	49%
Energy	31%
Financial Services and Investors	38%
Healthcare	15%
Information and Communications Technology	25%
Media, Entertainment, and Information	18%
Mobility	39%
Professional Services	22%

Source: World Economic Forum (2016).

Chapter 15: Global - Overview

Much of the data we share in this book relates to the changing dynamics within the United States. Globally, we are seeing some of the same gender disparity, and are also fighting a similar battle for wage equality outside of North America. This chapter gives a sense of the population around the world, its life expectancy, and the overall relationship these two factors have to the workforce. It shows different areas of the world that globally promote more women, shining a bright light on those global companies working to empower women. Some countries even have government protections for gender equality. More than 95% of the 56 national constitutions that have been adopted since 1995 include guarantees for gender equality, compared with just 79% enacted before then. Clearly, there's a worldwide push to secure equal rates of education and close the gender gap.

This chapter shows, however, that girls and women are far behind in the number of years of schooling. It shows government regulation and changing literacy rates. But maybe most important is the result of a study from 1970 to 2009 that used data from 219 countries, which found for every one additional year of education for women of reproductive age, child mortality rate decreased by 9.5%. On a global level, the development of women is literally a lifesaver.

Once again, organizations play a vital role in creating a framework, and building a program with executable goals. In this chapter, we name numerous organizations making a difference on a global basis for the advancement of women and girls. We name programs to support women entrepreneurs and women alike. The Goldman-Sachs 10,000 Women program, the Vital Voices program, the United Nations, and plenty of other initiatives are focusing on global leadership to advance women, particularly in different regions and countries. Globally, women's labor force participation rate decreased from 52.4% to 49.6% between 1995 and 2015. We need to reverse that downward movement.

Call to Action:

- Use this data to drive the numbers higher! Get involved and advocate for others. This is a call to action to globally advance women, to fill the boardrooms and CEO positions, to grow the entrepreneurs in small, medium, and large businesses, and to profile women on the front cover of every magazine so they can tell their stories. It is an opportunity to celebrate their success. We must equate the contributions to the economy and to the economies of the world to wage equality and opportunity.

- Women are flourishing as leaders, as those controlling wealth, and as philanthropists. As Maya Angelou said: "How important it is for us to recognize and celebrate our heroes and our she-roes!" It is incumbent on all of us to take the data and information from *Women's Quick Facts* and build upon each individual, organization, government entity, and business (and society) to make a difference. As we show, we're moving the needle, climbing the ladder, and propelling other women and girls up the mountainside. It takes an army, and we have one. Let's all ban together, join the movement, and work as a team to secure the balance and equality this world deserves.

CHAPTER 15: GLOBAL

Statistical Overview

Population

Estimated mid-year 2016:

- Total - 7,334,771,614
- Male - 3,693,280,349 - 50.353%
- Female - 3,641,491,265 - 49.647%
- Sex Ratio - 101.4

Source: U.S. Census Bureau (2014).

Life Expectancy

- Men - 68 years
- Women - 73 years

Source: World Health Organization (2015).

- Women's life expectancy rose from 69 years old to 73 years old and maternal mortality rates decreased by 40% in over 70 countries in the last decade.
- Globally, the total fertility rate reached 2.5 children per woman in 2015, a decline from three children in 1990.

Source: No Ceilings (2015).

Global Population

Life Expectancy

- In 2011, women's life expectancy at birth was more than 80 years in 46 countries, but only 58 years in the World Health Organization African Region.

Source: World Health Organization (2013).

Labor Force

- 55% of women globally are part of the labor force.
  - Compared with 82% of men.

Source: No Ceilings (2015).

- Since 2006, an extra one-quarter of a billion women have entered the labor force.

Source: World Economic Forum (2015).

- Overall participation in the labor market is only slightly lower in 2015, compared to 1995.
  - The gender gap in labor force participation remains especially large in northern Africa, western Asia, and southern Asia.
  - In Oceania, sub-Saharan Africa, and southern Asia, between 30 and 55% of employed women are contributing family workers, about 20 percentage points higher than men in the same regions.
  - Women and men ages 15 to 24 years have experienced a decline in participation.
    - This likely linked to expanding educational opportunities at the secondary and tertiary levels.
  - Older women ages 25 to 54 increased their labor force participation in most regions, while that of men in the same age group stagnated or declined slightly across regions.
  - The proportion of women ages 55 to 64 in the labor force has risen in most regions, reflecting changes in the statutory retirement age and pension reforms.

Source: U.N. Stats (2015).

- Globally, women's labor force participation rate decreased from 52.4% to 49.6% between 1995 and 2015.
- The odds that a woman will participate in the labor force remains almost 30% less than they are for a man.
- Still, an additional one-quarter of a billion women have entered the labor force since 2006.
- Over 60% of the world's employed women work in the services sector.
- Women face a gender wage gap globally, earning 77% of what men earn.
- Today, women earn what men were earning 10 years ago.
- Global average annual earnings for women are $11,000, compared to men's earnings of $21,000.
- Women hold only 12% of the world's board seats.

Source: Catalyst (2015).

- Globally women comprise 33.8% of our workforce. TCS employs over 119,000 women globally.

Source: TATA Consulting Services (2016).

Business

- Larger companies with revenues promote more women.
  - Globally the percentage that do so is 49%.
- The national percentage of tech companies with women in leadership roles is 45%.
  - Europe is at 50%.
  - Asia is at 56%.

Source: Forbes (2014).

- 14% of CTOs worldwide are women.
- This number has stayed static for the past decade.
- North America has women making up 18.1% of CIOs.

- Women make up only 11.5% of CIOs in Asia.
- 11.2% in Europe, Africa, and the Middle East.

Source: BizWomen (2014).

- The average membership rate for employee resource groups was approximately 8% of the total global employee population ranging from less than 1% to over 20%, depending on the organization.
- Budgets vary greatly between "$150 for every 100 members to over $37,000" with an "average of $7,023 per every 100 members."
- DiversityInc reports a yearly average of $15,000 for the employee resource groups represented by the organizations in the DiversityInc. Top 50.

Source: Boston College (2015).

- Globally women comprise 33.8% of our workforce.

Source: TATA Consulting Services (2016).

Government Protections

- More than 95% of the 56 national constitutions that have been adopted since 1995 include guarantees for gender equality.
  - Compared with just 79% enacted before then.

Political Rights

- 91% of constitutions adopted after the Beijing Declaration (1995) ensure women's right to legislative office.
  - Compared with 70% previously.
- 63% guarantee women's right to political association.
  - Compared with 53% previously.
- Finally, 95% of constitutions have been adopted since Beijing guaranteed women's right to vote.
  - Compared with 73% previously.

Source: No Ceilings (2015).

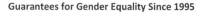

Guarantees for Gender Equality Since 1995

95%
of 56 national
constitutions
adopted

For more information on women in government, see Chapter 8 - Government.

Education

- A study using data from 219 countries from 1970 to 2009 found that for every one additional year of education for women of reproductive age, child mortality decreased by 9.5%.

Source: U.N. Women (2016).

Enrollment

- Today, girls and boys enroll in primary school at nearly equal rates globally, and the gender gap has closed in all regions.
  - Except sub-Saharan Africa, where it has narrowed from 85 girls for every 100 boys in 1995 to 93 in 2012.
- Today, girls and women ages 15 and over spend an average of 7.3 years in school, compared to 5.6 years in 1990.

Governmental Regulations

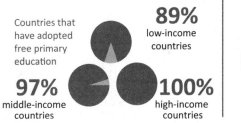

Countries that have adopted free primary education

89%
low-income countries

97%
middle-income countries

100%
high-income countries

22%
of national constitutions guarantee free secondary education

- 89% of low-income countries, 97% of middle-income countries, and 100% of high-income countries have made primary education tuition-free.
  - Seven countries still charge tuition for primary education.
- 22% of national constitutions guarantee the right to free secondary education.
- 14% of countries report charging tuition fees in the first year of secondary school.
  - This figure rises to 24% by the end of secondary school.

Source: No Ceilings (2015).

Literacy Rates

- While female literacy increased by three percentage points between 1995 and 2012, it had increased eight percentage points during the prior decade.
  - Reaching 80% literacy.
- Women today still account for nearly two-thirds of the 781 million adults who cannot read or write.

Source: No Ceilings (2015).

2/3
of adults who cannot read or write are women

Agriculture

- Women comprise an average of 43% of the agricultural labor force in developing countries, varying from
  - 20% or less in Latin America to
  - 50% or more in parts of Asia and Africa.
- Less than 20% of landholders are women.
- Women are responsible for household food preparation in 85% to 90% of cases surveyed in a wide range of countries.

Source: U.N. Women (2016).

Agricultural Labour Force

43%

agricultural labor force are women

Global Cooperation Examples

Convention on the Elimination of All Forms of Discrimination Against Women (CEDAW): The "women's bill of rights" is a cornerstone of all U.N. women programs. More than 185 countries are parties to the Convention.

Beijing Declaration and Platform for Action (PFA): Adopted by governments at the 1995 Fourth World Conference on Women, this document sets forth governments' commitments to enhance women's rights. Member states reaffirmed and strengthened the platform in 2000 during the global five-year review of progress, and pledged to accelerate its implementation during the 10-year review in 2005, the 15-year review in 2010, and the 20-year review in 2015.

U.N. Security Council Resolution 1325 on Women, Peace, and Security: This 2000 resolution recognized that war impacts women differently, and reaffirmed the need to increase women's role in decision-making with regard to conflict prevention and resolution. The U.N. Security Council subsequently adopted seven additional resolutions on women, peace, and security: 1820 (2008); 1888 (2009); 1889 (2009); 1960 (2010); 2106 (2013); 2122 (2013); and 2242 (2015). Taken together, the eight resolutions represent a critical framework for improving the situation of women in conflict-affected countries.

The Millennium Development Goals (MDGs): The MDGs, in effect, consolidated previous agreements, including those on women's rights, women's empowerment, and gender equality, into a single set of core goals, targets, and benchmarks for the development community. The Millennium Declaration from which they were drawn took a clear position, which has since been elaborated in multiple documents, that gender equality is both a right in itself and a driver of development.

U.N. Declaration on the Elimination of Violence Against Women: The 1993 Declaration on the Elimination of Violence Against Women is the first international human rights instrument to exclusively and explicitly address the issue of violence against women. It affirms that the phenomenon violates, impairs, or nullifies women's human rights and their exercise of fundamental freedoms. The Declaration provides a definition of gender-based abuse, calling it "any act of gender-based violence that results in, or is likely to result in, physical, sexual, or psychological harm or suffering to women, including threats of such acts, coercion, or arbitrary deprivation of liberty, whether occurring in public or in private life." The Declaration further states that gender-based violence takes many different forms and is experienced in a range of crisis and non-crisis settings. It is deeply rooted in structural relationships of inequality between women and men.

The International Conference on Population and Development (ICPD): The 1994 ICPD in Cairo was a milestone in the history of population and development, as well as in the history of women's rights. ICPD delegates reached a consensus that the equality and empowerment of women is a global priority. This issue was approached not only from the perspective of universal human rights, but also as an essential step toward eradicating poverty and stabilizing population growth. A woman's ability to access reproductive health and rights is a cornerstone of her empowerment. It is also critical to sustainable development.

Women, Peace, and Security Framework and Commitments: The U.N.'s guiding documents for women, peace, and security are Security Council Resolutions 1325 (2000) and 1889 (2009) on women, peace, and security and 1820 (2008), 1888 (2009), 2106 (2013), and 2122 (2013) on sexual violence in armed conflict. These resolutions have laid the foundation for the efforts of the U.N. community to expand the role of women in leadership positions in every aspect of prevention and resolution of conflicts, including peacekeeping and peacebuilding efforts, and to improve protection of women and girls within a framework of rule of law and respect for human rights. The U.N.'s primary road map for operationalizing its women, peace, and security agenda is the 2010 Seven-Point Action Plan on Gender-Responsive Peacebuilding, which specifies concrete commitments for the U.N. system in such areas as conflict resolution and economic recovery, and focuses on institutional reforms in relevant U.N. entities.

U.N. Framework Convention for Climate Change (UNFCCC): The Cancun Agreements emerging out of the UNFCCC COP-16 in 2010 was the first global climate change policy to include multiple references to gender equality. Since then, more gains have been made to foster women's participation in negotiations and entrench gender equality in UNFCCC outcome documents in such areas as guidelines for national adaptation plans, mitigation, capacity building, and technology and REDD+ safeguards. Gender considerations were also integrated in Green Climate Fund, the Adaptation Fund, and Climate Investment Funds.

The Hyogo Framework for Action (HFA): The 10-year HFA is the first plan to explain, describe, and detail the work that is required from all different sectors and actors to reduce disaster losses. It was developed and agreed on in 2005 with the many partners needed to reduce disaster risk—governments, international agencies, disaster experts, and many others—bringing them into a common system of coordination. The HFA, which aims to substantially reduce disaster losses by 2015 by building the resilience of nations and communities to disasters, provides a tool for integrating a gender perspective in all forms of disaster-risk management, including risk assessments and early warning mechanisms.

Aid Effectiveness Commitments: Policies on gender equality must be matched by the needed resources to implement them. The importance of gender equality in resource allocation was underscored in the 2008 Accra Agenda for Action (AAA), building on the 2005 Paris Declaration on Aid Effectiveness. Through the AAA, developing countries and donors commit to ensure that their respective development policies and programs are designed and implemented in ways consistent with their agreed international commitments on gender equality, human rights, disability, and environmental sustainability. The Busan Partnership for Effective Development Cooperation endorsed in 2011, recognizes that gender equality and women's empowerment are critical to achieving development results and agreed to accelerate and deepen efforts to: (1) improve information systems with disaggregating data by sex; (2) integrate targets for gender equality and women's empowerment in accountability mechanisms; and (3) address gender equality and women's empowerment in all aspects of development efforts, including peacebuilding and state building.

Other regional commitments: Numerous regional commitments also underscore the importance of and uphold gender equality, including the Protocol on the Rights of Women in Africa, adopted in 2003 by the African Union; the 1994 Inter-American Convention on the Prevention, Punishment, and Eradication of Violence Against Women (the Convention of Belem Do Para); the 2011 European Convention on Preventing Violence Against Women and Domestic Violence; and the Pacific Islands Forum Gender Equality Declaration of 2012.

U.N. Women: In 2015, U.N. Women developed a series of flagship programs to deepen its efforts and achieve transformative results. These high-impact, scalable initiatives build on and supplement U.N. Women's ongoing programming work.

- Using a human-rights-based approach focused on strengthening the voice of women and girls, they seek to remove structural barriers to gender equality and women's empowerment.
- Each program is guided by international human rights treaties and contributes to achieving U.N. Women's strategic plan.
- There are 12 flagships and 4 pipeline flagship programs.
- These included training courses such as Voces Mesoamericanas are provided as part of a U.N. Women project funded by the European Union in three countries (the Philippines, Mexico, and Moldova), which seeks to promote and protect the rights of female migrant workers during all stages of migration.

Sustainable Development Goals: In September 2015, governments united behind an ambitious agenda that features 17 new sustainable development goals and 169 targets that aim to end poverty, combat inequalities, and promote prosperity while protecting the environment by 2030. They were preceded by the MDGs from 2000 to 2015.

CONCLUSION

"The future belongs to those who believe in their dreams."

—Eleanor Roosevelt

This is the call to action to advance women. The clock is ticking so the time has arrived to set strong goals and deploy movement. Each and every one of us can play a role. Share copies of this book broadly and use it for discussion. Though these thousands of facts are compelling as we assess data today, and remind us it is crucial to remain proactive and act toward the future, we ask every sector to make a contribution as leaders of change by setting goals and elevating women and women of color in every area of our economy and society. We embrace a "Call to Action."

Together we can help women fill board rooms and CEO slots, grow entrepreneurs into billion dollar companies, gain cabinet positions, become governors and legislators, become presidents of colleges and universities, be recognized as top scientists and engineers, and be applauded as leaders. This is the manner in which we can reach gender pay equality. America certainly has talent on tap to advance. Our present call to action is to advance women and girls as talented leaders in every sector. Concurrently, we ask that every organization and leader move the bar higher and set a goal by 2020.

Recognize that today the field of the STEM is 80% of the available job opportunities and great paying jobs. This fact helps display how many women we need to join the field. It requires each and every one of us. We are all committed to drive the numbers upward—expeditiously!

Celebrate success and portray role models in ever section. Women on corporate boards has reached 19.9% in the United States, now we can focus on moving to 25% and eventually to 50%. Likewise, women and men alike, who have achieved status should be recognized and help pull up others. This nation in the 21st century can celebrate and achieve greater economic impact through positioning more women leaders.

The U.S. economy, and the economies of the world, flourish when women are given opportunities and professional development opportunities, and fill leadership positions. The more we not only learn but also act to champion women forward, the stronger our nation becomes as a competitive society. The numbers will demonstrate economic empowerment. All of this means that we can achieve a substantial economic impact for our world and the future of our children. Stand up as we control the purse strings.

The spirit of collaboration must be a clarion call for all of us. Driving change to move these numbers upward takes commitment. Identify what you can do and galvanize your colleagues. Help our girls aspire to be leaders in each sector.

We applaud all areas of women's advancement, and while this book focuses mainly on the business and economic world, we salute so many other areas, including the arts, architecture, labor, sports, entertainment, healthcare, etc. for bolstering women in the workplace.

Women's Quick Facts sets the stage for each of us to communicate broadly using social media, events, mentorships, and sponsorships at a rate that will take us to general parody and quickly help us reach our goal of equality. We live in an age of too much cynicism. We stand for optimism. In the words of Maya Angelou: "How important it is for us to recognize and celebrate our heroes and she-roes!" Together, let us work to make these dreams a new reality for generations to come.

Bibliography

2020 Women on Boards. "About Us." (2016). Accessed June 17, 2016, https://www.2020wob.com/about.

2020 Women on Boards. "Boardroom Diversity: When Women Lead." (2016). Accessed   June 17, 2016, https://www.2020wob.com/sites/default/files/2020GDI-2016Report.   pdf.

AAUW. "About AAUW." (2016). Accessed August 8, 2016, http://www.aauw.org/.

AAUW. "Why So Few?: Women in Science, Technology, Engineering, and Mathematics."   Access to Capital. "Accessing Capital for Women-Owned and Minority-Owned Businesses." (2013). Accessed June 17, 2016, http://accesstocapital.com/accessing-capital-for-women-owned-and-minority-owned-businesses/.

Access to Capital. "Let's Talk Access to Capital at the 2015 Entrepreneurial Women's Conference." (2015). Accessed June 17, 2016, http://accesstocapital.com/lets-talk-access-to-capital-at-the-2015-entrepreneurial-womens-conference/.

_____. "Women Entrepreneurs on the Rise." (2014). Accessed June 17, 2016, http://accesstocapital.com/women-entrepreneurs-on-the-rise/.

Advertising Women of New York. "About AWNY." (2016). Accessed August 8 2016, http://www.awny.org/about-awny/faqs#2.

ALL3DP. "30 Most Influential Women in 3D Printing."(2016). Accessed June 17, 2016, https://all3dp.com/20-influential-women-3d-printing/.

American Bar Association. "A Current Glance at Women in the Law." (2014). Accessed June 15, 2016, http://about.americanexpress.com/news/docs/2016x/2016SWOB.pdfasp.

American Express OPEN. "The 2016 State of Women-Owned Businesses Report." (2016). Accessed May 23, 2016, http://about.americanexpress.com/news/docs/2016x/2016SWOB.pdfasp.

American Medical Writers Association. "AMWA Membership." (2016). Accessed July 31, 2016, http://www.amwa.org/membership.

American Speech-Language-Hearing Association (ASHA). "Nonprofit Groups With an International Focus." (2016). Accessed July 31, 2016, http://www.asha.org/members/international/IntNonProfRes/.

Asian American Business Women's Association. "About Us." (2016). Accessed June 23, 2016, http://aabwa.info/about/about.htm.

Asian American Women's Alliance. "About AAWA." (2016). Accessed June 23, 2016, http://www.aawalliance.com/about/.

Association of Science Technology Centers. "About ASTC." (2016). Accessed June 23, 2016, http://www.astc.org/about-astc/.

Association for Women in Science. "About AWIS." (2016). Accessed June 23, 2016, http://www.awis.org/?page=AboutAWIS.

Association of Women's Business Centers. "About Us." (2016). Accessed June 23, 2016, http://awbc.org/about-us/.

Association for Women in Communications. "About WomCom." (2015). Accessed July 5, 2016, http://www.womcom.org/content.aspx?page_id=22&club_id=903060&module_id=193261.

Astia. "How It Works." (2014). Accessed July 4, 2016, http://astia.org/how-it-works/.

Babson. "Diana Report. Women Entrepreneurs 2014: Bridging the Gender Gap in Venture Capital." (2014). Accessed June 30, 2016, http://www.babson.edu/Academics/centers/blank-center/global-research/diana/Documents/diana-project-executive-summary-2014.pdf.

Barclays. "Shattering Stereotypes - Women in Entrepreneurship." (2015). Accessed June 30, 2016, https://wealth.barclays.com/content/dam/bwpublic/global/documents/wealth_management/shattering-stereotypes-women-in-entrepreneurship.pdf.

BIGinsight. "Shopping Behaviors and Strategies of Women's Clothing Shoppers by Select Retailers." (2012). Accessed June 2, 2016, http://www.biginsight.com/news/Reports/BIG-Consumer-APR12-Apparel.pdf.

BizWomen. "Aspire to Be a CIO? It's Still Hard to Get to the Top If You're a Woman." (2014). Accessed June 13, 2016, http://www.bizjournals.com/bizwomen/news/latest-news/2014/05/women-cio-roles-reman-flat-worldwide.html.

Black Girls Code. "About Black Girls Code." (2016). Accessed June 28, 2016, http://www.blackgirlscode.com/about-bgc.html.

_____. "What We Do." (2016). Accessed June 28, 2016, http://www.blackgirlscode.com/what-we-do.html.

Bloomberg. "Occidental 'Lifer' Vicki Hollub to Be First Female Oil Chief." (2015). Accessed June 28, 2016, https://www.bloomberg.com/news/articles/2015-05-05/occidental-exploration-boss-hollub-to-succeed-chazen-as-ceo

Boardroom Bound, „About Us" (2016) Accessed from http://www.boardroom-bound. com/about-us/.

Boardroom Diversity. "About Boardroom Diversity." (2016). Accessed June 20, 2016, http://www.boardroomdiversity.org/home/.

Boardroom Insiders. "Where Are the Women CIOs?" (2016). Accessed February 18, 2016, http://web.boardroominsiders.com/where-are-the-women-cios.

Boston College Center for Work & Family. "Employee Resource Groups: A Strategic Business Resource for Today's Workplace." (2015). Accessed June 22, 2016, https:// www.bc.edu/content/dam/files/centers/cwf/pdf/BCCWF%20EBS-ERGs.pdf.

Boston Consulting Group. "Bridging the Entrepreneurial Gender Gap: The Power of Networks." (2014). Accessed June 22, 2016, https://www.bcgperspectives. com/content/articles/business_social_sector_investing_impact_bridging_ entrepreneurship_gender_gap/.

Bringing Out Successful Sisters. "About BOSS." (2016). Accessed July 17, 2016, http:// bringingoutsuccessfulsisters.blogspot.com/p/about-boss-network.html.

Business Insider. "26 of the Most Powerful Female Engineers in 2016." (2016). Accessed June 6, 2016, http://www.businessinsider.com/26-most-powerful-women-engineers-in-2016-2016-2.

_____. "These Are the 15 most Successful CMOs in the United States." (2016). Accessed June 6, 2016, http://www.businessinsider.com/execrank-top-cmos-and-marketing-executives-netflix-ge-coke-apple-2016-2.

_____. "Lean In' Isn't Enough: Women's Progress in Leadership Has Stalled." (2014). Accessed June 6, 2016, http://www.businessinsider.com/why-women-arent-getting-more-c-suite-jobs-2014-9.

_____. "Meet the Top 50 Female CFOs in America." (2015). Accessed June 6, 2016, http://www.businessinsider.com/top-female-cfos-in-america-2015-9.

California Public Employees Retirement System. "Diversity and Inclusion." (2016). Accessed August 3, 2016, https://www.calpers.ca.gov/page/investments/targeted-investment-programs/diversity-inclusion.

Catalyst. "2015 Catalyst Census: Women and Men Board Directors." (2015). Accessed June 16, 2016, http://www.catalyst.org/knowledge/women-sp-500-companies.

_____. "Our Story." (2012). Accessed July 5, 2016, http://www.catalyst.org/who-we-are/our-history.

_____. "Pyramid: Women in S&P 500 Companies" (2016). Accessed May 25, 2016, http://www.catalyst.org/knowledge/women-sp-500-companies.

_____. "Statistical Overview of Women in the Workforce." (2016). Accessed June 26, 2016, http://www.catalyst.org/knowledge/statistical-overview-women-workforce.

_____. "Still Too Few: Women of Color on Boards." (2015). Accessed June 16, 2016, http://www.catalyst.org/knowledge/still-too-few-women-color-boards.

_____. "Who We Are." (2016). Accessed June 9, 2016, http://www.catalyst.org/who-we-are.

_____. "Women CEOs of the S&P 500." (2016). Accessed June 9, 2016, http://www.catalyst.org/knowledge/women-ceos-sp-500.

_____. "Women In Canadian, United States, and Global Financial Services." (2015). Accessed June 27, 2016, http://www.catalyst.org/knowledge/women-canadian-us-and-global-financial-services#footnote11_f3emfq2.

Center for American Progress. "Fact Sheet: The Women's Leadership Gap Women's Leadership by the Numbers." (2014). Accessed May 25, 2016, https://www.americanprogress.org/issues/women/report/2014/03/07/85457/fact-sheet-the-womens-leadership-gap/.

_____. "Women of Color and the Gender Wage Gap." (2015). Accessed August 5, 2015, https://cdn.americanprogress.org/wp-content/uploads/2015/04/WomenOfColorWageGap-brief.pdf.

Center for American Women and Politics. "Women Appointed Tt Presidential Cabinets." (2014). Accessed May 31, 2016, http://www.cawp.rutgers.edu/sites/default/files/library/womenapptdtoprescabinets.pdf.

Center for Disease Control. "Women with Disabilities." (2014). Accessed June 2, 2016, http://www.cdc.gov/ncbddd/disabilityandhealth/women.html.

Center for Women and Enterprise. "About CWE." (2016). Accessed July 16, 2016, http://www.cweonline.org/bAboutbOurWork/AboutOverview/tabid/208/Default.aspx.

Citigroup. "Citi Women." (2016). Accessed August 22, 2016, http://www.citigroup.com/citi/diversity/.

Corporate Women Directors. "2015 CWDI Report on Women Directors of Fortune Global 200: 2004–2014." (2015). Accessed June 17, 2016, http://www.cdc.gov/ncbddd/disabilityandhealth/women.html.

CNBC. "The Top 10 Highest-Paid Female CEOs." (2015). Accessed June 9, 2016, http://

www.cnbc.com/2015/05/29/the-top-10-highest-paid-female-ceos.html?slide=12.

CNN. "By the Numbers: Women in the U.S. Military." (2013). Accessed May 31, 2016, http://www.cnn.com/2013/01/24/us/military-women-glance/.

_____. "How Many Wmen Are in the C-Suite?" (2016). Accessed June 6, 2016, http://money.cnn.com/infographic/investing/female-ceo-leadership/.

_____. "Still Missing: Female Business Leaders." (2015). Accessed June 6, 2016, http://money.cnn.com/2015/03/24/investing/female-ceo-pipeline-leadership/.

Council on Veterans Employment Women Veterans Initiative. "Employment of Women Veterans in the Federal Government." (2015) Accessed June 11, 2016, https://www.fedshirevets.gov/pdf/Employment-of-Women-Veterans-in-the-Federal-Government.pdf.

Deloitte. "2015 Women in Manufacturing Study Exploring the Gender Gap." (2015). Accessed June 27, 2016, https://www2.deloitte.com/content/dam/Deloitte/us/Documents/manufacturing/us-mfg-women-in-manufacturing-2015-study.pdf.

_____. "Women in the Boardroom: A Global Perspective." (2015). Accessed June 17, 2016, https://www2.deloitte.com/content/dam/Deloitte/global/Documents/Risk/gx-ccg-women-in-the-boardroom-a-global-perspective4.pdf.

Demos. "The Retail Race Divide: How the Retail Industry Is Perpetuating Racial Inequality in the 21st Century." (2015). Accessed June 27, 2016, http://www.demos.org/sites/default/files/publications/The%20Retail%20Race%20Divide%20Report.pdf.

Disabled American Veterans. "Women Veterans: The Long Journey Home." (2016). Accessed July 4, 2016, https://www.dav.org/wp-content/uploads/women-veterans-study.pdf.

Diversity Best Practices. "20 Women's Organizations You Need to Know." (2011). Accessed July 3, 2016, http://www.diversitybestpractices.com/news-articles/20-womens-organizations-you-need-know.

Diversity Inc. "The Diversity Inc. Top 10 Companies for Employee Resource Groups." (2016). Accessed July 2, 2016, http://www.diversityinc.com/top-10-companies-employee-resource-groups/.

_____. "The Diversity Inc. Top 50 List: Companies for Diversity." (2016). Accessed June 22, 2016, http://www.diversityinc.com/the-diversityinc-top-50-companies-for-diversity-2016/.

Diversity Women. "About." (2016). Accessed June 23, 2016, http://www.diversitywoman.com/about/.

Easter Seals. "Call to Action Support Community Efforts to Improve the Transition to Civilian Life for Women Veterans." (2016). Accessed August 9, 2016, http://www.easterseals.com/shared-components/document-library/study-on-female-veteran.pdf.

Enterprising Women. "About Enterprising Women." (2016). Accessed August 5, 2016, https://enterprisingwomen.com/enterprising-women-magazine.

_____. "Enterprising Women Magazine Announces Its Class of 2015." (2015). Accessed August 9, 2016, https://enterprisingwomen.com/images/resources/press_releases/Enterprising_Women_announces_class_of_2015.pdf.

Ernst & Young. "Competition, Coexistence, or Symbiosis? The DNA of C-Suite Sales and Marketing Leaders." (2014). Accessed June 9, 2016, https://webforms.ey.com/Publication/vwLUAssets/EY-competition-coexistence-or-symbiosis/$FILE/EY-competition-coexistence-or-symbiosis.pdf.

_____. "Competition, Coexistence, or Symbiosis? The DNA of C-Suite Sales and Marketing Leaders: The COO Perspective." (2014). Accessed June 13, 2016, https://webforms.ey.com/Publication/vwLUAssets/ey-cco-perspective/$FILE/ey-cco-perspective.pdf.

_____. "Megatrends 2015: Making Sense of a World in Motion." (2013). Accessed June 3, 2016, https://webforms.ey.com/Publication/vwLUAssets/ey-megatrends-report-2015/$FILE/ey-megatrends-report-2015.pdf.

_____. "Women: The Next Emerging Market." (2013). Accessed June 3, 2016, https://webforms.ey.com/Publication/vwLUAssets/EY_Women_-_The_next_emerging_market/$FILE/EY_Women_the_next_emerging_market.pdf.

_____ and Kennesaw State University. "Women in Leadership: The Family Business Advantage." (2015). Accessed June 10, 2016, https://familybusiness.ey-vx.com/pdfs/ey-women-in-leadership-the-family-business-advantage.pdf.

Executive Leadership Council. "About ELC." (2014). Accessed July 15, 2016, https://www.elcinfo.com/information/who-we-are/elc-history.

_____. "Black Women Executives April 2016." (2016). Accessed June 17, 2016, http://elcinstitute.org/uploads/elc/pages/dcd069376dd15e17b621384e87b022ea.pdf.

eWomen Network. "About Us." (2016). Accessed June 17, 2016, https://new.ewomennetwork.com/aboutus.php.

EY. "Entrepreneurs' Hiring Plans Increase as Their Confidence in the Global Economy Holds Steady." (2016). Accessed June30, 2016, http://www.ey.com/GL/en/Newsroom/

News-releases/news-ey-entrepreneurs-hiring-plans-increase-as-their-confidence-in-the-global-economy-holds-steady.

Family Wealth Advisors Council. "Women of Wealth Study. Family Wealth Advisors." (2012). Accessed June 30, 2016, http://familywealthadvisorscouncil.com/women-of-wealth-study/.

Fast Company. "What the Gender Pay Gap Looks Like by Industry." (2015). Accessed November 5, 2015, https://www.fastcompany.com/3053226/strong-female-lead/what-the-gender-pay-gap-looks-like-by-industry.

Female Entrepreneurs. "10 Top Female Venture Capital Firms." (2015). Accessed June 30, 2016, http://femaleentrepreneurs.institute/female_venture_capital_firms/

Ferreira, Fernando and Joseph Gyourko. "Does Gender Matter for Political Leadership? The Case of U.S. Mayors." (2011). Accessed May 23, 2016, http://www.nber.org/papers/w17671.pdf .

Forbes. "After 20 Years, Women-Owned Small Businesses Finally Receive 5% of Federal Contracts." (2016). Accessed June 13, 2016, http://www.forbes.com/sites/eilenezimmerman/2016/03/03/after-20-years-women-owned-small-businesses-finally-receive-5-of-federal-contracts/#23746d425dfc.

_____. "C-Suite Sees More Female Leaders Reaching Top." (2013). Accessed June 6, 2016, http://www.forbes.com/sites/tatianaserafin/2013/03/08/c-suite-sees-more-female-leaders-reaching-top/#2a87661d3c90.

_____. "Five Reasons Why There Are More Women CIOs Than CEOs or CFOs." (2015). Accessed June 13, 2016, http://www.forbes.com/sites/peterhigh/2015/11/23/five-reasons-there-are-more-women-cios-than-ceos-or-cfos/#5789f0863123.

_____. "The Top States for Female Entrepreneurs." (2014). Accessed June 15, 2016, http://www.forbes.com/sites/hollieslade/2014/08/20/the-top-states-for-female-entrepreneurs/#45722ff45277.

_____. "United States Lags Europe in Women in Technology Leadership." (2014). Accessed June 15, 2016, http://www.forbes.com/sites/naomishavin/2014/07/21/the-latest-statistics-on-women-in-technology-leadership/#23e33a10a2e1.

_____. "Why The Force Will Be With Women Entrepreneurs in 2016." (2016). Accessed June 13, 2016, http://www.forbes.com/sites/geristengel/2016/01/06/why-the-force-will-be-with-women-entrepreneurs-in-2016/#409ed3694ce2.

Forté Foundation. "About Forté." (2015). Accessed June 19, 2016, http://www.fortefoundation.org/site/PageServer?pagename=about#.V3wCdZMrKAx.

Fortune Magazine. "10 Best Workplaces for African Americans." (2015). Accessed February 12, 2016, http://fortune.com/best-workplaces-for-african-americans/

_____. "10 Best Workplaces for Asian Americans." (2015). Accessed February 12, 2016, http://fortune.com/best-workplaces-for-asian-americans/.

_____. "58 Women CFOs in the Fortune 500: Is This Progress?" (2015). Accessed June 9, 2016, http://fortune.com/2015/02/24/58-women-cfos-in-the-fortune-500-is-this-progress/.

_____. "Meet the World's Greatest Female Leaders." (2016). Accessed August 4th, 2016, http://fortune.com/2016/03/24/greatest-female-leaders/.

_____. "Most Powerful Women." (2015). Accessed June 6, 2016, http://fortune.com/most-powerful-women.

_____. "These Are the 50 Fastest-Growing Women-Owned Businesses." (2016). Accessed June 17, 2016, http://fortune.com/2016/04/06/fastest-growing-women-business/?iid=sr-link1.

_____. "Women CEOs in the Fortune 500." (2016). Accessed August 2, 2016, http://fortune.com/2013/05/09/women-ceos-in-the-fortune-500/.

_____. "Women Make More Than Men in This C-Level Position." (2015). Accessed June 6, 2016, http://fortune.com/2015/12/18/women-men-cfo/.

The Financial Brand. "When Marketing to Women, Financial Brands Fall Way Short." (2013). Accessed June 2, 2016, http://thefinancialbrand.com/35365/marketing-financial-services-banking-to-women/.

Financial Women's Association. "The Value of Women's Internal Networks: Do Women and Companies Win With WINs?" (2015). Accessed June 22, 2016, http://fwa.org/pdf_2015/20150331_WIN_Report.pdf.

_____. "About Us." (2016). Accessed June 22, 2016, http://fwa.org/about-us/.

FONA. "The Purchasing Power of Women." (2014). Accessed June 28, 2016, https://www.fona.com/resource-center/blog/purchasing-power-women.

General Federation of Women's Clubs. "Memberships." (2016). Accessed August 2, 2016, http://www.gfwc.org/membership/.

Girl Start. "About Girl Start." (2011). Accessed August 8, 2016, http://www.girlstart.org/about-us/what-we-do-and-why.

Girls Inc. "About Girls Inc." (2016). Accessed June 28, 2016, http://www.girlsinc.org/

about/about-girls-inc.html.

Girls Who Code. "About Us - Girls Who Code." (2016). Accessed June 28, 2016, https://girlswhocode.com/about-us/.

Girlstart. "By the Numbers." (2011). Accessed June 29, 2016, http://www.girlstart.org/about-us/by-the-numbers.

Glenmede. "Adding Value With a Gender Investment Lens." (2016). Accessed August 4, 2016, https://www.glenmede.com/files/files/imce/june-2016-glenmede-gender-lens-investing.pdf.

The Global Entrepreneurship and Development Institute. "Female Entrepreneurship Index 2015 Report." (2015). Accessed June 28, 2016, https://thegedi.org/female-entrepreneurship-index-2015-report/.

Global Entrepreneurship Monitor. "GEM 2014 Women's Report." (2015). Accessed June 17, 2016, http://gemconsortium.org/report/49281.

Global Entrepreneurship Week. "GEW Women." (2015). Accessed June 17, 2016, http://gemconsortium.org/report/49281.

Global Women. "2015 CWDI Report on Women Directors of Fortune Global 200: 2004–2014." (2015). Accessed July 1, 2016, http://www.globewomen.org/CWDI/2015FG200KeyFindings.html.

Goldman Sachs. "10,000 Women." (2016). Accessed August 18, 2016, http://www.goldmansachs.com/citizenship/10000women/index.html?cid=PS_01_08_07_00_00_00_01&mkwid=Cxrf5D7p#overview.

Government Accountability. "Corporate Boards: Strategies to Address Representation of Women Include Federal Disclosure Requirements." (2015). Accessed June 20, 2016, http://www.gao.gov/assets/680/674008.pdf.

Grantspace. "Knowledge Base." Accessed June 3, 2016, http://grantspace.org/tools/knowledge-base/Funding-Research/Statistics/number-of-nonprofits-in-the-u.s.
Grant Thornton. "Women in Business: The Path to Leadership." (2015). Accessed June 2, 2016, http://www.grantthornton.global/globalassets/1.-member-firms/global/insights/ibr-charts/ibr2015_wib_report_final.pdf.

Harvard Business Review. "The Female Economy." (2009). Accessed June 3, 2016, https://hbr.org/2009/09/the-female-economy.

Hispanic Association on Corporate Responsibility. "2013 Corporate Governance Study." (2013). Accessed June 17, 2016, http://www.huffingtonpost.com/2015/03/27/women-in-tech_n_6955940.html.

_____. "2013 HACR Employee Resource Group Study." (2013). Accessed June 17, 2016, http://www.huffingtonpost.com/2015/03/27/women-in-tech_n_6955940.html.

_____. "About." (2016). Accessed June 17, 2016, http://www.hacr.org/about/.

The Huffington Post. "The Stats on Women in Tech Are Actually Getting Worse." (2015). Accessed June 9, 2016, http://www.huffingtonpost.com/2015/03/27/women-in-tech_n_6955940.html.

Human Resource Executive. "The Feminization of HR." (2012). Accessed June 9, 2016, http://www.hreonline.com/HRE/view/story.jhtml?id=533345673.

Inc. Magazine. "30 Surprising Facts About Female Founders." (2015). Accessed June 22, 2016, http://www.inc.com/lisa-calhoun/30-surprising-facts-about-female-founders.html.

_____. "The Top 50 Women Entrepreneurs in America." (2015). Accessed June 2, 2016, http://www.inc.com/magazine/201510/ss/inc-staff/impact-50.html.

Indiana University Bloomington. "Patent Filings by Women Have Risen the Fastest in Academia, IU Study Finds." (2015). Accessed August 4, 2016, http://news.indiana.edu/releases/iu/2015/07/women-patents.shtml.

Insurance Information Institute. "Careers and Employment." (2016). Accessed June 28, 2016, http://www.iii.org/fact-statistic/careers-and-employment.

Insurance Journal. "Agency Compensation: Unequal Pay for Women?" (2016). Accessed June 28, http://www.insurancejournal.com/magazines/coverstory/2016/02/22/398997.htm.

Inter-Parlamentary Union. "Women in National Parlaments." (2016). Accessed June 1, 2016, http://www.ipu.org/wmn-e/world.htm.

International Finance Corporation (World Bank Group). "SHE for SHIELD: Insure Women to Better Protect All." (2015). Accessed June 30, 2016, http://www.ifc.org/wps/wcm/connect/a2d8348049d01b0c82a5a3e54d141794/SforShield_Final-Web2015.pdf?MOD=AJPERES.

ION. "Annual Census of Women Board Directors and Executive Officers." (2014). Accessed June 20, 2016, http://www.ionwomen.org/wp-content/uploads/2014/11/ION.2014SummaryFINAL4RevMSCI.pdf.

IWEC. "About IWEC." (2014). Accessed June 20, 2016, http://iwecawards.com/about-iwec/.

Jacobson Insurance Talent. "Breaking Barriers: The Time Is Now for Women in Insurance." (2014). Accessed June 28, 2016, https://jacobsononline.com/uploadfiles/breakingbarriers-womenininsurancewhitepaper.pdf.

Jennifer Brown Consulting. "Executive Sponsors Fuel High-Performing ERGs." (2015). Accessed June 22, 2016, http://jenniferbrownconsulting.com/wp-content/uploads/2015/05/JBC_Executive_Sponsor_White_Paper-May-2015.pdf.

JP Morgan Chase & Co.. "Winning Women - Undergraduate." (2016). Accessed August 22, 2016, http://careers.jpmorgan.com/careers/programs/winning-women-ba.

KPMG. "Women in Alternative Investments: A Marathon, Not a Sprint." (2014). Accessed June 2, 2016, http://www.kpmg-institutes.com/content/dam/kpmg/kpmginstitutes/pdf/2014/women-in-alternative-investments.pdf.

LATINAStyle. "50 Women CEOs in the Fortune 500." (2016). Accessed August 2, 2016, http://latina50.latinastyle.com/the-2014-latina-style-50/2014-top-12-companies/.

Leadership Education for Asian Pacifics. "About." (2016). Accessed June 28, 2016, http://www.leap.org/about.

League of Women Voters. "About the League." (2016). Accessed June 28, 2016, http://lwv.org/content/about-league.

Lippe Taylor. "Women's Buying Behavior Index, April 2013." (2013). Accessed June 2, 2016, http://shespeaksinc.com/wp-content/uploads/2014/02/Womens-Buying-Behavior-Index-II.pdf.

Makers. "21 Facts You Never Knew About International Gender Inequality." (2015). Accessed June 30, 2016, http://www.makers.com/blog/21-facts-you-never-knew-about-international-gender-inequality.

Merrill Lynch. "Women Power." (2015). Accessed June 30, 2016, https://www.ml.com/articles/women-power.html.

Morningstar. "Morningstar Research Report, Fund Managers by Gender." (2015). Accessed June 2, 2016, https://corporate.morningstar.com/US/documents/ResearchPapers/Fund-Managers-by-Gender.pdf.

McKinsey Global Institute. "Women in the Workplace 2015." (2015). Accessed June 8, 2016, http://womenintheworkplace.com/ui/pdfs/Women_in_the_Workplace_2015.pdf?v=5.

_____. "Women Matter." (2016). Accessed June 19, 2016, http://www.mckinsey.com/global-themes/women-matter.

The Nation. "Why Does the United States Still Have So Few Women in Office?" (2014). Accessed June 8, 2016, https://www.thenation.com/article/why-does-us-still-have-so-few-women-office/.

National Association of Corporate Directors. "2015–2016 NACD Public Company Governance Survey." (2016). Accessed June 17, 2016, https://www.nacdonline.org/Store/ProductDetail.cfm?ItemNumber=19733.

_____. "About NACD: Overview." (2016). Accessed June 17, 2016, https://www.nacdonline.org/AboutUs/.

National Association of Female Executives. "About Us." (2016). Accessed June 20, 2016, http://www.nafe.com/about-us.

National Association of Women Business Owners. "About NAWBO." (2015). Accessed July 7, 2016, https://www.nawbo.org/about/history-timeline.

_____. "Access to Capital for Women-Owned Businesses." (2016). Accessed June 20, 2016, https://www.nawbo.org/advocacy/policies-and-positions/access-capital-women-owned-businesses.

_____. "Membership." (2016). Accessed August 8, 2016, https://www.nawbo.org/membership.

National Association of Women in Real Estate Business. "Most Wealthy Women Are Entrepreneurs." (2016). Accessed June 20, 2016, http://www.nawrb.com/2016/06/16/wealthy-women-entrepreneurs/.

National Center for Charitable Statistics. "Quick Facts About Nonprofits." (2013). Accessed August 8, 2016, http://nccs.urban.org/statistics/quickfacts.cfm.

National Center for Veterans Analysis and Statistics. "Profile of Veterans: 2014 Data From the American Community Survey." (2014). Accessed August 9, 2016, http://www.va.gov/vetdata/docs/SpecialReports/Profile_of_Veterans_2014.pdf.

National Coalition of 100 Black Women. "About NC100BW." (2012). Accessed August 8, 2016, http://www.100blackwomen.org/

National Conference of State Legislatures. "Women In State Legislatures for 2016." (2016). Accessed June 5, 2016, http://www.ncsl.org/legislators-staff/legislators/womens-legislative-network/women-in-state-legislatures-for-2016.aspx.

National Council of Negro Women. "About NCNW." (2016). Accessed June 13, 2016, http://ncnw.org/about/index.htm.

National Council of Nonprofits. "The National Council of Nonprofits." (2016). Accessed

June 28, 2016, https://www.councilofnonprofits.org/.

National Girls Collaborative Project. "About NGCP." (2016). Accessed June 30, 2016, https://ngcproject.org/about-ngcp.

NHBWA. "Who We Are." (2015). Accessed July 19, 2015, http://nationalhbwa.com/main/?page_id=2.

National Retail Federation. "Retail Insight: Spotlight on Retail Employees." (2013). Accessed June 30, 2016, https://9649c63edda9f03b02ad-c646b49aabec2270b315a9c86da372e0.ssl.cf1.rackcdn.com/Insight_Center_Spotlight_On_Retail_Employees.pdf.

National Science Foundation. "High Participation Fields for Women: Biosciences and Social Sciences, 1993–2012." (2015). Accessed June 9, 2016, http://www.nsf.gov/statistics/2015/nsf15311/digest/theme2.cfm#psychology.

_____. "Scientists and Engineers Working in Science and Engineering Occupations: 2013." (2015). Accessed June 9, 2016, http://www.nsf.gov/statistics/2015/nsf15311/digest/theme5.cfm#trends.

National Women's Business Council. "About the NWBC." (2016). Accessed June 16, 2016, https://www.nwbc.gov/about-the-nwbc.

_____. "The Economic Impact of Women-Owned Businesses in the United States." (2015). Accessed July 1, 2016, https://www.nwbc.gov/research/economic-impact-women-owned-businesses-united-states.

National Women's Law Center. "Women in the Federal Judiciary: Still a Long Way to Go." (2016). Accessed June 6, 2016, https://nwlc.org/resources/women-federal-judiciary-still-long-way-go/.

NCWIT. "Women and Information Technology - By the Numbers." (2015). Accessed June 7, 2016, https://www.ncwit.org/sites/default/files/resources/btn_04032015_web.pdf.

NerdWallet. "Small-Business Grants for Women: 10 Go-To Spots." (2015). Accessed June 13, 2016, https://www.nerdwallet.com/blog/small-business/small-business-grants-for-women/.

Network of Executive Women. "Women 2020: The Future of Women's Leadership in Retail and Consumer Goods." (2013). Accessed June 27, 2016, https://www.nerdwallet.com/blog/small-business/small-business-grants-for-women/.

The New York Times. "Childless Women to Marketers: We Buy Things Too." (2016). Accessed June 3, 2016, http://www.nytimes.com/2016/07/10/business/childless-women-to-marketers-we-buy-things-too.html?_r=0.

No Ceilings. "The Full Participation Report." (2015). Accessed June 27, 2016, http://noceilings.org/report/report.pdf.

Oliver Wyman. "Women in Financial Services." (2014). Accessed June 27, 2016, http://www.oliverwyman.com/content/dam/oliver-wyman/global/en/2014/dec/OW-Women-in-Financial-Services-04_12_14_FINAL-v3.pdf.

_____. "Women in Financial Services." (2016). Accessed June 27, 2016, http://www.oliverwyman.com/content/dam/oliver-wyman/global/en/2016/june/WiFS/WomenInFinancialServices_2016.pdf .

OpenMind. "10 Facts About Female Leadership in 2016." (2016). Accessed June 8, 2016, https://www.bbvaopenmind.com/en/10-figures-you-need-to-know-about-female-leadesrship/.

Payscale. "The Truth About the Gender Pay Gap." (2015). Accessed June 8, 2016, http://www.payscale.com/data-packages/gender-pay-gap.

Pelosi, Nancy. "Biography - Congresswoman Nancy Pelosi" (n.d.)." Accessed May 23, 2016, https://pelosi.house.gov/biography/biography.

Pew Research Center. "Women and Leadership. Pew Research Centers Social Demographic Trends Project." (2015). Accessed May 24, 2016, http://www.pewsocialtrends.org/2015/01/14/women-and-leadership/.

Pitchbook. "5 VCs That Invest in Female Entrepreneurs." (2016). Accessed June 28, 2016, http://pitchbook.com/news/articles/5-vc-investors-that-target-female-entrepreneurs.

Powder Room Diaries. "DC's Top Ten Networking Groups for Women." (2009). Accessed July 21, 2016, https://powderroomdiaries.wordpress.com/2009/06/21/dcs-top-ten-networking-groups-for-women/.

PNC. "About Us." (2016) Accessed July 21, 2016, https://www.pnc.com/en/about-pnc/company-profile/corporate-overview.html.

Prudential Research. "Financial Experience and Behaviors Among Women." (2011). Accessed June 28, 2016, http://www.prudential.com/media/managed/Womens_Study_Final.pdf.

Quartz. "Harvey Mudd College Took on Gender Bias and Now More Than Its Computer Science Majors Are Women." (2016). Accessed August 24, 2016, http://qz.com/730290/harvey-mudd-college-took-on-gender-bias-and-now-more-than-half-its-computer-science-majors-are-women/.

Rehman. "Accounting and Wealth Management Services for the Grand Rapids Area."

(2014). Accessed June 17, 2016, http://www.rehmann.com/locations/michigan/grand-rapids

Russell Reynolds Associates. "Minority and Female Representation on Fortune 250 Boards and Executive Teams." (2014). Accessed June 9, 2016, http://www.russellreynolds.com/insights/thought-leadership/minority-female-representation-on-fortune-250-boards-executive-teams.

Rutgers, Center for American Women and Politics. "Fact Sheet: Women of Color in Elective Office 2015." (2015). Accessed May 23, 2016, http://www.cawp.rutgers.edu/women-color-elective-office-2015.

_____. "Fact Sheet: Women in State Legislatures 2015." (2015). Accessed May 23, 2016, http://www.cawp.rutgers.edu/women-state-legislature-2015.

_____. "Fact Sheet: Women in Statewide Elected Executive Offices 2015." (2015). Accessed May 23, 2016, http://www.cawp.rutgers.edu/women-statewide-elective-executive-office-2015.

_____. "Fact Sheet: Women in the U.S. Congress 2015." (2015). Accessed May 23, 2016, http://www.cawp.rutgers.edu/women-us-congress-2015.

_____. "Women Presidential and Vice Presidential Candidates: A Selected List." (2016). Accessed May 23, 2016, http://www.cawp.rutgers.edu/levels_of_office/women-presidential-and-vice-presidential-candidates-selected-list.

Savor the Success. "About Savor the Success." (2015). Accessed March 4, 2015, http://join.savorthesuccess.com/become-a-member/.

_____. "Join Savor." (2016). Accessed August 8, 2016, http://join.savorthesuccess.com/.

SigFig. "Gender and Investing: Let's Set the Record Straight." (2015). Accessed June 29, 2016, https://blog.sigfig.com/wp-content/uploads/2015/02/SigFig-Report-Gender-and-Investing-2015.pdf.

Skilledup. "Organizations That Empower Women in Business." (2015). Accessed May 2, 2016, http://www.skilledup.com/articles/organizations-empower-women-business.

Smart Politics. "Minnesota: Where Female Lieutenant Governors Reign." (2014). Accessed May 29, 2016, http://editions.lib.umn.edu/smartpolitics/2014/01/16/minnesota-where-female-lieuten/.

Spencer Stuart. "Progress or Plateau? The State of Women in IT Leadership." (2015). Accessed June 29, 2016, https://www.spencerstuart.com/~/media/pdf%20files/research%20and%20insight%20pdfs/womenit_dec2013_final.pdf.

STEAM Magazine. "Summer/Fall 2016." (2016). Print.

STEMconnector. "100 CIO/CTO Leaders in STEM." (2015). Print.

The Suit Magazine. "Only 14 Percent of CEO Positions Nationwide Filled by Women." (2015). Accessed June 29, 2016, http://www.thesuitmagazine.com/business/small-business/22503-only-14-percent-of-ceo-positions-nationwide-filled-by-women.html.

Syracuse University. "Women Military Veterans, Disability, and Employment." (2015). Accessed June 29, 2016, http://vets.syr.edu/wp-content/uploads/2016/03/Prokos-2015-IVMF-Research-Brief.pdf.

TechCrunch. "About." (2016). Accessed June 25, 2016, https://techcrunch.com/about/#about-tc.

_____. "The First Comprehensive Study on Women in Venture Capital and Their Impact on Female Founders." (2016). Accessed June 28, 2016, http://time.com/3821006/time-100-women-scientists/.

_____. "Venture Capital's Next Venture? Women: Where Do We Go After Ellen Pao?" (2015). Accessed June 5, 2016, https://techcrunch.com/2015/06/03/venture-capitals-next-venture/.

Time. "Meet the Women Scientists of TIME 100." (2015). Accessed June 9, 2016, http://time.com/3821006/time-100-women-scientists/.

_____. "Top Female Leaders From Around the World." (2015). Accessed August 4, 2016, http://content.time.com/time/specials/packages/completelist/0,29569,2005455,00.html.

Time Labs. "Men Prefer Flashy or Brawny Vehicles; Women Prefer Import Brands and Smaller Vehicles According to TrueCar.com Study." (2012). Accessed June 3, 2016, http://labs.time.com/story/women-in-military/.

Traackr. "The Top 10 Most Influential CMOs – Who Are Also Moms." (2016). Accessed May 31, 2016, http://wp.traackr.com/blog/2016/05/top-10-influential-cmos-also-moms/.

TrueCar. "See Women's Progress in the U.S. Military." (2015). Accessed May 31, 2016, http://www.truecar.com/blog/2012/04/23/men-prefer-flashy-or-brawny-vehicles-women-prefer-import-brands-and-smaller-vehicles-according-to-truecar-com-study/.

United Nations. "Facts and Figures: Economic Empowerment." (2015). Accessed June 25, 2016, http://www.unwomen.org/en/what-we-do/economic-empowerment/facts-and-figures.

_____. "Gender Equality Strategy 2014—2017." (2014). Accessed June 22, 2016, http://www.undp.org/content/undp/en/home/librarypage/womens-empowerment/gender-equality-strategy-2014-2017.html.

_____. "The World's Women 2015. Chapter 4: Work." (2015). Accessed January 1, 2016, http://unstats.un.org/unsd/gender/chapter4/chapter4.html.

U.N. Development Programme. "Human Development Reports - USA." (2016). Accessed June 22, 2016, http://hdr.undp.org/en/countries/profiles/USA.

U.N. News Centre. "FEATURE: A Conversation With Female Ambassadors About the U.N. Security Council." (2016). Accessed August 24, 2016, http://www.un.org/apps/news/story.asp?NewsID=53474.

U.N. Women. "Facts and Figures: Economic Empowerment." (2016). Accessed May 23, 2016, http://www.unwomen.org/en/what-we-do/economic-empowerment/facts-and-figures.

_____. "Facts and Figures: Leadership and Political Participation." (2016). Accessed May 23, 2016, http://www.unwomen.org/en/what-we-do/leadership-and-political-participation/facts-and-figures.

_____. "Women Migrant Workers in Mexico Organize for Their Rights." (2016). Accessed June 23, 2016, http://www.unwomen.org/en/news/stories/2016/7/women-migrant-workers-in-mexico-organize-for-their-rights.

University of Illinois at Urbana-Champaign. "Women's Milestones in U.S. Government." (2016). Accessed June 25, 2016, http://www.library.illinois.edu/doc/researchtools/guides/subject/womengov.html.

USAID. "Strengthening Women's Rights And Political Participation." (2016). Accessed June 9, 2016, https://www.usaid.gov/what-we-do/gender-equality-and-womens-empowerment/addressing-gender-programming/strengthening-women

U.S. Bureau of Labor Statistics. "Current Population Survey, Annual Averages Table 39: Median Weekly Earnings of Full-Time Wage and Salary Workers by Detailed Occupation and Sex 2014." (2015). Accessed June 2, 2016, http://www.bls.gov/cps/cpsaat39.htm.

_____. "Employed Persons by Detailed Industry, Sex, Race, and Hispanic or Latino Ethnicity." (2015). Accessed June 28, 2016, http://www.bls.gov/cps/cpsaat18.htm.

_____. "The Employment Situation — May 2016." (2016). Accessed June 16, 2016, http://www.bls.gov/news.release/pdf/empsit.pdf.

_____. "The Employment Situation of Veterans." (2016). Accessed June 16, 2016, http://www.bls.gov/news.release/pdf/vet.pdf.

_____. "Median Weekly Earnings of Full-Time Wage and Salary Workers by Detailed Occupation and Sex 2015." (2016). Accessed June 2, 2016, http://www.bls.gov/cps/cpsaat39.pdf.

_____. "Persons With a Disability: Labor Force Characteristics Summary." (2015). Accessed June 3, 2016, http://www.bls.gov/news.release/disabl.nr0.htm.

_____. "Women in the Labor Force: A Databook." (2015). Accessed May 23, 2016, http://www.bls.gov/opub/reports/womens-databook/archive/women-in-the-labor-force-a-databook-2015.pdf.

U.S. Census Bureau. "2014 National Population Projections." (2014). Accessed June 16, 2016, http://www.census.gov/population/projections/data/national/2014.html.

_____. "A Look at the U.S. Population in 2060." (2012). Accessed June 27, 2016, https://www.census.gov/newsroom/cspan/pop_proj/20121214_cspan_popproj.pdf.

_____. "America's Families and Living Arrangements: 2015: Adults (A Table Series)." (2015). Accessed June 15, 2016, http://www.census.gov/hhes/families/data/cps2015A.html.

_____. "Census Bureau Reports Majority of STEM College Graduates Do Not Work in STEM Occupations." (2014). Accessed June 9, 2016, http://www.census.gov/newsroom/press-releases/2014/cb14-130.html.

_____. "Female Persons, Percent, July 1, 2014, (V2014)." (2014). Accessed May 20, 2016, https://www.census.gov/quickfacts/table/SEX255214/00.

_____. "Fertility of Women in the United States: 2014." (2015). Accessed June 15, 2016, http://www.census.gov/hhes/fertility/data/cps/2014.html.

_____. "FFF: Women's History Month: March 2016." (2016). Accessed June 9, 2016, http://www.census.gov/newsroom/facts-for-features/2016/cb16-ff03.html.

_____. "Income and Poverty in the United States: 2014." (2015). Accessed June 15, 2016, http://www.census.gov/content/dam/Census/library/publications/2015/demo/p60-252.pdf?cssp=SERP.

_____. "International Data Base World Population by Age and Sex." (2016). Accessed May 24, 2016, http://www.census.gov/population/international/data/idb/worldpop.php.

_____. "Los Angeles County a Microcosm of Nation's Diverse Collection of Business Owners, Census Bureau Reports." (2015). Accessed June 9, 2016, http://census.gov/

newsroom/press-releases/2015/cb15-209.html.

_____. "Majority of STEM College Graduates Do Not Work in STEM Occupations." (2014). Accessed June 9, 2016, http://www.census.gov/newsroom/press-releases/2014/cb14-130.html.

_____. "QuckFacts From the U.S. Census Bureau." (2012). Accessed May 20, 2016, https://www.census.gov/quickfacts/table/SEX255214/00.

_____. "Statistics for All US Firms by Industry, Gender, Ethnicity, and Race for the United States, States, Metro Areas, Counties, and Places: 2012." (2015). Accessed June 9, 2016, http://factfinder.census.gov/faces/tableservices/jsf/pages/productview.xhtml?src=bkmk.

_____. "Wives' Earnings Make Gains Relative to Husbands', Census Bureau Reports." (2015). Accessed June 15, 2016, http://www.census.gov/newsroom/press-releases/2015/cb15-199.html.

U.S. Department of Defense. "2013 Demographics Profile of the Military Community." (2014). Accessed August 4, 2016, http://download.militaryonesource.mil/12038/MOS/Reports/2014-Demographics-Report.pdf.

_____. "2014 Demographics Profile of the Military Community." (2015). Accessed August 4, 2016, http://download.militaryonesource.mil/12038/MOS/Reports/2014-Demographics-Report.pdf.

U.S. Department of Justice - Bureau of Justice Statistics. "Crime Against Persons With Disabilities, 2009–2012 - Statistical Tables." (2014). Accessed June 3, 2016, http://www.bjs.gov/content/pub/pdf/capd0912st.pdf.

U.S. Department of Labor. "Equal Pay - 78 Cents." (2015). Accessed August 4, 2016, https://www.dol.gov/sites/default/files/documents/featured/equalpay/EqualPay-78cents.pdf.

_____. "Women Veterans in the Workforce." (2015). Accessed July 23, 2016, https://www.dol.gov/vets/womenveterans/Women_Veterans_in_the_Workforce_Transcript.pdf.

_____. "Women Veterans Profile." (2016). Accessed July 23, 2016, https://www.dol.gov/wb/resources/women_veterans_profile.pdf.

U.S. Department of Veterans Affairs. "2014 Minority Veterans Report." (2016). Accessed June 23, 2016, http://www.va.gov/vetdata/docs/SpecialReports/Minority_Veterans_2014.pdf.

_____. "Women Veterans Healthcare." (2015). Accessed May 23, 2016, http://

www.womenshealth.va.gov/WOMENSHEALTH/latestinformation/facts.asp.

U.S. Equal Employment Opportunity Commission. "2013 EEO-1 National Aggregate Report by NAICS-3 Code: 525: Funds, Trusts, and Other Financial Vehicles, 2013 Job Patterns for Minorities and Women in Private Industry." Accessed June 2, 2016, https://www.eeoc.gov/eeoc/statistics/employment/jobpat-eeo1/index.cfm.

U.S. Small Business Administration. "Empowering Women Veterans: An Overview of Programs Available to Women Veterans Through SBA's Women's Business Centers and Veterans Business Outreach Centers." (2016). Accessed January 18, 2016, https://www.sba.gov/sites/default/files/resources_articles/Report_to_Congress_Empowering_Women_Veterans.pdf.

_____. Office of Advocacy. "Profile of Veteran Business Owners: More Young Veterans Appear to Be Starting Businesses." (2013). Accessed May 27, 2016, https://www.sba.gov/sites/default/files/Issue%20Brief%201,%20Veteran%20Business%20Owners.pdf.

_____. "Women's Business Center." (n.d.). Accessed June 17, 2016, https://www.sba.gov/tools/local-assistance/wbc.
_____. "Women-Owned Small Businesses." (2016). Accessed June 13, 2016, https://www.sba.gov/contracting/government-contracting-programs/women-owned-small-businesses.

USA Today. "New Wall Street Movie 'Equity' Opens a Dialogue for Women, Finance." (2016). Accessed August 3, 2016, http://www.usatoday.com/story/money/personalfinance/2016/07/29/equity-movie-women-wall-street-premiere/87295292/.

USPAACC. "About USPAACC." (2016). Accessed March 21, 2016, http://uspaacc.com/about.

Vital Voices. "About Vital Voices." (2015). Accessed August 8, 2016, http://www.vitalvoices.org/about-us/about.

Vocativ. "Female U.N. Ambassadors Represent Only 16% of the World's Population." (2015). Accessed July 17, 2016, http://www.vocativ.com/243914/female-un-ambassadors-represent-only-16-of-the-worlds-population/.

The Wall Street Journal. "Women, Minorities, Continue CFO Gains in 2015: Study." (2016). Accessed June 9, 2016, http://blogs.wsj.com/cfo/2016/02/02/women-minorities-continue-cfo-gains-in-2015-study/.

_____. "Male Investors vs. Female Investors." (2015). Accessed June 29, 2016, http://www.wsj.com/articles/male-investors-vs-female-investors-how-do-they-compare-1430709406.

The Washington Post. "8 Major Firms Still Lack Women in Boardroom." (2016). Accessed June 16, 2016, http://www.pressreader.com/usa/the-washington-post/20160615/282123520791218.

_____. "The Number of White Dudes Becoming Federal Judges Has Plummeted Under Obama." (2016). Accessed June 16, 2016, https://www.washingtonpost.com/news/wonk/wp/2016/02/18/the-number-of-white-dudes-becoming-federal-judges-has-plummeted-under-obama/.

_____. "There Are 77 Women in Statewide Executive Office, but Only Five Governors. Why?" (2015). Accessed June 25, 2016, https://www.washingtonpost.com/news/the-fix/wp/2015/01/22/there-are-77-women-in-statewide-executive-office-but-only-five-governors-why/.

Wechsler, Pat. "58 Women CFOs in the Fortune 500: Is This Progress?" *Fortune*, February 24, 2015. Accessed June 2, 2016, http://fortune.com/2015/02/24/58-women-cfos-in-the-fortune-500-is-this-progress/.

The Williams Institute. (2014). "LGBT Demographics: Comparisons Among Population-Based Surveys." Accessed June 20, 2016, http://williamsinstitute.law.ucla.edu/wp-content/uploads/lgbt-demogs-sep-2014.pdf.

Women Impacting Public Policy. "2015 National Survey of Women Business Owners on Top Issues." (2015). Accessed June 6, 2016, http://women2.com/2015/10/13/female-ctos-to-watch/.

_____. "WIPP Statements." (2016). Accessed August 9, 2016, http://www.wipp.org/?page=WIPP_Statements.

Women 2.0. "12 Female CTOs to Watch in 2016." (2016). Accessed June 6, 2016, http://women2.com/2015/10/13/female-ctos-to-watch/.

Women Corporate Directors. "About WCD." (2016). Accessed June 6, 2016, http://www.womencorporatedirectors.com/?page=_AboutWCD.

Women in Technology International. "Demographics." (2016). Accessed August 1, 2016, https://www.witi.com/demographics/.

Women Presidents' Organization. "About WPO." (2016). Accessed March 12, 2016, https://www.womenpresidentsorg.com/about.

_____. "WPO Fact Sheet." (2016). Accessed June 17, 2016, https://www.womenpresidentsorg.com/about/facts.

Women's Business Enterprise National Council. "About WBENC." (2016). Accessed August 8, 2016, http://www.wbenc.org/about-wbenc/

Sources & Resources

2020 Women on Boards
AAUW
Academy Women
Accenture
Accounting MOVE Project Report
Ada Initiative
Advancing Women in Technology
Advertising Women in NY
All3DP
American Bar Association
American Church Lists
American Community Survey
American Medical Women's Association (AMWA)
American Women Veterans
AMEX Open
Anita Borg Institute
ASHA
Asian American Business Women Association
Aspen Institute
Association for Women in Communications
Association for Women in Science
Association of Women Business Centers
ASTIA
AXA Group
Babson
Bad Girls Ventures
BBG Ventures
Belle Capital USA
Biz Women
Black Girls Code
BlogHer
Bloomberg
BMO Financial Group
Boardroom Bound
Boardroom Insider
Boston College
Boston Consulting Group
BP
Bringing Out Successful Sisters (BOSS) Network
Business Insider

CALPERS
Catalyst
Center for American Progress
Center for Women's Business Research
Center for Women and Enterprise (CWE)
Chevron
Chronus
CitiGroup
CNET
CNN
CodeEd
Commercial Real Estate Women (CREW Network)
Corporate Women Directors International
Council of Nonprofits
Creating IT Futures
CW Developers (Chicago)
D&B (Access to Capital)
DC Web Women (Washington, D.C.)
DDI World
Deloitte
DEMOS
Disabled American Veterans
Discover.org
Diversity Inc.
Diversity Woman
Drug Store News
Enterprising Women
eWomenNetwork
Executive Leadership Council (ELC)
EY
Fast Company
Female Entrepreneurs
Female Entrepreneurship Index
Female Founders Fund
Feminist Approach to Technology
Ferreira
Financial Women's Association (FWA)
Finomial
FONA International
Forbes
Fortune
Geek Girls Blogs
GEM Women's Report
General Federation of Women's Clubs (GFWC)
GEW Women - Global Entrepreneurship Network

Girl Develop
Girl Geek Dinners
Girl Scouts
GirlGeeks
Girls in Tech
Girls Who Code
Girlstart
Glenmede
Golden Seeds
GoldieBlox
Goldman Sachs & 10,000 Women
Government Accountability Office
Grant Thornton
Hackbright Academy
Harvard Business Review
Harvey Mudd
Hewlett
Higher Education Today
Hispanic Association on Corporate Responsibility (HACR)
How Tech Companies Compare in Employee Diversity
Huffington Post
Human Resource Executive
IFC
Illuminate Ventures
Inc. Magazine
Increasing Diversity in the STEM Pipeline
Indiana University
Insurance Information Institute
Insurance Journal
Inter-Parliamentary Union
International Federation of Business and Professional Women (BPW)
International Women's Entrepreneurial Challenge Foundation (WEC)
ION
Iowa (Lt. Governor)
IPEDS
Jacobson Insurance Talent
Jennifer Brown Consulting
JP Morgan Chase & Co.
Kennesaw State
KPMG
LA Times
LATINAstyle
Leadership Education for Asian Pacifics (LEAP)
League of Women Voters
LinkedIn

Lippe Taylor
Makers
McKinsey Global Institute
MCM
Merrill Lynch
Military OneSource
Million Women Mentors (MWM)
Minorities and Women in Private Industry
Morningstar
MSCI USA Index
My College Options
MYWIT (WITI)
National Association for Female Executives (NAFE)
National Association of Black Military Women
National Association of Corporate Directors
National Association of Women Business Owners (NAWBO)
National Association of Women in Real Estate Businesses (NAWRB)
National Business Women's Council
National Center for Charitable Statistics
National Center for Veterans Analysis and Statistics
National Coalition of 100 Black Women
National Council of Jewish Women (NCJW)
National Council of Negro Women (NCNW)
National Girls Collaborative Project (NGCP)
National Hispanic Business Women Association (NHBWA)
National Organization for Women (NOW)
National Retail Federation (NRF)
National Science Foundation (NSF)
National Women of Color Technology Conference
National Women's Business Council (NWBC)
National Women's Law Center (NWLC)
National Women's Veterans United
NCCS Business Master File
National Center for Women & Information Technology (NCWIT)
NerdWallet
Network of Executive Women
New York Times
NewMe Accelerator
Nielsen
No Ceilings
NTEN
NWBOC
OECD Gender Initiative
Ohio State University
Oliver Wyman

Open MIND
Payscale
PBS News
Pelosi, Nancy (Biography)
PepsiCo Inc.
PEW Research Center
Pewinternet
Philly Women Tech (Philadelphia)
Pitchbook
PNC
Powder Room Diaries
Prudential Research
Quartz
Rehman
Russell Reynolds Associates
Rutgers
S Hour Women STEM Careers
SAIS Center-Boardroom Diversity
Savor the Success
Scientific American
She's Geeky
She++ (Stamford)
SigFig
Skillcrush
Skilledup
Smart Asset
Smart Politics
Society for Women Engineers (SWE)
Sodexo
Spencer Stuart
Springboard (SB.com)
STEAM Magazine
STEMconnector®
Syracuse University
Systers
TCS
Tech Girls
Tech novation Challenge
Techbook
Techbridge
TechCrunch
TechRepublic
The Kauffman Foundation
The Nation
The Purchasing Power of Women

The RAISE Project
The State of Women and Girls in STEM
The Suit Magazine
The Williams Institute
Time
Time Labs
Traackr
TrueCar
United Nations
U.N. Development Programme
U.N. News Centre
U.N. Women
University of Illinois at Urbana-Campaign
University of Minnesota
University of Pennsylvania
U.S. AID
U.S. Bureau of Labor Statistics
U.S. Census Bureau
U.S. Department of Defense
U.S. Department of Education
U.S. Department of Justice
U.S. Department of Labor
U.S. Department of Veteran Affairs
U.S. Equal Employment Opportunity Commission (EEOC)
U.S. News
U.S. Pan Asian American Women's Alliance (USPAACC)
U.S. Small Business Administration (SBA)
U.S. Small Business Administration Office of Advocacy
USA Today
USPTO - AllinSTEM
VBE Certification
Virginia Department of Veterans Sources
Vital Voices
Vocativ
Wall Street Journal
WAMDA
Washington Post
Walmart
WBE and WBE Certification
Web Start Women (Boston)
WebChick
Webgrrls
Wechsler
Wells Fargo
WEST

WIRED
Women & Hi Tech
Women 2.0
Women as Veteran Entrepreneurs (WAVE)
Women Business Enterprise National Council (WBENC)
Women Corporate Directors
Women Impacting Public Policy (WIPP)
Women in Business (Teresa Meares)
Women in Leadership and Development
Women in Leadership and Philanthropy
Women in Tech: The Facts
Women in Technology (U.K.)
Women in Technology (WIT)
Women in Technology International "Demographics" (WITI)
Women in the Boardroom
Women in Wireless
Women Innovate Mobile
Women Kind
Women Presidents' Organization (WPO)
Women Who Tech
Women's Rural Entrepreneurial Network (WREN)
Women's Sports Foundation
Women's Venture Fund
Womenable.com
Workforce Strategies Initiative at the Aspen Institute
Working Mother
World Economic Forum
World Health Organization
World Library
World Public Library
Zonta International

A free eBook edition is available with the purchase of this book.

To claim your free eBook edition:

1. Download the Shelfie app.
2. Write your name in upper case in the box.
3. Use the Shelfie app to submit a photo.
4. Download your eBook to any device.

Shelfie

A **free** eBook edition is available with the purchase of this print book.

CLEARLY PRINT YOUR NAME ABOVE IN UPPER CASE

Instructions to claim your free eBook edition:
1. Download the Shelfie app for Android or iOS
2. Write your name in **UPPER CASE** above
3. Use the Shelfie app to submit a photo
4. Download your eBook to any device

Print & Digital Together Forever.

Snap a photo

Free eBook

Read anywhere

The Morgan James
Speakers Group

www.TheMorganJamesSpeakersGroup.com

We connect Morgan James published
authors with live and online events
and audiences whom will benefit
from their expertise.

Morgan James makes all of our titles available
through the Library for All Charity Organization.

www.LibraryForAll.org